Burning Country

Burning Country

Syrians in Revolution and War

Robin Yassin-Kassab and Leila Al-Shami

PlutoPress
www.plutobooks.com

First published 2016 by Pluto Press
345 Archway Road, London N6 5AA

www.plutobooks.com

British Library Cataloguing in Publication Data
A catalogue record for this book is available from the British Library

ISBN 978 0 7453 3627 5 Hardback
ISBN 978 0 7453 3622 0 Paperback
ISBN 978 1 7837 1800 9 PDF eBook
ISBN 978 1 7837 1802 3 Kindle eBook
ISBN 978 1 7837 1801 6 EPUB eBook

This book is printed on paper suitable for recycling and made from fully managed and sustained forest sources. Logging, pulping and manufacturing processes are expected to conform to the environmental standards of the country of origin.

Typeset by Stanford DTP Services, Northampton, England

Simultaneously printed in the European Union and United States of America

Contents

List of Abbreviations

ANA	Activists News Association
ASP	Arab Socialist Party
CDF	Committees for the Defense of Democratic Freedoms and Human Rights in Syria
FSA	Free Syrian Army
GCC	Gulf Cooperation Council
HRAS	Human Rights Association in Syria
ISI	Islamic State in Iraq
ISIS	Islamic State of Iraq and Sham (Daesh)
KNC	Kurdistan National Council
KRG	Kurdish Regional Government
LCCs	Local Coordination Committees
NCB	National Coordination Body for Democratic Change
PFLP-GC	Popular Front for the Liberation of Palestine-General Command
PKK	Kurdistan Workers' Party (Partiya Karkerên Kurdistanê)
PLO	Palestine Liberation Organization
PYD	Democratic Union Party (Partiya Yekîtiya Demokrator)
SHRIL	Syrian Human Rights Information Link
SNC	Syrian National Council
SSNP	Syrian Social Nationalist Party
SRCU	Syrian Revolution Coordinators Union
SRF	Syrian Revolutionaries Front
SRGC	Syrian Revolution General Commission
SRY	Syrian Revolutionary Youth
UAR	United Arab Republic

Acknowledgements

We would like to thank all those, named or anonymous, who shared their stories with us.

For various kinds of logistical help, we thank Razan Ghazzawi, Lina Sergie (Amal Hanano), Yassin al-Haj Saleh, AbdulRahman Jalloud, Wassim al-Adel, and Olmo.

For their reading and comments on sections of the text, we thank Hassan Hassan, Thomas Pierret, Yasser Munif, Rime Allaf, and particularly Muhammad Idrees Ahmad. Our friend and trusty IT expert Alasdair MacPhee of macpheeit.co.uk made the maps. We thank everybody at Pluto Press, most of all our editor David Shulman, who initiated this project as an act of solidarity with the Syrian revolution. His support throughout the process of researching and writing the book has been invaluable.

Preface

Bristol, June 2014. A compact old lady in red hair and a flowery dress is attending an evening of Syrian texts. As a description of Damascus is read out, she preserves her bright smile but begins nevertheless, quietly, to weep. Afterwards she comes up to talk. She's a Damascene herself, she says. 'I've lived in England for over thirty years, and I didn't realise until the revolution that I had a fear barrier inside. Then I noticed I'd never talked about Syria. I'd tried not to even think about it. But those brave youths gave me courage; they gave me back my identity, and my freedom.'

This is where the revolution happens first, before the guns and the political calculations, before even the demonstrations – in individual hearts, in the form of new thoughts and newly unfettered words. Syria was once known as a 'kingdom of silence'. In 2011 it burst into speech – not in one voice but in millions. On an immense surge of long-suppressed energy, a non-violent protest movement crossed sectarian and ethnic boundaries and spread to every part of the country. Nobody could control it – no party, leader or ideological programme, and least of all the repressive apparatus of the state, which applied gunfire, mass detention, sexual assault and torture, even of children, to death.

Revolutionary Syrians often describe their first protest as an ecstatic event, as a kind of rebirth. The regime's savage response was a baptism of horror after which there was no going back. Not silenced but goaded into fiercer revolt, the people organised in revolutionary committees and called not just for reform but for the complete overthrow of the system. Eventually, as soldiers defected and civilians took up arms to defend their communities, the revolution militarised. And then where the state collapsed or was beaten back, people set up local councils, aid distribution networks, radio stations and newspapers, expressing communal solidarity in the most creative and practical ways.

For a few brief moments the people changed everything. Then the counter-revolutions ground them down. The regime's scorched earth strategy drove millions from the country; those who remained in the liberated zones were forced to focus on survival. Syria became the site of proxy wars, of Sunni–Shia rivalries, of foreign interventions. Iranian and transnational Shia forces backed the regime; foreign Sunni extremists flocked to join the organisation known as 'Islamic State'. (Or 'the Islamic State in Iraq and the Levant', or ISIS, or even 'the Caliphate'. Syrians call it 'Daesh', by its Arabic acronym.)

Nobody supported the revolutionaries. Abandoned by the ill-named 'international community', usually ignored or misrepresented in the media, these people have been our chief informants. Their voices and insights make the core of this book. Their input was sought not only because it goes so often unheard, but because they have made history, and in the hope that we may learn from them.

If one woman in particular illuminates these pages, it is Razan Zaitouneh. In the years before the revolution Leila worked closely with Razan. She knew her as so many others did for her honesty and self-effacing modesty. Razan was softly spoken, penetratingly intelligent and uncompromisingly independent. She worked 16-hour days, chain-smoked Gitanes and had a will of steel.

In those days she was a human rights lawyer who advocated for political prisoners and befriended these damaged souls after their release. In the revolution she became a leading light. She attended some of the uprising's first protests in Damascus, and was a founding member of the Local Coordination Committees. She was also the driving energy behind the Violations Documentation Centre, recording and transmitting information to the world. For two years she lived underground; then in April 2013 she came into the open, basing herself in Douma, a liberated suburb in the Ghouta area outside Damascus. There she worked with the Douma Council and other revolutionary administrative structures, offered human rights training to armed groups and fearlessly criticised anyone who abused the people's freedoms. She witnessed the regime's bombardment and starvation siege on the Ghouta suburbs, and in August 2013 its massive sarin gas attacks.

Then on 9 December 2013, Razan and three others were abducted by armed men. Her husband Wael Hamada was taken, and the lawyer and poet Nazem Hamadi, as well as the activist Samira Khalil. Most blame Zahran Alloush's Jaysh al-Islam, Douma's strongest militia, for the abduction. Nothing has been heard of the four since.

Samira Khalil is married to Yassin al-Haj Saleh, a former political prisoner and a key revolutionary thinker. Now exiled in Istanbul, deprived of his wife and his homeland, Yassin describes Razan Zaitouneh in these terms:

> Razan is of a younger generation. She is a very courageous woman, a very good writer, a great ethical agent in our struggle for freedom. Razan is the person who revolutionized and radicalized the field of human rights activism in Syria, and brought it to the people, the persecuted, the impoverished and the invisible population. Before Razan, human rights activism in Syria was confined to well-educated middle class people and the narrow circles of political activism.
>
> Samira and Razan's abduction symbolizes the two-fold character of the battle imposed on Syrians: Against the Assadist necktie fascists and against the Islamist long-bearded fascists. Both women are great heroes in the Syrian struggle for freedom on the political level and on the social and cultural level.[1]

In many ways, Razan's fate mirrors Syria's. This book is dedicated to her, and to every free Syrian.

Leila al-Shami and Robin Yassin-Kassab
March 2015

TURKEY
Gaziantep
Kobani
Qamishli
Afrin
Manbij
Hasakeh
Atmeh
Aleppo
Idlib
Saraqeb
Raqqa
Jisr al-Shughour
SYRIA
Lattakia
Jableh
Deir al-Zor
Banyas
Hama
Selemmiyeh
Rastan
Tartous
Homs
Aal Bu Kamal
al-Qusayr
Palmyra
LEBANON
Yabroud
Zabadani
Damascus
IRAQ
Quneitra
Sweida
Deraa
JORDAN
Israeli-Occupied
Golan Heights

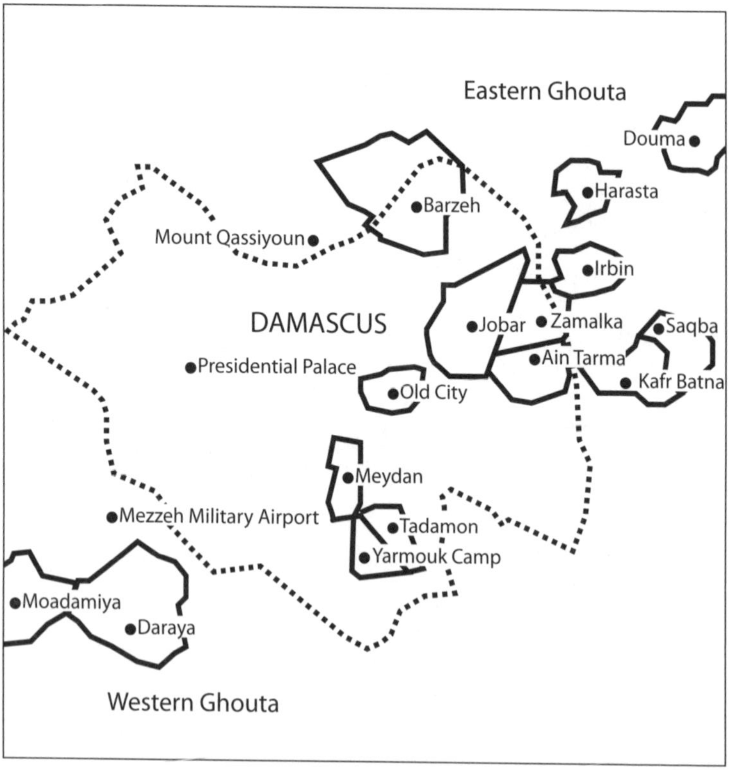
Eastern Ghouta
Douma
Harasta
Barzeh
Mount Qassiyoun
Irbin
DAMASCUS
Jobar
Zamalka
Saqba
Presidential Palace
Ain Tarma
Kafr Batna
Old City
Meydan
Mezzeh Military Airport
Tadamon
Yarmouk Camp
Moadamiya
Daraya
Western Ghouta

1

Revolution from Above

O Sultan, my master, if my clothes
are ripped and torn
it is because your dogs with claws
are allowed to tear me.
And your informers every day are those
who dog my heels ...
the reason you've lost wars twice
was because you've been walled in from
mankind's cause and voice.

Nizar Qabbani, 'Notes on the Book of Defeat'[1]

Geography bestowed diversity on Syria.[2] Unlike Egypt, with its central river and ancient tradition of central government, the lands to the east of the Mediterranean consist of mountains, forests, plains and deserts, and have housed plural and sometimes fiercely independent peoples.

This topography of division made cooperation necessary, and encouraged the free interchange of goods and ideas. For millennia, Syria's various communities have argued and traded in the Levant's great cities. Both Damascus and Aleppo claim the title of oldest continuously inhabited city on earth. Before the Umayad Mosque in Damascus was a mosque it was a cathedral (it still houses the head of John the Baptist); before it was a cathedral it was a Roman-style temple to Jupiter; before that, a temple to Haddad, the Aramean thunder god.

As part of the fertile crescent, Syria was the site of the first agricultural revolution; the plants and animals domesticated here became staples for much of the world. The world's first alphabet (Phoenician) was excavated north of Lattakia. And the country is pocked with tells, hills made over millennia of human habitation – the pebbles beneath your feet are not pebbles but the shards of ten million pots manufactured and discarded generation after generation.

It's been a land of invasions – Hittite, Egyptian, Assyrian, Macedonian, Crusader, Mongol, among many others – and was once, under the Islamic Umayad dynasty, briefly the seat of a world empire. It's welcomed peaceable immigrants too, pilgrims and poets, and refugees from countries including the Balkans, the Caucasus, Turkish Armenia, and most recently from Palestine and Iraq.

And it's always been a trading zone, once – before Europe developed and dominated the sea routes – one of the world's most important, on the caravan route through Jerusalem to Mecca and Yemen, and on the Silk Route linking Europe and Africa to India and China. Aleppo's textile industry still provided underwear to Harrods until the revolution and war.[3]

The country was crucial in the development of the three main varieties of Abrahamic monotheism, and has been a site of constant contestation between religions, sects and ideologies, and more violently, between warlords and armies harnessing religious rhetoric. Its sectarian composition shifted with time and according to the dominant power structures. Christians remained a majority in the first centuries of Muslim rule. Later heterodox Shia groups, particularly the Nizari Ismailis, prospered alongside the Crusader states. Saladin's Ayyubid dynasty and then the Mamluks re-established orthodox Sunni rule, which the Ottomans continued for 400 years.

Today about 65 per cent of Syrians are Sunni Arabs. Alawi Arabs are 10 to 12 per cent. The mainly Arab Christians, mostly Orthodox and Eastern Catholic, but also Assyrian, Chaldean and Armenian, including a small Aramaic-speaking community at Maalula, constitute 10 per cent. Kurds, almost all Sunnis, speaking two main dialects, account for another 10 per cent. The remainder are Druze, Ismailis, Twelver Shia, and Turkmen. The Bedouin, their circulation blocked by postcolonial borders, are mostly settled now. Of course, these categories fail to reflect the enormous diversity within each group. Sunni Arabs, for instance, are differentiated by urban–rural, regional, tribal, familial, and of course gender and class cleavages, and then by individual temperament and experience.

Social differences often count a great deal, but sometimes don't matter at all. Tolerance and purist bigotry are two of the poles of any country's life. Even today, with battle lines drawn, common interests, alliances and love affairs cross political and sectarian divides. Generalisations are sometimes necessary, but it's most accurate to think of Syria as a collective of 23 million individuals.

* * *

The Ottoman Empire ruled Syria from 1516 until 1917, first as a thriving multicultural Caliphate, later as Europe's 'sick man' struggling at once to keep more vigorous imperialisms at bay and to resist internal nationalisms.

The Ottoman 'millet' system, whereby the major religious communities applied their own jurisprudence to their own affairs, provided some local, if patriarchal, balance to the central state and allowed for a continuing cosmopolitanism. But the system had its limits. The Alawis, deigned a heretical group, were not recognised as a millet. (The Druze were also considered heretics, but they enjoyed a level of autonomy in recognition of their actual power in the Lebanon mountains.) The technological limits of the pre-modern state meant that the Sultan cast very little shadow on most Syrians. Immediate government was local and traditional; Istanbul lay in a distant land. The dramatic exceptions to this general rule were the armed taxation and conscription convoys which periodically made their way around the increasingly poor villages demanding grain, gold and men who'd disappear in unheard-of wars.

Syria's economy stagnated. Samuel Lyde, an Anglican clergyman on a hopeless mid-nineteenth-century mission to convert the Alawis of the coastal mountains, described 'the increasing desolation and depopulation, which in the neighbourhood of Ladikeeh are going on at the present moment, in the burning of villages, and the death, in perpetually recurring petty fights, of their inhabitants ... scenes of blood and desolation which must ... end in the utter ruin of the country and extirpation of the population.'[4]

In the late nineteenth and early twentieth centuries, conditions of poverty, famine and recurrent epidemic spurred a wave of emigration to South and North America, the Caribbean, and west Africa. A couple of hundred Syrian-Lebanese drowned with the Titanic. The 'Street of the Turks' in Gabriel Garcia Marquez's fictional Macondo is so called because the people were Ottomans when they arrived in Colombia, but they were Syrian Ottomans, Arabs. Today millions describe themselves as Syrian-Brazilians. Guyana's richest family is the Maqdeesis. Carlos Menem, former Argentinian president, is of Syrian origin too. Beyond South America, the Argentinian drink Yerba Maté is best known on the Syrian coast.

By now the Islamic aspect of Turkish rule was relegated to the propaganda department. Turkish chauvinism – a response to European national and colonial models – was the governing ideology. The result was a stirring of cultural nationalism in the Arab provinces, involving the revival of classical Arabic as a language of education and politics, and a rediscovery of its literature. Various reformist attempts to decentralise the empire ultimately failed, and the Ottomans met nationalist agitation with harsh repression.

For decades the ailing empire had been kept intact only by European agreement – the competing states hadn't wanted their profitable power balance upset. World War I, and Turkey's alliance with Germany, changed that. In 1917 the British-assisted Arab Revolt ended Turkish rule in Syria.

The agreement between Sharif Hussain of Mecca and Sir Henry McMahon appeared to grant British support for 'the freedom of the Arab peoples' in return for armed action against Turkey. What Sharif Hussain and the nationalists understood from this was a promised Arab independence (in the eastern Arab world) and unity through federation, but the British and the French had already signed the Sykes–Picot agreement, which carved up the Arabs into British and French zones, and the British, with the Balfour Declaration, had granted a section of Palestine to Zionism.

At the post-war conferences of Versailles and San Remo, Sykes–Picot was readjusted and then implemented against the clearly formulated wishes of the people of the region. In July 1919, delegates had attended a Pan-Syrian Congress in Damascus which specifically called for the unity of 'bilad al-sham', a cultural and quasi-administrative unit under the Ottomans containing the current states of Syria, Lebanon, Israel-Palestine, Jordan and parts of southern Turkey.

Sharif Hussain's son Faysal, now king of Syria, was pressured to accept a French Mandate. He conceded, but his Chief of Staff Yusuf al-Azmeh, refusing to accept the surrender, led a small army to Maysaloon, where 2,000 were killed by French warplanes.

The Arabs called 1920 – the year of San Remo, of French occupation in Syria and British occupation in Iraq – *aam al-nakba*, the Year of Catastrophe. In July an intifada broke out in Iraq. Then in 1947 and 1948 a new Nakba – the ethnic cleansing of Palestine – drowned the memory of the old.

Under the French, the Maronite statelet on Mount Lebanon was expanded into a larger Lebanese state including reluctant Orthodox Christians, Shia and Sunni Muslims, and Druze. Next, Arab-majority areas north of Aleppo were ceded to Turkey, and in 1939 the entire Iskenderoon governorate was handed over in return for Turkish neutrality in the approaching global war. Cities lost their hinterlands, markets and water supplies.

The French made further, unsuccessful efforts to dismantle the country, envisaging an Alawi state in the mountains around Lattakia and a Druze state based on Sweida in the south. 'Autonomous' puppet governments were set up in Aleppo and Damascus.

To some extent the origins of the Arab–Israeli conflict, the Lebanese civil wars, and the current chronic instability in Iraq and Syria can be traced to this early twentieth-century bout of imperialist map-making and sectarian engineering. The Kurds – split between Syria, Turkey, Iraq and Iran – inherited no state whatsoever from the ruins of Ottomanism; the Arabs were embittered by the imposition of mini-states. For Syrians in particular, the dismemberment of *bilad al-sham* was a primal trauma. Because the truncated postcolonial state had no historical legitimacy, Syrians tended to affirm either more local identities or supra-state allegiances – to *bilad al-sham*, or the Arab Nation, or the global Islamic community.

Alongside the political-geographical cutting came a deliberate economic stunting. The French 'open door' policy flooded the country with cheap imports, while Syrian exports were heavily taxed. Consequences included a diminishment of gold reserves by 70 per cent, a depreciation of the currency, mushrooming unemployment, and a collapse in traditional skilled manufacturing. Throughout the French occupation, when 40 per cent of children died before the age of five, less than 3 per cent of the state budget was spent on health care. And crippling collective punishments caused grievous social as well as economic ramifications. For example, the gold fine imposed after an Alawi rebellion in 1921 made the mountain peasants for the first time hire their daughters out as domestic servants to the urban rich, which led to mutual resentments, which in turn intensified sectarianism when an Alawi-dominated army (developed from the French 'Army of Minorities') later took over the country's political life.[5]

Resistance to the occupation was constant, and from 1925 to 1927 it flared into a large-scale uprising. The Druze rose under the anti-sectarian slogan 'Religion is for God and the Homeland For All', while the peasants of the Ghouta, aflame with the nationalism of nearby Damascus, also acted. The French bombarded the Ghouta's villages – today these are towns ravaged by Assad's bombardment – and brought in colonial troops from Morocco and Senegal to put down the rebellion. A residential quarter of Old Damascus was burned to the ground by French bombing. Rebuilt, the area is now called Hareeqa or 'Fire'. This is where the first Damascene mass protest of 2011 would occur.

The French finally evacuated in April 1946, and power was inherited by the nationalist elite. The Mandate-era National Bloc split along regional lines into the Damascus-based National Party and the Aleppo- and Homs-based People's Party, but both represented the same merchant-landlord oligarchy. The big landowners had only established absolute private control over their territories during the Mandate and were often themselves city dwellers, as unresponsive to peasant needs as they were distant from their lands.

The bourgeois democracy which Syria at this stage enjoyed was incapable of redressing the popular grievances of the deprived social classes. Elections were held, but there was no secret ballot to protect dependent peasants, nor any non-elite parties to vote for. After the disastrous 1948 defeat in Palestine, the ruling class was utterly discredited among Syrians of all backgrounds. The calls that would be raised within a decade for an independent socialist economy were stirred not by workers' action but by outraged nationalism.

Colonel Husni al-Zaim's CIA-backed coup in March 1949, the first such coup in the modern Arab world, was rapidly followed by two more. Democracy was briefly re-established in 1954, but by then the centre of gravity in the Syrian polity had shifted irretrievably to the army – now both a vehicle of advancement for hitherto marginalised rural and minority groups and a vanguard of nationalist opinion to pressure civilian decision makers.

Soon the ideological and factional battles fought within the army would determine the fate of the country, but in the 1950s there was still space for political and social action beyond the armed forces. Throughout the decade, urbanisation and industrialisation created new opportunities as well as further dislocations. Trades unions were set up by the small but growing working class. School and university education expanded greatly; this as well as employment by the military explains the upward mobility of rural minority groups. The mechanisation of agriculture, on the other hand, led to widespread rural unemployment.

The most important response was a powerful peasants' movement harnessed and directed by Akram Hawrani, a key figure whose story illustrates the interconnection of nationalist and class politics. A descendant of the fifteenth-century *shaikh* who established the Rifa'i Sufi order in Hama, Hawrani grew up resentful of the town's *zawaat*, the big landlords who called themselves 'the flower of God's elect'. His Arabism was fired in 1915 when his friend Ali al-Armanaazi was hanged by the Turks in Beirut's main square. Hawrani fought to expel the French garrison from Hama in 1945, and commanded perhaps the greater portion of Syrian raids on Zionist forces in Palestine in 1948. He blamed the Palestine defeat on social backwardness and 'feudalism', and held that, given the peasants were a majority of Arabs, peasant emancipation was a prerequisite of Arab national success.

Hawrani was the prime mover in the Arab Socialist Party (ASP), which had strong grassroots cross-sectarian support. A famous ASP slogan was 'Hatu al-quffah wal-kreik lin'ash al-agha wal-beik', or (in nearly rhyming translation) 'Bring shovel and brush to bury lord and boss'. In 1951, amid peasant protests across northern Syria expanding into incipient revolt, 20,000 people attended a three-day peasant congress in Aleppo, and Hawrani launched a 'land to the peasant' movement.

The ASP called for the secret ballot, which became law in 1954, when Hawrani sat in parliament. In that election the oligarchy still won a majority, but the new middle class parties made a breakthrough to gain 20 per cent of the seats. Hawrani was also behind the Ghab marshes reclamation project launched in 1952 to turn the malarial swamp between Hama and Idlib into fertile agricultural land. In 1957, thanks to his efforts, it became illegal to eject peasants from their holdings.

Hawrani was a democrat who vehemently opposed the 1951 to 1954 Shishakli dictatorship which suspended parliamentary life, repressed the peasant movement, and for the first time installed the presidential system. Yet the ASP merged with the Baath Party in 1952, bringing it much of its popular base. Hawrani was influenced by the pro-peasant statements of foundational Baathists such as Michel Aflaq, who wrote: 'the struggle can only be based on the generality of the Arabs, and these will not take part in it if they are exploited'.[6]

The Baath (its name means 'Resurrection') linked the battle against the oligarchy to a romantic version of Arabism, a term which requires brief examination. The definition of 'Arab' has expanded over the last 150 years from describing tribal nomads (as opposed to townsmen), to the people of the Arabian peninsula, and finally to those peoples, from the Atlantic Ocean to the Gulf, brought together by the Arabic language and culture.

Egypt's Abdul Nasser appealed to the Arabs in the latter sense, as peoples connected by historical forces, for the purposes of strategic strength; the Baath Party, however, reached far beyond the traditional nationalist picture and saw the Arabs as a nation outside history, as an eternal creative force embodying a unified will (Henri Bergson's philosophy was important). That Baathism found religious significance in the Arab identity is evident from its slogan 'One Arab Nation Bearing an Eternal Message'. The word used for message here (*risala*) is the term for the message revealed to the Prophet (more often called 'Messenger' in Arabic) Muhammad. And the word used for nation is *umma* – a word previously used to denote the international

Muslim community. In this respect Baathism (like, in a very different way, activist Salafism) should be seen as one of the twentieth century's many attempts to compensate for the collapse of traditional religion and to channel religious energies to political ends. Michel Aflaq was clear on this: 'Europe is as fearful of Islam today as she has been in the past. She now knows that the strength of Islam, which in the past expressed that of the Arabs, has been reborn and has appeared in a new form: Arab nationalism.'[7]

In its effort to spiritualise and mythologise the Arabs, Baathism surely takes nationalism to absurd extremes, but it is significant that the Baath Party was founded by a Damascene Christian, and that it often appealed to minority communities. Arab nationalism's potential strength was its inclusive nature, the possibility that Sunni and Shia, Christians and Muslims, urban and rural populations would all identify together as members of the Arab Nation.

The Baath called for a unified Arab state from Morocco to Iraq, from Sudan to Syria. Economically, it opposed 'feudalism' and the oligarchy, but not small or medium business. It had a lower middle class base and in its first stage was a party of schoolteachers (leadership) and schoolboys (mass membership). Itinerant doctors and intellectuals too spread Baathism to the provincial towns and countryside.[8]

The Party's pan-Arabism stood midway, 'geographically' speaking, between the Greater Syrian nationalism of the Syrian Social Nationalist Party (SSNP) and the internationalism of the Syrian Communist Party. The radically secularist SSNP's quasi-fascist vision of the Syrian homeland included Iraq and Cyprus as well as *bilad al-sham*. It attracted support particularly in minority communities, but was ruthlessly suppressed after it assassinated the Baathist officer Adnan al-Malki in 1955. The Communist Party never recovered from its disastrous decision to follow Moscow's line and recognise the partition of Palestine, but it did build a significant base, especially among Kurds excluded from Arabist politics.

In the wake of Nasser's 1956 nationalisation of the Suez canal and the consequent British-French-Israeli attack on Egypt, a surge of anti-Western nationalist sentiment benefitted Syria's middle class and leftist parties. The influence of Baathist and Communist ministers in cabinet was buttressed by support from the army and on the streets.

The nationalist tide – and dissatisfaction with truncated Syria – was such that in 1958 Syria's rulers voluntarily ceded power to Nasser and the country became part of the United Arab Republic (UAR). The UAR redistributed some land and offered social provision to the poor. On the other hand, it repealed the right to strike and banned independent trades unions. The only legally permitted party was Nasser's Arab Socialist Union. The Syrian Baath therefore dissolved itself in 1959.

The dream of union was wildly popular in Syria, yet the UAR failed miserably. In effect, Syria became a colony of Egypt, its government, economic planning, and security controlled by Egyptians. Worse, this period installed (and to some extent normalised) a police state on a grander scale than before. In any case, the UAR fell apart in 1961 and so, more or less, did the Baath Party. Opposing reunification, Akram Hawrani broke away to refound the ASP. The remnants squabbled over the correct response to Nasser's version of unity.

The secessionist coup of 1961 was led by conservative officers who immediately reprivatised nationalised businesses and served redistributed land back to the landlords. Meanwhile a clandestine Baathist Military Committee, including Salah Jadid and Hafez al-Assad, had been founded in 1959, aiming first to prevent secession from Egypt, then to seize power in Syria. On 8 March 1963, the Military Committee staged a successful coup, at first in coalition with Nasserist and independent officers. For the rest of the decade various factions jostled for control within government; the losers were killed, exiled or imprisoned. The first victims were hundreds of conservatives, then Nasserists of the urban Sunni communities. The still-vocal pro-Nasser street presence was violently repressed, the media brought under absolute state control, and a new influx of rural and minority recruits were brought into the army to replace those pushed out. Akram Hawrani went into exile.

Within the Baath, the pro-Aflaq wing favoured an accommodation with the bourgeoisie and an expanded democratic space, but Salah Jadid's leftists won out, and at the Sixth National Congress, top-down revolution in Syria was prioritised over pan-Arab unification. During the dictatorship of what is sometimes known as the neo-Baath, nationalisations and agrarian reforms accompanied Soviet-style economic planning. Meanwhile Jadid demanded, but didn't prepare for, a 'people's war' to liberate Palestine.

Then came Israel's June 1967 defeat of the Syrian, Egyptian and Jordanian armies. Syria lost its air force and, shockingly, the entire Golan Heights, including the city of Qunaitra. Syrian soldiers fought fiercely to defend the city, but panicked and fled when they heard the infamous Communique No. 66, issued by the defence minister himself, which stated that Qunaitra had fallen before it actually did. The defence minister in question was Hafez al-Assad. The bitter notion that Assad *père* had deliberately given up Syrian territory persisted in whispers for decades, and in 2011 spurred a chant which illustrated the gulf between state propaganda and popular perceptions of the regime's nationalism: *ibn al-haram/ba'a al-jowlan* (The Bastard Sold the Golan). But there are other, more convincing, explanations for Assad's blunder. Perhaps by announcing the fall of Qunaitra he hoped to spur the Soviet Union into action on Syria's behalf; or perhaps he hoped the UN would pressure Israel into a ceasefire. Most likely the key problem was amateurism. Assad failed to double-check reports from the front of an Israeli tank column near Qunaitra, assumed the city had fallen, and scrambled to save his forces. In any case, the army, profoundly weakened by its politicisation and the years of recurrent purges, suffered from poor communications.

The defeat sharpened the struggle within the Baath, now one between the partisans of Assad and those of Jadid. Power decisively shifted to Assad during the 1970 'Black September' conflict between the Jordanian monarchy and Palestine Liberation Organization (PLO) guerrillas. Jadid had sent a Syrian-Palestinian tank column to support the PLO, but this was forced to retreat when Assad refused to provide air cover. In November Assad seized full control in an internal coup called the Correctionist Movement. Salah Jadid lived for a further 23 years, until his death in Mezzeh prison, Damascus.

Combining pragmatism with ruthlessness, Hafez al-Assad proceeded to build an absolutist regime which would end the age of coups and dominate the country's life until 2011. He ended Jadid's 'revolutionary' foreign policy and patched up relations with the Gulf monarchies, winning large amounts of Gulf aid and investment for Syria as a 'frontline state', particularly after the 1973 war against Israel (and again much later, when Syria joined the US-led coalition in the 1991 Gulf War).

Even as he centralised power in the presidency, Assad sought to broaden the regime's narrow base. He reached an accommodation with Sunni clerics – declaring that 'the Corrective Movement is necessary to preserve the Islamic identity of the country'[9] – and with the bourgeoisie, pursuing more liberal economic policies which benefitted some families from the old mercantile elite as well as parasitic new entrants. Gradually an Alawi/military-Sunni/business ruling class began to coalesce. Meanwhile a savage new purge of party and army, this time targeting radical leftists, and their replacement by Alawis loyal to Assad, further sharpened sectarian competition in society as a whole. Under Assad, loyalty was prized above all; corruption and incompetence therefore flourished.

The Baath was refashioned as a mass party carefully controlled from the top. By 1984 it would contain over half a million members, very few of them ideologically motivated. Party Congresses were suspended, and the Baath became not a formulator of policy but a patronage machine, a vehicle for personal gain. Membership offered job opportunities and eased promotion and access to state funds. The party was also an organised proclaimer of the Assadist cult of personality. Grim statues of the Leader watched over squares and campuses; his name was painted on walls and hillsides.

Assad's 'revolution from above' involved a general infrastructural modernisation as well as grand and ultimately failed projects like the Assad dam on the Euphrates.[10] Most significantly, Assad presided over a massive expansion of the Syrian state. By the 1980s one in every five workers would be employed in the bureaucratic or public sector. The army would grow to over 200,000 men, in addition to the police, various state-Party militias, and at least twelve overlapping security agencies.

The president's declared focus was on reorganising economy and army in order to recapture the Golan Heights, and in the first days of the October 1973 war Israel was indeed driven back. The war ended in another defeat, but Assad won credibility for Syria's improved performance. Thereafter he became known for his strategic and diplomatic gifts. Domestically and internationally, the perception was established that Syria was punching above its weight.[11]

Ultimately, however, in foreign as in domestic policy, the regime's only abiding interest was self-preservation. Assad's nationalist honeymoon came to an abrupt end in 1976 when, in stark contradiction to his rhetoric, the Syrian army first prevented a Palestinian-Leftist victory in Lebanon, then proceeded to slaughter Palestinians in the Lebanese camps. Assad further outraged his Arabist constituency by supporting Iran against Arab Iraq after 1980, and by joining the US-led coalition to drive Iraq from Kuwait in 1990.

Economically, though Syria retained its bureaucratic-socialist character, further waves of liberalisation were pushed through in response to recurrent debt crises. These policies, alongside an entrenchment of the crony capitalist elite, meant that by the 1990s 'an upper class [had] emerged both greater in number and wealthier than the bourgeoisie of the pre-Baathist era.'[12]

All regimes must rule through a combination of coercion and consent; when either one fails, the regime must transform or die. Hafez al-Assad's regime won the at least partial consent of a cross-sectarian peasant constituency by redistributing land and improving rural conditions. (Bucking the developing-world trend, Syria may have even experienced a migration of people from the cities to the countryside in the 1990s.[13]) Previously marginalised groups, particularly Alawis, found employment in the new army and security services, while the urban working and middle classes benefitted from subsidised goods and jobs in the bureaucracy. And although the regime failed to liberate either Palestine or the Golan Heights, a precarious and seemingly dignified stability was maintained. For a while Syria looked like an island of calm, surrounded as it was by chaos in Lebanon and Iraq and insurgencies and repression in Palestine and Turkish Kurdistan. It avoided war with Israel, but without surrendering. People could live in relative peace, and businessmen could make money – so long as they kept out of politics. This was the 'security bargain', and the final plank of consent.

Coercion was just as important. The Baathist army suppressed urban uprisings in 1963, 1964, 1965, 1967, 1973, 1980 and 1982, culminating in the massacre at Hama, the most traumatising of repressions, when much of the Old City was destroyed and up to 20,000 people were killed. The opposition of the late 1970s and early 1980s started as leftist as well as Islamist, but degenerated under harsh repression into a sectarian assassination campaign by the armed wing of the Muslim Brotherhood which alienated the minorities and most Sunnis. By the time the Brotherhood staged their armed uprising in Hama, the rebellion had been isolated there. Still, the fact that the regime felt the need to make such a terrible example of the city shows how little it could trust the consent of the masses. Descriptions of 1982 which have the peasant-worker-Baath on one side and the bourgeois-clerics on the other are far too simplistic. The Baathist Nur al-Din Atassi, for instance, a president before Assad, was a scion of Homs' most prominent clerical family, while most clerics since the fall of the Ottomans had emerged from lower middle class backgrounds. In Hama the regime was fighting Akram Hawrani's old constituency more than the foot soldiers of the old bourgeoisie.

More haunting for Syrians than the numbers of dead were the whispered stories of specific abuses during 'the events' – tales of rape and torture, of men dragged from their homes at night and kept rotting in dungeons for decades.[14] In the post-Hama years Syria became a kingdom of silence, a realm of fear. The *mukhabarat* (secret police) presence increased again, and the regime developed a post-ideological character.

'Assad's Syria' (as state propaganda called it) was fascist in the most correct sense of the word. It sought to replace class conflict with devotion to the absolute state. Following the fascist corporatist model, the peasants and workers unions, the professional associations, the youth and women's unions, as well as Party and army, were entirely absorbed into the state machinery. A facade of pluralism was provided by the National Progressive Front, set up in 1976, comprising the Baath and nine smaller parties which accepted the Baath's leadership – and by the People's Assembly, where two-thirds of seats were reserved for Baathists. Beneath the froth, Syria's was a one-party system, and the party was controlled by one man. The state cultivated a surveillance society, everyone spying on everyone else and no one secure in position, not even the top generals and security officers. Hafez stood alone at the apex – the Struggling Comrade, the Sanctified One, the

Hero of War and Peace – a rarely seen yet omnipresent leader who governed by telephone.

By the end of Hafez's reign all organised political opposition had been crushed and civil society, where it existed, was co-opted and quiescent. The business that remained was to appoint a successor. Hafez's eldest son, Bassel, was the initial choice. Presented as a virile figure, often on horseback, he rose through the military and was introduced to foreign leaders. But he died in a car accident in 1994.

So the succession fell on his younger brother Bashaar, who seemed an unlikely candidate. The gawky, slightly geekish ophthalmologist was brought back from the London hospital where he was working, and over the next few years his support base was carefully nurtured. Bashaar appointed friends to the military and security apparatus while his father retired those officers who might challenge him. In 1998 the new heir was given charge of the crucial Lebanon file.

The Eternal Leader's death was announced on 10 June 2000. In the following hours an atmosphere of barely suppressed panic oppressed the country. The fear was that Assad's generals would fight in the streets for power, or that his brother Rifaat would make a violent challenge. Neither threat materialised. As the organised crowds mourning Hafez turned to celebration of Bashaar, the constitution was amended to reduce the head of state's minimum age from 40 to 34 (Bashaar's age). The Baath Party met and unanimously elected him leader. Then came the people's turn in the theatre; standing unopposed in referendum, Bashaar won an unremarkable 99.7 per cent of votes, with a turnout of 94.6 per cent. On 17 July he became president, and a republican monarchy was born. The dictatorship passed smoothly from father to son. Otherwise put, the Eternal Leader would rule from the grave for another eleven years.

2

Bashaar's First Decade

Silence is the only thing left for Syrian society to express its existence and its refusal of the status quo. Thus, silence is taken here as a position, but it cannot last indefinitely, and society must, with its vital force, produce new forms of expression under the register of declarations, public statements and actions.

Riad al-Turk, interview with *Al-Hayat*, 17 January 2000[1]

The Damascus Spring is a pure media term with which the Syrian government does not deal. It only deals with reality.

Bashaar al-Assad, 4 June 2008[2]

Bashaar's personable image was skilfully projected. His pre-presidential role as head of the Syrian Computer Society – credited with introducing the Internet to the country in 2001 – suggested an outward-looking moderniser. Six months after assuming the presidency, he married Asma al-Akhras, daughter of a Sunni family from Homs. Brought up in London, briefly an international investment banker, Asma was now refashioned as a sort of Lady Diana for Damascus, heading development charities and speaking on women's rights – or as a 'desert rose', in the style of a Vogue Magazine puff piece.[3] The first couple made seemingly spontaneous trips to theatres and ice cream parlours, unaccompanied by security, Bashaar himself driving. The people around the young leader – such as Imad Moustapha, ambassador to the US, who wrote a blog on subjects including visual art and classical music – often seemed culturally sophisticated and intellectually open.[4]

Inside and outside Syria, therefore, people expected a new age. At his inauguration, the president called on 'every single citizen to participate in the process of development and modernisation', and for 'constructive criticism' towards this end. Checking all the boxes of liberal democratic discourse, he spoke of greater transparency and accountability, of shaking up the bureaucracy and fighting against corruption. But he emphasised that his priority was economic, not political, and he framed this as a continuation of his father's trajectory towards a competitive market economy. As for politics, he rejected 'Western' democracy as an inappropriate model, in favour of Syria's own type of 'democratic thinking'. It was necessary, he added, 'to develop the method of the work of the National [Progressive] Front in a way that responds to the needs of development'.[5]

This beginning could be interpreted in various ways; and, naturally, people hoped. Soon after the first speech, a decree prohibited the public display of the president's image – surely a stirring and evident break with the past. (The decree was later retracted.) Among the optimists who believed it would now be possible to revive the suffocated public space were a small number of intellectuals, professionals and cultural figures who organised public meetings, both to discuss the way forward and to disseminate democratic concepts. A key figure was Michel Kilo, a leftist writer of Christian background who had been imprisoned in the 1980s, part of the democratic opposition crushed alongside the Muslim Brotherhood. Riad Seif, a businessman and independent member of the People's Assembly, was also important – he established the Forum for National Dialogue, a weekly meeting to debate political, social and economic issues. The longest-lived group was the Jamal Atassi Forum, founded by Suheir al-Atassi and named after her father, a Baathist who eventually opposed Hafez al-Assad.

By the end of 2000 a number of forums (*muntadiyat*) had been established in and beyond Damascus, often in private homes, in which reform ideas were hotly debated. This was by no means a radical movement, and its demands were modest, but still it represented a significant change in a polity where for decades all criticism had been brutally suppressed. Before long the international media was talking of a 'Damascus Spring'.

The first statement giving voice to the movement was the Statement of the 99, published by the pan-Arab daily *Al-Hayat* on 27 September 2000.[6] Signed by 99 intellectuals, it called for an end to martial law and the state of emergency; for an amnesty for political prisoners; for the rule of law, including a recognition of political pluralism, freedom of assembly, the press, and expression; and for the freedom of citizens to participate in the country's development.

The state of emergency, in place since the 1963 Baathist coup, was a constant source of disquiet. Its official justification was the Israeli security threat; in reality it was a basic tool of the state's repressive apparatus, effectively suspending constitutional rights, legalising surveillance and media censorship, and awarding the security services the right to detain those deemed to 'threaten public security and order'. Special courts were established to deal with issues 'relating to national security'. Those accused by these courts had no right to representation and no right to appeal. Furthermore, civilians could be tried in military courts. Such exceptional powers had led to the incarceration of thousands.

In January 2001 came the Statement of the 1,000. This one was much bolder than the last. In Assad's Syria, it declared, 'Citizenship was reduced to the narrow concept of belonging to one party and to personal loyalty ... Patronage replaced law, gifts and favours replaced rights, and personal interests replaced the general interest. Society was desecrated, its wealth plundered and its destiny commandeered by those who became symbols of oppression.'[7] It directly challenged authoritarianism, encouraging a revival of 'societal and social institutions free of domination by the executive authority and ... security apparatus'. It called for a review of the Baath's position as 'the leading party in society and the state', calling instead for a multi-party system. It demanded too an end to social injustice, a more equitable distribution of the national wealth, and the abolition of legal discrimination against women.

Women were disadvantaged by the sharia-based Personal Status Laws in areas such as the marriage age, the right to divorce, inheritance and child custody. Marital rape was not criminalised, and reduced sentences were given to men who committed honour killings. Of course, gender discrimination was embedded within the deeply patriarchal mores of society at large. The women's rights movement, meanwhile, composed largely of the educated upper class, had little to say to ordinary women and had anyway been co-opted into the state apparatus in the form of the General Union of Syrian Women. Any women's organisations working independently of this framework faced harassment and repression. A number of women were nevertheless prominent in the Damascus Spring.

The easing of repression, however slight, released an enormous amount of energy. One result was the formation of independent civil society organisations. The Human Rights Association in Syria (HRAS), headed by dissident lawyer Haitham al-Maleh, was established in 2001. Al-Maleh had spent seven years in jail for agitating against the state of emergency and special courts, and for judicial independence, during his time at the Syrian Lawyers Union. The intricate beaded art work which decorated HRAS's office, an old stone building in Damascus' Baramkeh neighbourhood, was testimony to his time in prison.

Razan Zaitouneh was another HRAS founding member. Razan at this time was a young lawyer who advocated passionately for the rights of the persecuted, whether they were civil society activists, leftists, Kurds, or Islamists (for while the state was busy co-opting the clerical establishment, it continued to repress Islamist dissidents; membership of the outlawed Muslim Brotherhood remained a crime punishable by death). In the spirit of human solidarity for which she would come to be known, Razan also provided material and emotional support to the families of detainees, and often befriended former political prisoners whose long incarceration made it difficult for them to adapt to the outside world.

The Committees for the Defense of Democratic Freedoms and Human Rights in Syria (CDF), was re-established, and in 2004 the Syrian Center for Media and Freedom of Expression, headed by Mazen Darwish, was set up.[8] Although these and similar organisations worked openly, they operated in a legal black hole. The Law of Associations (1958) prevented the formation of any civil society organisation without government permission, and permission was never granted to a dissenting organisation.

Yet the regime initially tolerated the nascent movement, and took a number of further steps to nurture the reformers' optimism. By the end of the year 2000, hundreds of political detainees had been released. These were mainly associated with the Muslim Brotherhood, but also included communists, human rights activists from the CDF, and a number of Palestinians and Lebanese. In December, the National

Progressive Front member parties were for the first time permitted to open regional offices and issue public newspapers. One of the first to publish was the pro-regime Communist Party, whose *Sawt al-Shaab* (*Voice of the People*) was quick to denounce proposed reforms, declaring that civil society contravened communist principles.[9] A licence was also issued for the publication of Syria's first independent newspaper in almost 40 years – the satirical weekly *Al-Domari* (the Lamplighter), managed by renowned cartoonist Ali Farzat. The paper addressed taboo issues like unemployment and corruption, but steered clear of direct criticism of the regime's upper echelons. It was hugely popular, the first edition selling 75,000 copies in a few hours.

But the regime's tolerance was short-lived. In February 2001, senior officials were despatched to the universities and provinces to denounce the discussion forums. Vice President Abdul Halim Khaddam and Defense Minister Mustafa Tlass accused forum participants of serving foreign agendas – the same smear would be amplified during the 2011 uprising. With customary clumsiness, Bashaar joined in: 'When the consequences of any action affect stability at the level of a country there are two possibilities: one that the actor is an agent who is working against the interests of the state and he is either ignorant or doing it without intending to do so. The result is that in both cases the person will be serving the enemies of his country.'[10]

Now activists were obliged to request permission from the Ministry of Social Affairs 15 days before a meeting, detailing the names of all attendees (a near impossibility) and the topics for discussion. The forums in any case were infiltrated by *mukhabarat* who noisily praised the regime and intimidated the participants. The forums quickly lost momentum, and one after another they closed.

By autumn 2001, the Damascus Spring had turned to winter. Key figures of the movement were arrested, including Riad Seif, who had continued, without seeking permission, to attract hundreds to his Forum for National Dialogue (FND). He had also announced plans to set up an independent political party, and had questioned a corrupt mobile phone deal involving the president's cousin Rami Makhlouf.[11] Riad al-Turk was also detained after an Al Jazeera interview in which he proclaimed 'the dictator is dead'. Al-Turk was secretary-general of the unauthorised Syrian Communist Party (Political Bureau) – later called the Democratic People's Party – a group which split from the Syrian Communist Party when the latter joined the regime's National Progressive Front. Sometimes known as 'Syria's Mandela', al-Turk had been imprisoned in 1980 for 18 years. He refused repeated attempts to co-opt him in return for his release. The price was spending most of his time in solitary confinement, only allowed books and newspapers in the final two years, and being repeatedly tortured. He preserved his sanity by making artworks from lentils picked from his meals.

Others arrested included Habib Salih, who headed the Tartous Forum for National Democratic Dialogue; Habib Isa, a founding member of HRAS and spokesperson for the Jamal Atassi Forum; and Hassan Sa'dun, also a HRAS member. All were sentenced to between two and ten years on charges such as 'weakening national sentiment', 'spreading false information', 'attempting to change the constitution', and 'inciting sectarian strife'.[12]

In September 2001, Decree No. 50 intensified media censorship. Under increasing pressure, Ali Farzat's *Al-Domari* closed in 2003. While Internet access as a whole increased during Bashaar's first decade (from 30,000 users in 2000 to almost four million in 2010),[13] many websites (including Hotmail and Facebook) were blocked. Young Syrians became experts in the use of proxy servers to navigate the restrictions. Critical bloggers and journalists, meanwhile, were targeted. The Committee to Protect Journalists would name Bashaar's Syria as the third worst country in the world to be a blogger.[14] Travel bans were slapped on prominent human rights activists, including Razan Zaitouneh, who was also prevented from practising in court. Yet Razan was one of the very few to continue documenting the regime's abuses. Despite the rising intimidation, she went on to establish the Syrian Human Rights Information Link in 2005.

As the crackdown continued, civil society resisted with a handful of protests and sit-ins. One was held by families and friends of the Damascus Spring prisoners in front of the Supreme State Security Court in April 2002; another was provoked by the closure of the Jamal Atassi Forum in 2005.[15] But the movement struggled to convey its message to a broader audience.

* * *

Kurdish activists participated in the Damascus Spring by founding their own forums. One of the largest was the Bedir-Xan Forum in Qamishli, led by Meshaal Temmo. Then the Kurdish activist Habib Ibrahim tried to establish a cultural club in 2001: 'The goal of the club was to organise readings and lectures with well-known Arab writers and other public figures in order to promote dialogue between Kurds and Syrian Arabs. During one of the lectures, the authorities came and closed the event – arresting and torturing two members and putting and end to the club.'[16] Many other forums were shut down. Kurds remained a key target of the 'Arabist' regime which, despite its opportunistic support for Kurdish movements in Iraq and Turkey, had always repressed its own Kurdish minority. The arms of the police state were regularly raised against Kurds, striking heavily against political and cultural expression.

The 1962 exceptional census had stripped 120,000 Syrian Kurds of their nationality (around 20 per cent of the total), rendering them and their descendants (approximately 300,000 people by 2011) stateless. Those affected were categorised as either foreigners (*ajanib*) or unregistered (*maktoumeen*). The latter faced the worst discrimination, prevented from voting, travelling or accessing higher education or health care. They were barred from many professions and from owning land, housing or businesses. 'A *maktoum* friend of mine,' one Kurdish student reported, 'who had the grades to study medicine now sells tea to passers-by in the streets.'[17]

Institutionalised racism extended too to those Kurds considered Syrian citizens. Kurdish-language publications and cultural festivals were banned, as was the use of Kurdish as a language of instruction. A Kurdish mathematics graduate who wished to teach complained that the only employment available to him was restaurant work. 'Most of the teachers in Hasakeh are Arab Syrians, despite the three million Kurds who live there. The Kurds who do teach are usually members of the Baath and those who help the *mukhabarat*.'[18]

In 2004, a Kurdish intifada burned briefly. It was sparked when clashes at a Qamishli football match between supporters of rival Kurdish and Arab teams were suppressed by live fire. Thirty-six people

– mainly Kurds – were killed, and over a hundred injured. Protests and riots spread across the regions of Jazeera, Afrin and Ayn al-Arab (called Kobani in Kurdish). Regime symbols were attacked, police stations, courts and Baath Party buildings set alight. In Aleppo and Damascus, where they constitute a sizeable minority, Kurds mobilised in solidarity, and rioted when attacked by security.

This mass uprising was quite new, not only because of its size and spread, but also because it didn't result from party mobilisation. Rather, it was a spontaneous eruption of anger against long-term ethnic and economic marginalisation. The Syrian-Kurdish desire for autonomy was also bolstered by developments in Iraq, where the March 2004 transitional constitution granted Kurds control over three northern provinces.

The uprising was crushed after only a week when the army moved its tanks into Qamishli and other towns. More than 2,000 Kurds were detained, often without charge. Many were tortured in prison, including children as young as twelve. Five detainees died.[19]

* * *

In Bashaar's Syria as in his father's, the prison and the entire security apparatus it implied acted as the primary means of social control. The torture and ill treatment of dissidents were systematic and systemic. Torture was particularly widely practised in the detention centres of the security services, where people would be held, often without anyone's knowledge, for weeks or months of interrogation. Torturers acted with impunity, protected by Legal Decree No. 14, a 1969 law which prohibited the prosecution of any General Intelligence Division employee for crimes committed in an official capacity. In 2008, Bashaar extended the law to cover all members of the security and police apparatus.

Preferred methods of torture included beating, electrocution and suspension from the ceiling. The 'German chair' method strapped the prisoner in a metal seat whose moveable parts restricted breathing, often causing loss of consciousness, or severe spinal damage. The 'flying carpet' involved strapping the victim face down on a board and bringing the ends together to bend the spine. A former detainee of the al-Fayhaa Political Security Branch in Damascus describes his experience:

> I was detained in a cell at the end of a cellar, about thirty metres away from fresh air. During the first week we weren't allowed any medicine, even though one of us was suffering from heart disease. We were tortured with the 'flying carpet'. They tried to insert rods into our anuses. They swung us from our feet by thick cords, and from our hands by iron trammels. They used electric shocks together with the 'flying carpet', and they deprived us from sleep for the period of our initial detention [July 2003] until the middle of August. They even threatened to bring my wife! The torture went on every day from 9 am to 2 pm, with 15 to 20 minutes of interrogation, and again from 6 pm to 4 am.[20]

One more story will serve to illustrate the mind-bending extremes of humiliation and pain meted out to perceived opponents. When he was 19, Aziz Asaad was an IT student with a passion for aeroplanes. By chance he met an Iraqi ex-pilot, and was spurred to research and write an article on the role of air power in the Iran–Iraq war. He managed to publish the article in *Avions*, a specialist magazine in France.

Next he was arrested and tried for the crimes of 'seeking to undermine national unity' and 'disclosure of military information'. He still doesn't understand why, but thinks something in the article must have upset the Iranians, Assad's closest allies. He was sentenced to two and a half years' imprisonment – much of it spent in Seydnaya prison, where he met some of the Salafist extremists who would be released in 2011 (while the regime was rounding up moderate and non-violent activists). After the first year, and after paying a $1,000 bribe, his parents were able to pay him a two-minute visit. During this agonisingly brief encounter they were roundly insulted by the guards.

Aziz spent four months of his detention in solitary confinement, in the dark. Mercifully, he forgot his sense of smell. The cell was 90 cm wide and 180 cm long. It included a toilet and a tap. The humidity caused mould to grow on his skin. He caught scabies from his filthy blanket. Pus-filled sores developed all over his body.

One day (he had no way of distinguishing morning or evening), he awoke in great pain to find insects emerging from his skin. For a timeless stretch after that he was gripped by panic. He threw himself against the walls, trying to die.

The revolution erupted less than a year after his release. Aziz became a member of the Local Coordination Committee in Selemmiyeh, and a media activist after that.[21]

* * *

Despite the regime's sadism, Bashaar retained his personal popularity. Many believed it was the old guard, those who had built their fortunes on the cronyism nurtured by Hafez, and who had the most to lose from reform, who stood in the way of change. In addition, Bashaar's pro-Arab and anti-Western, anti-Zionist rhetoric worked well on the Syrian and wider Arab street – unlike the stances of other Arab dictatorships, it fell in line with popular sentiment. Bashaar was also credited domestically with maintaining stability in a region that was subject to the ambitions of global and regional powers. The 2003 American invasion and occupation of Iraq (which the Syrian regime vocally opposed) and the 2006 July War between Lebanon's Hizbullah (which it supported) and Israel were felt keenly by neighbouring Syrians. Syria hosted around 500,000 Iraqi refugees and more than 200,000 Lebanese.[22] Posters of Bashaar beside a triumphant Hassan Nasrallah – Hizbullah's leader – were pasted on shop walls and car windows.

On closer examination, the regime's vocal anti-imperialism was no more than populist opportunism. Bashaar had no qualms about colluding with the US-led 'war on terror'; Syria was a popular destination for terror suspects illegally extradited by the US to third countries for 'torture by proxy'. In 2002 Maher Arar, a Canadian citizen of Syrian origin, was arrested at an American airport while in transit to Canada from a holiday in Tunisia, and sent to Syria, where he was repeatedly tortured during a year of detention. 'I can't describe in words what I experienced', he said:

> Only a person who has been tortured can understand what it means to feel so helpless and defenceless ... I can tell you that during the first couple of days of the interrogation I was beaten with a thick cable all over my body, especially on my palms, my back and my hips. They beat me with the cable three or four times and then asked a question; if I hesitated to answer quickly they beat me again. This continued on and off for sometimes 18 hours. In between interrogation sessions I was placed in a waiting room where I could hear screams of other detainees who were being tortured. After three or four days they mostly used slapping, punching and hitting me on the back of my neck. They also threatened me with 'the chair' and electric shocks. At the end of every day they told me the next day would be worse so I could not sleep. I was placed in an underground dark cell, one metre by two metres, for ten months and ten days. The food was very dirty and of poor quality and as a result I always had diarrhoea. I lost about 20 kilos before they transferred me to Seydnaya prison.[23]

Despite its collaboration, the regime's international isolation intensified in the Bush years. In 2004 further American sanctions were imposed, citing Syria's support for militant Islamist groups, its occupation of Lebanon, the pursuit of weapons of mass destruction and the undermining of security in Iraq. Prominent neoconservatives boasted about how easy it would be to destroy the regime, describing it as 'low-hanging fruit'. The widespread fear that Syria was next on the list for American imperial ambition probably shored up domestic support for Bashaar. But the debacle which followed the 14 February 2005 assassination of Lebanese Prime Minister Rafiq al-Hariri – a crime in which the Syrian regime was deeply implicated – threatened seriously to damage the young president. The assassination triggered enormous protests in Lebanon – an 'independence uprising' which led to Syria withdrawing its troops in April, ending a three-decade occupation. The anti-Syrian, March 14 coalition won elections. For Syria, this was more than a domestic humiliation; significant income was lost as migrant workers – whose families often depended on their remittances – were forced home from Beirut.

The Lebanese events reinvigorated calls for change.

* * *

In October 2005 came the Damascus Declaration for Democratic National Change (more simply, the Damascus Declaration). Its signatories were oppositional figures and groupings from secular and religious, Arab and Kurdish backgrounds.[24] The Declaration made a clear call for democracy based on free periodic elections. Five months later, several hundred Syrian and Lebanese signed the Beirut-Damascus Declaration; this spoke of Lebanese sovereignty, and was the first declaration to challenge Syria's foreign policy. Ten Syrian signatories – including Michel Kilo – were arrested in the days and weeks following, although some were later released without charge. Kilo, human rights lawyer Anwar al-Bunni, and teacher and translator Mahmoud Issa, a dissident leftist, were sentenced to between three and five years on charges of 'weakening national sentiments at times of war' and 'spreading false information harmful to the state'.

The Damascus Declaration was a serious attempt to create a unified front, but the opposition remained fragmented. Splits came to the fore during elections for a national council in 2007, particularly between the nationalist/leftist camp, including Hassan Abdul Azim and Haytham Manna, and the liberal/civil society camp, including Riad Seif and Riad al-Turk. The division is perhaps better described as between those following traditional, party-led grand narratives on the one hand, and the new oppositional forces emerging from the Damascus Spring on the other. At the time, the independent leftist intellectual Yassin al-Haj Saleh argued that:

> the opposition must change itself first in order to be an example of change to society ... Neither communism nor Arab nationalism can solve the problem. The democratic opposition needs new ideas about Syrian patriotism and the current economic and social transformation taking place in Syria ... It must be independent from the outside. The only way to exit this crisis of failure is to focus on ... developing knowledge of Syrian society which the opposition in all its different branches lacks completely.[25]

Tensions also existed between the Arab and Kurdish opposition, and between the Kurds. While some Kurdish groupings joined the Damascus Declaration, seeing its explicit recognition of Kurdish rights as an important step forward, others felt it didn't go far enough in addressing Kurdish self-determination. The Kurdish and Assyrian parties which did join the Damascus Declaration felt marginalised in leadership elections.

The Muslim Brotherhood, in Europe, added its voice to the Declaration. Undergoing internal transformation, it hoped to take advantage of the more open climate to return to the domestic scene. Its inability to build a grassroots support base from exile made it reliant on an alliance with the overwhelmingly secular domestic opposition. And some secular oppositionists, lacking a mass base, believed the Brotherhood might one day provide one. The distance between the camps had been narrowing. In the 2001 Charter of National Honour, the Brotherhood had renounced violence and sectarianism – thus distancing itself from its tactics during the 1980s uprising – and committed itself to building a democratic state. These principles were affirmed in December 2004 in the much more ambitious Political Project for the Future Syria. And a meeting was held in London in August 2002, gathering about 50 Islamists, leftists and independents. It was the first of a number of such consultations.

While the Damascus Declaration (possibly to appease the Brotherhood) recognised the cultural importance of Islam in society, it also called for a civil state.[26] This may have alienated some of the Brotherhood's traditional support base at a time when the Syrian street, in tune with the regional trend, was tending more and more towards public expressions of Islamic identity, with a visible rise in the number of women wearing the hijab. Political Islam was winning victories in the immediate vicinity. In January 2006, Hamas won elections in Palestine, and the July War between Israel and Hizbullah later that year was widely seen as a victory for the latter – a Shia Islamist group. But the Syrian Muslim Brotherhood lost much of its credibility when it entered into alliance with former Vice President Abdul Halim Khaddam (who'd defected after the Hariri assassination), establishing the National Salvation Front in 2006.[27] Khaddam had been Hafez's strong man during terrible periods of repression, and was remembered too for his recent attacks on the Damascus Spring. Damascus Declaration members also feared the National Salvation Front was acting under American patronage. They stood firmly against foreign intervention, calling instead for a broad domestic coalition to bring down the regime peacefully. The alliance between Khaddam and the Brotherhood broke down in 2009 in any case; in deference to the regime's support for Hamas, the Brotherhood then suspended oppositional activities.

* * *

It must be emphasised that all this oppositional activity, though brave and in some ways groundbreaking, involved only a tiny section of the population. Plagued by infighting and boxed in by continual bouts of repression, the opposition failed to galvanise the street. It certainly failed to attract young people to its ranks, and almost 60 per cent of Syrians were under 24 years of age. The population in general was far larger than when political life was frozen by Hafez al-Assad's coup; by 2011 it reached 22 million, compared to six million in 1970. Society was now more complex, and more linked up, than ever before. Despite the factionalism and censorship of the 'Arabist' dictatorship, Syrians were more connected to the Arabs elsewhere – through migrant work, satellite TV and the Internet – than at any other time in their history.

Unlike the now ageing opposition leaders, Syrian youth had never witnessed a period of struggle. They'd only known the Assad regime; and their parents' generation was one of defeat, both domestic (in the crushing of the opposition) and international (in the loss of the Golan Heights and a series of nearby Arab disasters). Many were disillusioned by the traditional political ideologies which had been so distorted in the pursuit of power and profit. The three discourses to have grown from the anti-colonial struggle – nationalism, socialism and Islamism – had only served to facilitate the transfer of power from colonial masters to local elites across the Arab world.

Youth unemployment stood at a staggering 48 per cent, with young women four times more likely to be unemployed than young men.[28] The education system did not encourage free thinking, school children were made to join the Baath's Revolutionary Youth Union, and textbooks endlessly extolled the virtues of party and president. Overcrowding meant that many university students, particularly of popular subjects such as economics, never saw inside a classroom. Instead they bought copies of lectures to be memorised by heart and regurgitated at exam time. University access was expanding, but graduates very often failed to find work. The establishment of private universities under Bashaar, meanwhile, provided greater opportunities for the elite.

Political organising on campus was of course suppressed, and the Students' Union fully incorporated into the state apparatus. In Aleppo University's 2004 student elections, Mohammed Arab, a medical student, defeated the Baath Party candidate. His reward was to be suspended from studies. Later – after attending a Damascus protest against his suspension – he was arrested and sentenced to three years in prison for 'support of goals contrary to the [Baathist] revolution'. He was released after eight months, having been tortured.

Despite these conditions, more seemed possible in the years leading up to the 2011 rupture than in the past. According to a young Damascene, 'We were fed up with insults and humiliation in the army and corruption in the university system. After the Hariri assassination in 2005, there was something of a political opening. Young people became more critical in conversation.'[29]

* * *

Another reason why the traditional opposition failed to build a popular base was its focus on political reform rather than on the increasingly desperate economic situation of ordinary people. The pro-democracy coalition was comprised of nationalists, communists, Marxists, Islamists and liberals. It would have been difficult, therefore, to formulate an economic programme on which all could agree. But one was needed, and no serious effort was made to produce it.

Bashaar's declared focus was on economic reform – a perestroika without a glasnost, Chinese-style – but Syria was no China. The economy was in a mess. A major source of funding had been lost in 1991 when the Soviet Union collapsed. Syria's oil reserves, still an important income source, were rapidly dwindling. And economic growth was dramatically outstripped by population explosion.

Now the regime was attempting to move away from the predominantly state-controlled model of the Hafez years towards a supposed 'social' market economy. In a final abandonment of the Baath's traditional constituencies, it implemented wide-ranging neo-liberal reforms.[30] In 2000, the state farms were privatised, increasing intensive commercial farming and leading to a wave of peasant evictions. A private banking system was introduced, the foreign exchange regime was liberalised, private investment was encouraged, with key industrial sectors brought under private control, and subsidies – including for food and fuel, a life-line to the poor – were reduced. International investment flooded in, particularly from the Gulf. The economy was also kept afloat by an illicit oil trade with Iraq (in violation of UN sanctions) and by selling tenders in 2003 allowing US and EU oil companies to drill. In search of new trading partners, the regime continued negotiations on an EU Association Agreement intended to create a free trade area through tariff dismantlement.

Ultimately, high levels of corruption, nepotism and bureaucratic inertia stifled Bashaar's economic reforms. Their main consequence was an entrenchment of the business monopolies of powerful regime loyalists in place since Hafez, and a further integration of the state and private capital. The most notorious crony capitalist was Bashaar's maternal cousin, Rami Makhlouf, estimated to control some 60 per cent of the economy.[31] He owned SyriaTel, one of the country's two mobile phone companies, as well as ventures in tourism, real estate, banking, construction, media, advertising, the oil sector, duty-free shops and in the newly created free trade zones along the Lebanese border. The Shaleesh family, related to Bashaar on his father's side, not only owned such major commercial interests as SES International, important in the construction and automobile sectors, but were also powerful in the security apparatus. They were rumoured to be involved in smuggling and money laundering too. Former Defense Minister Mustafa Tlass's family (Sunni Muslims) also had major business holdings. Mustafa's son Manaf was a member of Bashaar's inner circle and a brigadier general in the Republican Guard. Manaf's brother Firas, a tycoon, was thought to be the second richest person in

Syria after Rami Makhlouf.[32] Former Vice President Khaddam's family (also Sunnis) enjoyed similarly substantial riches until Khaddam's defection in 2005.[33]

Crucially, the neo-liberal reforms were accompanied by the dismantling – by cutting subsidies – of the economic safety net for the poor. Inequality grew, until 50 per cent of the country's wealth was concentrated in the hands of 5 per cent of the population.[34] High unemployment, underemployment and low wages made it harder and harder to make ends meet. In 2004, just over 30 per cent of the population (5.3 million people) lived in poverty, rising to 62 per cent in rural areas. Those living in extreme poverty (that is, unable to meet their basic needs) were 11.4 per cent of the population (two million people).[35] According to Riad al-Turk:

> The issues that concern people are the issues that affect their daily lives. The average salary, for example, is less than 6,000 lira (about $115) per month. It's not enough; they need to pay rent and put food on the table and most families have at least five people. At best, it can cover only the most modest expenses like food. With that salary, at least three people in the family have to work, but how often do you find a family with three people who can work? ... The average citizen may work two or three jobs and there is no time for anything else. How is he supposed to get involved in politics? It's not possible because the mafia-like rulers have continuously impoverished the people of this country.[36]

In the cities, the liberalisation of real estate sent property prices through the roof, and new laws made it easier to evict tenants. This, and a lack of affordable formal housing to accommodate the rapidly expanding population, contributed to the growth of substandard informal housing on the urban periphery.

At the same time, luxury residential and tourist developments were being built for the urban elite and wealthy visitors. As the migration of poor and middle class families to the suburbs speeded up, new cafés, restaurants and boutique hotels crowded Damascus's Old City. People grumbled that a cup of coffee in the Four Seasons hotel – built on demolished Ottoman houses and owned by Saudi prince Waleed bin

Talal – cost an astounding 600 lira (about $11.50, or more than a tenth of an average monthly salary). Supermarkets (a new phenomenon for Syria) and glossy car showrooms sprouted in the ramshackle outskirts. Tax cuts on car imports without improvements to the transport infrastructure turned the city to grey choking gridlock.[37]

The situation was made worse by the severe drought plaguing much of the country since 2006. Rural areas such as the Jazeera (in the east) and the Hawran (in the south) were particularly hard-hit. By 2010 the drought had pushed between two and three million Syrians into extreme poverty, destroying the livelihoods of around 800,000 farmers and herders, and forcing hundreds of thousands off their lands.[38] Food supplies ran low as a result of crop failure and the death of livestock. The effects of the drought were exacerbated by poor water management, wasteful irrigation practices, and a focus on water-intensive cotton and wheat farming. According to Yassin Swehat, a young leftist forced to leave Syria in 2009 after winning a Deutsche Welle prize for his blogging: 'Bashaar's years were a fine example of the "shock doctrine". The UN had to distribute flour to the people. By 2011, 60 per cent of Damascenes were living in unofficial housing. A million Syrians had fled the Jazeera. Yes, there was a drought, but the regime "spent" $20 billion in 20 years on irrigation. This money was stolen.'[39]

The drought caused massive internal displacement. In their desperate search for work, many moved to makeshift urban camps in now overcrowded cities such as Deraa and Homs. This influx meant that water shortages plagued the cities too – during the hot summer months the taps sometimes only flowed once a week in poorer areas, while the lawns of the rich remained lush and green.

By 2011, Bashaar's regime had alienated the key constituencies that his father's had at least partly won over. The cross-sectarian peasant constituency, once the beneficiary of land redistribution, now suffered drought, mismanagement and neglect. The urban working and middle classes were impoverished by a particularly corrupt version of neoliberalism. And the regime's nationalist and 'resistance' justification was seriously compromised by the Lebanese retreat and repeated rounds of peace negotiations with Israel. The dictatorship had lasted more than four decades, but had produced no national victory to compensate for its repression of the people. Hundreds of thousands of Syrians had been directly affected by state terror; millions suffered the state's daily humiliations.

The regime's failure to fulfil a set of bargains – economic, political and national – set the scene for the uprising. When it came, the system proved itself incapable of containing and absorbing the dissent. The regime's immediate descent into barbarity would rapidly transform calls for reform into cries for revolution.

Still, in early 2011, the masses apparently remained depoliticised. The workers' movement was emasculated, the public space devalued. This made what happened next all the more remarkable.

3

Revolution from Below

When we revolt it's not for a particular culture. We revolt simply because, for many reasons, we can no longer breathe.

Frantz Fanon[1]

It was called the Dignity Revolution. What does dignity mean? It means being able to feed your children.

Yassin Swehat[2]

We all suffered from the grip of the security forces. I was interrogated thrice before the revolution began, and I had nothing to do with politics. The revolution came from the people's will for democracy. At the start we only wanted reform.

Monzer al-Sallal[3]

March 15th was my birthday, and the first demonstration. It was the most wonderful moment in my life.

Basel al-Junaidi[4]

On 28 January 2011, in the north-eastern town of Hasakeh, Hassan Ali Akleh set himself alight in protest against the regime. His final act – which went largely unremarked – mirrored that of Mohamed Bouazizi, whose self-immolation six weeks earlier in Tunisia was the spark that ignited a transnational revolutionary uprising known as the Arab Spring. Unprecedented demonstrations erupted in Tunisia, Egypt, Yemen, Oman and Morocco; they would quickly expand to Libya and Bahrain, and find international echoes in movements such as Occupy and Los Indignados. This mass revolt raged against state repression, elite corruption, poverty and inequality. The mobilisations were decentralised and spontaneous; they were neither led by political parties nor defined by the traditional narratives of socialism, nationalism, or Islamism. They were 'creating a new geography of liberation, which is no longer mapped on colonial or cast upon postcolonial structures of domination', a 'restructuring [which] points to a far more radical emancipation'.[5] They united people (overwhelmingly young people) across class, gender and religious divides. The slogan 'al-Shaab Yureed Isqat al-Nizam' ('The People Want the Fall of the Regime') reverberated through the region's streets and squares. The moment of insurrection entailed the temporary suspension of absolutist ideology, and what exactly was to follow the regime was not articulated – but civil disobedience, strikes, protests and the occupations of public space spread, networks and alliances were built, and tactics of struggle shared, not least through social media. By the end of January, the 23-year regime of Tunisian dictator Ben Ali had indeed fallen, and around the globe, people watched live images of Cairo's Tahrir Square packed with hundreds of thousands chanting for Egypt's three-decade pharaoh President Hosni Mubarak to step down.

The Syrian revolution arrived in this context. According to Assaad al-Achi, 'It was a direct result of the Arab Spring. People started gathering around the Tunisian, Egyptian and Libyan embassies in Damascus. People travelled there from Aleppo and Homs. They got to know each other, and the question of "Why not us?" began to be asked. These gatherings were tolerated up to a certain degree.'[6] Calls were made for a Syrian 'Day of Rage' on 4–5 February, but no one showed up. 'People just wanted to see how the police would respond. Nobody protested, but the riot police came out in force. This was the first message from the state to the people that protest wouldn't be tolerated. People took a step back.'[7]

But something had changed in the public mood. On 17 February, 1,500 people gathered to protest in Damascus's Hareeqa – that central neighbourhood named 'Fire' since the French colonial bombardment – when traffic police beat up the son of a local trader.[8] 'The Syrian People Won't Be Humiliated!' they chanted. The Interior Minister was quickly sent to the scene. 'Is this a demonstration?' he asked testily. 'No, no!' the men replied – but it obviously was. A couple of plain clothes men shouted, 'We're at your service, Bashaar!' A few in the crowd joined in half-heartedly. Most didn't. That evening Syrians sat around their screens, some open-mouthed, wondering what it meant.

It clearly wasn't a call for revolution, but it was certainly something entirely new.

A second Day of Rage was called for 15 March. This time thousands gathered in simultaneous demonstrations across the country, in the central city of Hama, in Hasakeh in the north and Deir al-Zor in the east, and in Deraa in the south. In the Damascus Old City, 200 mainly young people chanted 'God, Syria, Freedom and that's all', a play on the pro-regime slogan 'God, Syria, Bashaar and that's all'. They also shouted 'Selmiyyeh, Selmiyyeh', or 'Peaceful, Peaceful', words that would soon be heard across Syria.[9] The response was anything but peaceful. The demonstration was violently dispersed, and the *mukhabarat* made several arrests.

The next day a protest calling for the release of political prisoners was held outside the Interior Ministry. It brought the families of the detainees together with activists known from the Damascus Declaration and the new human rights organisations. Among those gathered were Suhair Atassi, who would soon lead the General Commission of the Syrian Revolution, and Razan Zaitouneh, who would help found the Local Coordination Committees. The demonstrators were attacked and around 30 were arrested, including Atassi, who was detained for ten days – but the conversation conducted at the protest led to results which the state was unable to suppress. 'Most of the big names of the civil resistance were present', says Assaad al-Achi. 'And it was from this gathering that the Local Coordination Committees (LCCs) were born. Everyone was charged with returning to their own area and starting a committee. So Anas Shughri returned to Banyas, Manhal Bareesh to Saraqeb, Omar Edelbi to Homs, Ahmed Tomeh to Deir al-Zor, Khalil al-Haj Saleh to Raqqa, and so on. Razan, Omar Aziz and Mazen Darwish stayed to work in Damascus.'[10]

Protests continued around the country in the following days, each met by assaults and arrests. The protestors' demands remained centred on the kind of reforms that people had hoped the Damascus Spring would deliver a decade earlier. According to Ziad Homsi, a tall, slight young man from Douma: 'We didn't ask for unrealistic things. We wanted a prisoner release, a repeal of the emergency law, a new parties law, and so on.'[11]

* * *

It was the southern city of Deraa that would catalyse the revolution. The city's conservative Sunni population had traditionally supported the Baath, but suffered increasing hardship as a result of state neglect and the influx of drought refugees. The city was ripe for unrest. Again, it was police brutality that triggered it.

Fifteen schoolboys, all under the age of 15 and all from prominent families, had been arrested on 6 March for graffitiing walls with the revolutionary slogans they'd heard chanted on Tunisian and Egyptian streets. The children were tortured in detention, their fingernails ripped out. When their parents went to plead with the local head of political security, a cousin of the president called Atef Najib, they were told: 'Forget your children. Go sleep with your wives and make new ones, or send them to me and I'll do it.'[12] Several thousand family members and their supporters responded by gathering in front of the Omari Mosque in the city's Balad district on 18 March, demanding the children's release and the resignation of Atef Najib and the city's mayor.[13] Security replied with water cannons and live ammunition, killing at least four people, the first deaths of the uprising.[14] The next day, the funeral for the victims turned into a mass demonstration chanting 'He Who Kills His People is a Traitor'. More were killed. In a tactic which would become routine, security forces occupied the nearby hospital, and any wounded who arrived there were detained or shot. Residents used the Omari Mosque as a makeshift hospital instead.

Briefly, the regime adopted a conciliatory tone. On 20 March, Assad sent a delegation to offer condolences to the bereaved families and to promise that those responsible would face justice. On the same day, thousands gathered again at the Omari Mosque. Now their demands were somewhat more expansive: an end to corruption, the release of all political prisoners and the repeal of the Emergency Law.[15] This time 15 were killed, immediately proving the emptiness of Bashaar's words. The enraged protestors refused to be cowed. They set fire to the Baath Party headquarters and the SyriaTel building – SyriaTel was owned by Rami Makhlouf. Seven police officers were killed in the riot.

At last Assad took some remedial action, ordering the children's release and removing Faisal Kulthum, Deraa's governor, from his post. But it was too late to erase the effects of the earlier provocation. Hundreds continued to gather in and around the Omari Mosque, its walls now plastered with posters of the dead.

On 23 March, security stormed the mosque with heavy gunfire. There were a number of deaths and numerous casualties; many of the wounded were abducted by the army. Still the protests continued. In the days and weeks that followed, hundreds were rounded up from their homes, the city's mobile phone coverage was cut, and military and police checkpoints were set up in the streets.[16] Two years later the ancient minaret of the Omari Mosque, built by Caliph Omar ibn al-Khattab in the seventh century, would crumble under bombardment.

* * *

The regime's violent repression outraged Syrians; as a result, the protests grew rapidly in numbers and in geographical spread. On 25 March, a second 'Friday of Dignity', tens of thousands protested furiously in Deraa; this time they tore down a statue of Hafez al-Assad. The nearby towns Jasim, Dael, Inkhil and Sanamayn also staged mass protests; in the latter, up to 20 were killed by live fire. Thousands gathered in Hama and in Homs, Syria's third largest city, as well as in the north and along the coast – in Saraqeb, Jableh, Amouda, Baniyas – and in Raqqa and Deir al-Zor in the east. In Lattakia, home to many regime figures, several protestors were killed. Demonstrations were also held in central Damascus and its suburbs, and in Aleppo too. Everywhere protestors chanted their solidarity with the people of Deraa.[17]

On the same day pro-regime rallies were held in Damascus, the first of a series of official shows of support. Many participants, wearing Bashaar T-shirts and kissing his image, seemed to be genuinely passionate in their love for the leadership; many others – schoolchildren and civil servants – were bussed in by the state for the occasion.[18]

From the outset, the regime's public response to the protests was couched in security discourse and conspiracy theory. At the start, as later on, it refused to acknowledge the existence of the popular protest movement. When state media reported the first deaths, it spoke of 'infiltrators' and 'armed gangs' causing chaos and damaging property, of 'foreign parties' inciting riots, and of 'Salafist terrorists' aiming to establish an Islamic emirate.[19] When the Omari Mosque was stormed, state TV aired footage – denounced by locals as fabricated – of guns and ammunition supposedly found inside.[20] Clashes elsewhere were reported as the work of external agitators. Later names would be attached to these phantoms – Saudi Arabia's Prince Bandar, for instance, or Israel's Mossad. But the grainy images taken on mobile phones and shared on social media – of unarmed Syrians being beaten and shot – told an entirely different story.

As the uprising spread the regime worked carefully to control and manipulate the flow of information. Nationalist songs were played day and night in ministries and other public buildings. State TV interviewed pro-regime religious leaders and intellectuals alongside members of the public who praised the army and president and bayed for the blood of the 'terrorists'. When the struggle militarised, TV endlessly repeated pictures of regime 'martyrs' (later, when they became an embarrassment, it stopped highlighting, or releasing the numbers, of military deaths). Al-Dunya TV, meanwhile, a private channel owned by Rami Makhlouf, specialised in frequently absurd conspiracy theories to support the regime's narrative of victimhood. It claimed, for instance, that Al Jazeera had constructed mock-ups of Homs and other Syrian cities in the Qatari desert, where it filmed scenes to discredit the Assad regime. It alleged that Barcelona Football Club was part of the anti-Assad plot, and that player formations during a match against Real Madrid were a code providing information on arms smuggling routes to Syrian rebels.[21] Another memorable al-Dunya moment was the supposed discovery of thousands of LSD 'pills', each branded with the Al Jazeera logo. A less crude PR campaign involved the erection of billboards depicting a raised hand alongside the words: 'I am with the law'. Revolutionaries soon pasted up posters of their own with the same raised hand but with slogans such as 'I am with the law, but where is it?' or simply 'I am free'.

The presence and movement of foreign journalists was severely restricted. Many international media outlets pulled out as their reporters failed to have visas renewed or were otherwise pressured to leave. Those permitted to stay were assigned a government minder and could only visit areas of unrest on state-organised visits.

White-skinned, red-haired Reem Haddad served as the regime's English-language spokesperson during the uprising's early days. When 10,000 refugees were driven across the Turkish border by the Syrian army in June, she claimed they were simply 'visiting relatives'. Her delusional comments earned her the nickname 'Comical Sally' (in reference to Saddam Hussein's 2003 spokesman Mohammed al-Sahaf, or 'Comical Ali'). She was later replaced by the much more effective Jihad Makdissi, until his defection (though he didn't join the revolution) in December 2012.

It was in this context – of shaping the narrative the regime would doggedly stick to in the years that followed – that Bashaar addressed the People's Assembly on 30 March.[22] His speech was eagerly awaited by Syrians. Vice President Farouq al-Sharaa, formerly a long-standing foreign minister and one of the more respected members of the governing elite, had prepared the way, promising that Syrians would hear things from the president that would please them all.[23] Many Syrians had remained on the fence until this point. 'Wait for Bashaar to speak,' they said, 'then we'll see.' People expected an apology for the killings and a declared intention to undertake serious reform. Some even thought the popular protests would be welcomed by Bashaar as ammunition in his presumed struggle against regime hardliners. After all, the man was genuinely popular. Perhaps – after allowing non-sectarian and non-ethnic parties to operate openly – he could even have won a real election, and gone down in history as hero of the democratic transition. For a moment, this seemed conceivable. Syrians inside the country and abroad, therefore, gathered around their screens for the televised address.

Less than an hour later, all wishful thinking had been dashed. Bashaar's speech demonstrated not only an unwillingness to compromise, but an absolute refusal to acknowledge reality. The president detailed the extent and depth of 'the continued conspiracy', which was aimed at Syria as a whole, not at his regime. He warned that Syria's 'enemies work every day in an organised, systematic and scientific manner in order to undermine Syria's stability'. Protests, therefore, though some innocents might be mixed up in them, were treacherous. The threat to the nation came from countries near and far, as well as from fifth columnists who incited violence and sectarianism; already in this flagging of potential sectarian conflict the strategy of frightening minority communities into loyalty was apparent. The Syrian state was cast throughout the speech in the role of victim – although of course it was the state that held the absolute monopoly on violence.

The speech was broken up by waves of applause and chants of adoration from the tame MPs. Frequently one rose to his feet, shaking his fist and shouting a slogan; then the rest would join in. At one point the delegates burst into 'God, Syria, Bashaar, That's All!' 'To which I reply,' beamed Bashaar, 'God, Syria, my people, that's all.' The crowd went wild, as if divine wisdom had spilled from the presidential lips.

Worst of all were the giggles. Preserving his habitual monotone, Bashaar laughed at his own jokes. This was probably intended to demonstrate confidence; most Syrians read it as further worrying proof of the president's disengagement from reality, and as an insult to those killed.[24]

The speech was followed by triumphant waves and smiles. In the street beyond the Assembly, a woman rushed Bashaar's car – it wasn't clear if she was protesting or seeking to petition the president. Security dragged her away. According to Monzer al-Sallal, later the commander of a Free Army battalion, 'Bashaar himself created the Syrian revolution, in his first speech. Then the people who had hope in him despaired of him.'[25]

An enormous sense of anti-climax was followed by a surge of unprecedentedly open discussion in Syrian homes, workplaces and cafés. Previously apolitical people were suddenly politicised. On 'Friday of the Martyrs', two days after the speech, tens of thousands marched all over the country, and were again confronted by clubs, tear gas and live ammunition.[26] In Lattakia people expressed their disgust with the sycophants of the People's Assembly, chanting, 'The People's Assembly is Pathetic and Sick.'

* * *

Violence continued to escalate through April, particularly in Deraa and Homs. On the 18 April, a funeral cortege of tens of thousands brought the corpses of protestors murdered in Bab Sbaa in Homs's Old City to the funeral prayer at the al-Kabeer Mosque. The Christian residents of al-Hamidiyeh threw rice down on the revolutionaries as the cortege passed through. After the burials, calls were raised to head for the central Clock Square, where the crowds only grew.

An eye-witness known as 'Ibn Homs' describes the diverse atmosphere at the square:

> More people flooded in. Freedom is like a magnet; it attracts the people that have been silenced for too long ... The chance is now available to speak up about the duty, to scream in the face of the suppresser, to prove all these identities that have been concealed by a tyrannical iron fist. Speeches were then delivered from the Clock's platform; a woman takes a turn, then an activist, then a sheikh, then an enthusiastic young man ... [at dusk] Preparations for another type of prayer began to take place, for a prayer very well done, for a Quran recited smoothly on the crowds ... All along the understanding of the true essence of freedom the way God the most almighty wants it, not like what tyrants want it.[27]

An engineering student known by the pseudonym 'Joly' corroborates the account. 'All the sects were present', she reports. 'People from all over the city and the suburbs ... until then people had been calling for the fall of the city's mayor. At the square they called for the fall of the regime. Of course the regime wouldn't tolerate it.'[28] As night fell, revolutionaries allocated tasks among themselves – food distribution, for instance, or banner preparation. They erected tents so people could stay the night and set up barricades to check those coming in. It seemed Syrians had managed to liberate a public space, that the Clock Square would become the country's Tahrir (indeed, they renamed the square so).

Military vehicles began to mass in nearby streets, and warning shots were fired. The protestors responded with chants emphasising their non-violence, 'Selmiyyeh, Selmiyyeh', as well as their anti-sectarianism, 'One, One, One, the Syrian People are One'. Religious leaders succeeded in persuading some men and many women to leave. But thousands were still present at around 2 am on 19 April, when the sit-in was assaulted. By then Joly was back home in the suburb of al-Wa'er, but 'we smelled the weapons and heard the shots five kilometres away. It was a terrifying, terrible and a transformative moment. That night we didn't know how many were dead, but we heard of very many bodies on the ground in the square.'[29]

Deraa's central Balad district, meanwhile, was now under complete lock-down. Snipers positioned on rooftops and government buildings shot at anyone attempting to enter the neighbourhood. The 15,000 residents trapped inside were starting to run out of baby milk, food and even water as snipers shot holes in roof tanks. Electricity, telephone and the Internet were cut off.

At dawn on 25 April, tanks rolled into the city, firing indiscriminately, even into people's homes as they slept. They were accompanied by thousands of troops, most from the army's elite Fourth Division, commanded by the president's younger brother Maher. The same Syrians that Bashaar had accused of following treacherous foreign-led agendas were enraged to see these tanks, which had done nothing since 1973 to liberate Israeli-occupied territory, turning their guns on Syrian civilians. Deraa's courageous young men jumped from the shelter of alleyways to chant 'Maher, you Coward, Take your Dogs to the Golan!'[30]

Snipers prevented ambulances from reaching the injured. Soldiers arrested medical personnel, set fire to pharmacies and prevented medical supplies from entering the city. The power outage had disabled the morgue, so the accumulating corpses were being stored in grocery refrigerators run on generators.

There were reports of soldiers refusing shoot-to-kill orders and surrendering to the protestors; this was perhaps a factor in the extension of the crackdown to nearby towns and villages. Thousands of homes were raided, thousands were taken and held in makeshift detention centres including schools, stadiums and fenced-off football fields. Many were tortured; some were executed.[31] Some were later discovered in mass graves.[32] On 29 April, thousands marched on Deraa from neighbouring towns to try and break the siege. They carried food, medicine and olive branches to show their peaceful intent. Up to 62 were killed, most shot in the head and chest. 'There were bodies lying in the streets,' one resident reported. 'People were injured, we could see them from our home but we couldn't reach them because of snipers. They died alone in the street. We couldn't leave our homes, not even to go to the market. We couldn't bury the dead.'[33]

* * *

While the state engaged in bloody repression, it also paid lip service to reform. At first glance, the nature of these reforms seemed to demonstrate that the regime had woefully misunderstood the causes and composition of the protest movement. Measures were taken in early April to placate two constituencies which had little to do with the developing unrest. First, 220,000 stateless Kurds were finally granted nationality.[34] Second, school teachers who wore the *niqab* (or face veil), and who'd been moved from teaching to administrative duties as a result, were reinstated. Damascus's casino was also closed (Islam forbids gambling).

Kurds and Islamists were the traditional sources of subversion and popular unrest, but not in this case. Perhaps the most remarkable feature of the protest movement at this time was its ability to unite people across religious, sectarian and ethnic boundaries. The language of protest was neither religious nor secular; the demands as expressed on the street were for political rights to be applied in general, not to specific groups. In retrospect, however, it seems the regime's appeal to Islamist and Kurdish constituencies was a wilful misinterpretation rather than a simple misunderstanding. In the years to come, the regime would stick to reading the revolution through ethnic and religious categories; largely as a result of its own efforts, these categories would indeed eventually grow in importance until they dominated the field of struggle. The regime's priority was to refuse any recognition of the non-Islamist civil activists, because these represented the greatest threat. There was nothing about them that could terrify minority communities or secularists; nor would their spectre encourage Western support for Assad. Even as security pulled these peaceful activists from their beds, and tortured many to death, a series of amnesties for political prisoners favoured Islamists, including the violent Salafist extremists who would come to dominate the armed uprising.

As for the Kurds, the regime was perhaps speaking over their heads, directly to the Democratic Union Party (Partiya Yekîtiya Demokrator, or PYD), which would later inherit control of Kurdish-majority areas. At the same time it moved to foreclose potential Kurdish–Arab alliances. On 7 October, Kurdish leader Meshaal Temmo, recently released from prison, would be shot dead by masked men. Temmo had described the Kurds as 'an inseparable part of the Syrian people', opposed negotiating with the regime and was organising anti-regime protests in Qamishli when he was murdered. The regime was most likely responsible.[35]

In March the regime had awarded a pay increase of up to 30 per cent for around two million civil servants. Then, on 16 April, in a televised address to his newly formed cabinet, Assad pledged the lifting of the Emergency Law alongside further economic reforms to tackle unemployment and the problems of the rural areas. He spoke too of steps to tackle corruption and reform the media, and called for dialogue with 'trade unions and organisations which represent professionals and interests throughout the country'.[36] On 21 April the Emergency Law was actually cancelled, and the hated Supreme State Security Court abolished. But the decisions were immediately rendered meaningless by two new pieces of legislation. The Emergency Law was substituted by a Counter-Terrorism Law which would soon be used to detain tens of thousands of activists, and the Supreme State Security Court was replaced by a special Counter-Terrorism Court. Also on the 21 April, a decree was issued which seemed to allow peaceful protest so long as permission was sought in advance.

The next day – named Great Friday by protestors, for the Christian Easter – a lawyer asked permission to hold a protest in Hasakeh. He was detained. Large demonstrations went ahead without permission in every region of the country, and at least 88 people were murdered by security forces. Once again, regime rhetoric was shown to be entirely unrelated to realities on the ground.

After weeks of abuses, people were increasingly demanding the fall of the regime; soon they'd be chanting 'The People Want the Execution of the President'. Young Syrians were refusing to be silenced as their parents had. 'The Syrian People Won't Be Humiliated' and 'The Syrian People Won't Be Insulted' were two of their most widespread slogans. 'I'm not an animal!' one protestor declared to camera, his face shocked, as if it were a new realisation. The recording was uploaded and shared on the Internet, as they all were. Perhaps this was one reason for the persistence of protest in the face of such violence – people didn't (yet) feel alone; their hopes and sufferings were immediately shared across the country and internationally. But the regime was behaving as if this were the 1980s.

The Canadian Ella Wind was living in Damascus at the time. 'The nonchalant dismissal by Assad of the people's suffering,' she wrote later, 'the arrests of friends and family members and an inexorably expanding awareness of the grim reality of Syrian prisons, as well as the deaths of popular and beloved civil society figures, all contributed to the rapid downturn in Assad's popularity. No conspiracy theory is required to make sense of the speed with which Assad went from being one of the most popular leaders in the Arab world to being so despised by his own people.'[37]

Why did the regime resort so immediately and wholeheartedly to violence? Why, once it became clear that violence only redoubled popular outrage, did it not change tack? According to blogger Yassin Swehat:

> The response seemed stupid at the time, but it was in fact very clever. They'd learnt lessons from Eastern Europe – for instance from the Solidarity organisation in Poland. Solidarity was allowed to survive and to work, and the end result was the fall of the regime. If the protests in Syria had been safe, everybody would have joined them. There would have been a real public space, and the expression of anger would have transformed into political dialogue. This is what the regime didn't want. They know how to play politics with foreign states, but not with the Syrian people.[38]

The regime was a long-standing expert in one form of domestic politics – the stirring of communal tensions for divide-and-rule purposes. Regime propagandists (and some commentators abroad) made much of the fact that most demonstrations started from mosques. This was indeed true – because places of worship were the only spaces where people were permitted to gather. Revolutionary Christians, Alawis, Druze and atheists had begun attending Friday prayers with the sole purpose of joining the protest afterwards. In any case, activists were doing their best to diversify the protest locations. People tried and failed – as in Homs – to lay claim to public squares, and students also mobilised on campus. On 11 April, Fadi al-'Asmi was the first student to be killed at Damascus University when a combination of security and Baathist students attacked around 500 protesting at the Faculty of Science.

From the very start, the regime also resorted to a campaign of rumours and false-flag operations to divide Sunnis from Alawis on the Syrian coast, the home region of top regime figures and at least half of the total Alawi community. In March, armed gangs were unleashed on the port city of Lattakia. They drove around shooting from their cars, screaming threats of rape and murder. In Sunni areas they declared themselves as vengeful Alawis; in Alawi areas they posed as vengeful Sunnis.[39] These thugs were *shabeeha*, a term with several etymologies, but certainly connected to the word *shabha*, meaning 'ghost', after the Mercedes Ghost, a car popular with the *mukhabarat*. Before 2011, *shabeeha* used to refer to the smuggling gangs based in the Alawi mountains who worked for lesser members of the Assad family. During the revolution, the term came to refer to the substate thug militias, financed by Rami Makhlouf and other pro-regime businessmen, to which much of the repression was subcontracted. (Later on, revolutionaries and rebel fighters would often attach the label pejoratively to anyone fighting for Assad.) In most of the country the *shabeeha* comprised paid goons of all backgrounds; in some regions, however, they had an exclusively Alawi or Shia composition. The massacres committed by these men at a later stage would play a key role in sectarianising the conflict.

Local communities very often acted to minimise the effects of such provocations. The Alawi writer Samar Yazbek describes an example from Jableh, her home town, where in an atmosphere formed by days of anti-regime protests met by pro-regime marches, and of *shabeeha*-spread rumours that each sect was about to slaughter the other, dirt barricades were thrown up between their respective neighbourhoods.

At this point activists and elders launched a mediation effort, and even succeeded in organising a demonstration in which members of both communities (including religious leaders) chanted 'Sunnis and Alawis are One'.[40]

But the most basic and frequently used weapon in the regime's arsenal could be named 'shock and awe'. On 3 June the UN reported that 1,000 people had died in the first three months of the uprising.[41] Nearly 3,000 (at a very minimum) had been detained.[42] More horrifying than the actual numbers were the details. Increasingly, the corpses of activists and protestors were returned to their families bearing the marks of horrific torture. Children were not spared. Videos were either smuggled out or deliberately leaked of *mukhabarat* taunting, whipping and electrocuting even primary school-aged children.[43]

On 25 May, the mutilated body of Hamza al-Khateeb, a pudgy 13-year-old from rural Deraa, was returned to his parents. Hamza had been arrested by Air Force Intelligence during the 29 April march to break the siege of Deraa. His parents posted pictures on the Internet – in his final hours the boy had suffered gunshot wounds, broken bones and cigarette burns. His penis had been severed.[44] Hamza's case provoked intense outrage. On 3 June, dubbed 'Friday of the Children' – the names of protests were now being chosen by vote on Facebook – there were still larger demonstrations. Scores more were murdered.[45]

The Syrian population was shocked, but not awed. 'Bashaar al-Assad is the leader of the revolution', remarked one young Damascene. 'Every time he kills someone, every time he tortures, he creates ten more men determined to destroy him.'[46]

But the horror was not evenly applied. Kurds in the north-east were rarely met by bullets, and demonstrations in central Damascus were dispersed by clubs and tear gas rather than live fire. The sons and daughters of the rich, and areas with large minority populations, were treated more gently. In the years to come, this pattern would greatly contribute to Sunni resentment.

* * *

AbdulRahman Jalloud, an activist in his twenties, was arrested on the very first Day of Rage. He was held in the capital's State Security Branch

251, and spent 53 days in solitary confinement. He was tortured every day. His first session began when an officer declared, 'I want to see blood on the walls'. This triggered a beating with a nail-studded club. Other torments included being hung from his wrists for hours on end, and being beaten while pushed inside a tyre. Often he was woken by a bucket of cold water followed up by an electric shock. The beatings and shocks were concentrated on his left knee and left shoulder. Over three years later, he still suffers pain and stiffness in these joints. He believes his torturers were on Captagon – an amphetamine-type drug very popular today among fighters on both sides. The worst torturer was called Abu al-Mowt, or Father of Death, and this man was clearly enjoying himself. But AbdulRahman found the psychological torture of solitary confinement the most difficult to deal with. He shivered in his underwear (these were the bitterly cold winter months), under a permanent strong light which broke his sleep. 'After a while you feel the torture is just your daily work. I used to spend an extra minute in the toilet so they'd punish me with torture – I wanted to be tortured to have a break from solitary.'

Later he was transferred through a series of group cells. One was two metres by one, in which 13 people were crammed; another was four metres by two, and fitted 30 to 50. On Fridays – protest day – he was held in a six metres by four cell with up to 200 others. It was forbidden to speak, and a *mukhabarat* mole was always with them. They could tell who he was quite easily – 'He was the only one who was clean and healthy. Who is clean and healthy in prison?'

The usual food – always dirty – was boiled potatoes and bitter olives, two things he's unable to look at now. But one guard was kind. When the other guards were absent he passed him small gifts – salt to gargle when his throat was infected, once a falafel sandwich.

One day he was summoned to meet an officer. Genuinely interested, this man engaged him in a four-hour conversation on the causes of the protests. AbdulRahman learned some of what was happening outside from their discussion. Later on, when there was a huge influx of new prisoners, and continuous sounds of torture in the distance, he understood a revolution was underway.

Finally he was moved to Adra prison, where he met people from all over Syria, from every sect and ethnicity. 'The regime's biggest mistake was to bring us all together', he says. 'The prison was full – at least 11,000 people inside. Riad Seif and George Sabra were there. So was Meshaal Temmo.[47] Meshaal learnt news of outside from Kurdish guards and relayed it to us. He also organised us. So for instance I taught computer skills to those who didn't have them. We memorised each other's phone numbers.'

AbdulRahman was released in July. He immediately chased up his prison contacts, and they began working. 'We blocked roads with fire and ran. When they shot at us, we decided to resist. We bought 300 slingshots and distributed them to the fastest runners. We spread information to revolutionaries in other areas – how to make and throw Molotovs for example.'[48]

* * *

The protests were growing exponentially. In July some of the biggest were in the city of Hama, scene of the Muslim Brotherhood's 1982 armed uprising and of the regime's retaliatory slaughter of between ten and twenty thousand. Hama had been traumatised for a generation by that episode. The 2011 protests grew slowly in the city, then more quickly after tens of protestors were shot dead. But by July the army, security forces, police and even traffic police had withdrawn, and activists were declaring Hama liberated. Checkpoints and barricades were thrown up to prevent security from re-entering, and neighbourhoods began to organise themselves, directing traffic, allocating drinking water and collecting waste. Activists distributed leaflets calling on the people to shun sectarianism and violence, and to avoid damage to property. During these days, no armed gangs emerged from the shadows to terrorise and loot. Christians and Alawis were not rounded up and shot. Nobody was whipped for wearing an un-Islamic haircut. All that happened was that demonstrations day and night swelled into crowds of hundreds of thousands – men and women, adults and children.[49] There was a festival atmosphere of song and dance. US ambassador Robert Ford travelled to Hama on 8 July and witnessed that day's protest – much to the chagrin of the regime (and of some activists too, who knew the regime would use the American presence to discredit them). It was 'the Friday of No Dialogue', and protestors were expressing their rejection of negotiations with the regime until it ended its military and security crackdown.

Perhaps Hama's governor, Khaled Abdul Aziz, was the reason the city was left alone. By the end of the month he was replaced by Anas Naim, and the army returned. Ramadan was coming; many Syrians hoped increased mosque gatherings in the holy month would finally bring down the regime. On Ramadan's eve, a new nationwide crackdown saw hundreds killed across the country, at least 100 in Hama alone. Hospitals overcrowded with dead and wounded were beginning to run out of supplies.

* * *

In comparison, Damascus and Aleppo, Syria's largest cities and economic centres, had remained relatively quiet. There were two reasons for this. The first was the intense security presence. Always thick with informers, the capital's streets were suddenly crowded by even more plain clothes men. As a result, protests in the city centre lasted only a few minutes before the *mukhabarat* and *shabeeha* turned up.[50] A massive police presence, and the positioning of snipers on roofs, meant that Damascenes were unable to occupy public spaces as the Egyptians had done (and the people of Homs and Hama too, briefly), though crowds from the eastern suburbs tried Friday after Friday to reach the central Abbassiyeen Square, at the cost of many lives.

Beyond that, many of the most influential Damascenes, particularly the merchant and industrial classes, had benefitted from the regime, either directly (through bought loyalties) or indirectly (through neo-liberal reforms). While they may have resented their exclusion from power, they remained nervous of an uprising that was raging most fiercely in disadvantaged rural areas and working class suburbs. The capital, by contrast, had been prioritised by the centralising Baathist regime in terms of resources and infrastructural development.

Although predominantly Sunni, the city contains many Alawis living in government housing and employed in the military or security services. Many (though by no means all) bought into the regime's sectarian propaganda and were fearful of losing their perceived privilege or, worse, falling prey to revenge attacks if the regime collapsed.[51] Damascus has a sizeable Christian community too. Less vehemently supportive of the regime than the Alawis, Christians in general shared their suspicions. The hierarchies of the various churches, like the best-known Muslim clerics, had long been co-opted by the regime, and advised their flocks to remain loyal. Even among the Sunni working and lower middle classes, there were many for whom the famous 'fear barrier' never broke. 'Um Bassam', a pseudonymous hijab-wearing retiree from Damascus, put it like this: 'These people aren't going anywhere. The young people don't understand that. They'll kill millions of us before they go. There's no use in protesting. At the end, we'll all be dead, and they'll still be on top.'[52] If protests in Damascus had gained a critical mass in 2011, events might have swung early in the revolution's favour, and the apocalypse predicted by Um Bassam might not have come to pass. But central Damascus and Aleppo didn't slip regime control, even as war flared elsewhere.

Yet claims that these cities didn't produce courageous and daring protests in the first few months are simply untrue. For a start, revolutionary Damascenes avoided the security in the central zone by travelling to protest in the suburbs; those originally from outside Damascus returned to their home towns and villages.[53] Even so, protests were sometimes held in the centre, including at the Umayyad Mosque, the fourth holiest site in Islam. Protests in the centre usually happened at night, or were flash mobilisations lasting just a few minutes but repeated again and again in different locations to exhaust security and *shabeeha*. Later on large protests were held in the Meydan and Kafr Souseh neighbourhoods.

And protests raged in the overcrowded and impoverished suburbs where migrants from other regions settled alongside Palestinian refugees and those forced by high rents to leave the city centre. Places like Douma and Harasta in the eastern Ghouta, Moadamiya and Daraya in the western Ghouta, and Tall in the hills north of the city, were protest hubs which suffered a militarised response very quickly.[54] As early as April, security forces had surrounded Douma, setting up checkpoints and raiding homes, arresting dozens. Similar raids were launched in Moadamiya, Daraya and Barzeh. Ziad Homsi describes his experience:

> On 25 April there was a huge detention campaign in Douma. The roads were closed. I'd been told at the internet café that my name was on their wanted list. They arrested me at home. They smashed our possessions and beat me in front of my parents; they beat me and shocked me with an electric prod as they dragged me down the stairs. In the car I was blindfolded and my beard was ripped out. Someone held a knife to my throat and told me he was going to kill me. He ordered me to say the *shahada* [the Muslim profession of faith], but I refused ... My little brother was also arrested. They used to torture me in front of him and him in front of me. They threw us into walls, and beat us, and used electricity.[55]

Aleppo was a similar story.[56] Syria's largest city and industrial centre accounted for more than half of the country's manufacturing employment and an even larger export share.[57] The city's merchant and business classes had benefitted from Bashaar's economic liberalisation as well as from the trade opportunities afforded by proximity to Turkey. They didn't want to upset the stability on which their prosperity depended. Workers feared losing their jobs, or worse, if they protested.

Yet the rural periphery, an agricultural region ravaged by drought and now a source of cheap labour, was raging, as were working class city neighbourhoods such as Salahudeen, Fardous, Sakhour and Marjeh, where factory and office workers, shopkeepers, street vendors and minor civil servants lived. Students also demonstrated on campus and within 'the University City' where the dormitories are located. (In 2012, the regime would close the University City, leaving thousands of students homeless just before the end of term exams, and in January 2013 Aleppo University would be targeted by a regime airstrike.) And Aleppo's lawyers protested too, holding a sit-in at the Palace of Justice to condemn the state's violence.[58] By 2012, shortly before armed revolutionary forces took control of half the city, protests in the centre were growing inexorably.

* * *

> *Now the street has spoken. The young revolutionaries have spoken. Those who have created the events have spoken. It is the people who*

> *have emerged from their silence today, and undermined the walls of the kingdom of silence.*
>
> Riad al-Turk[59]

Many Syrians speak of their first protest as a moment of personal liberation. Joly, for instance, the engineering student from Homs:

> At first I was scared to join in. But one day there was a very big demonstration which came from two directions – from the old part and the new part of al-Wa'er. When I heard the chanting – The People Want ... – and the singing, I started crying. Suddenly I was filled with courage, and I picked myself up and walked out to join in. My mother tried to stop me, but I went anyway. It was a beautiful experience. I felt at last I was participating in the effort to lift the oppression off us. Before that I used to be scared to talk even in front of my friends. I even cheered for Bashaar at the university, during his first speech to the People's Assembly. Can you imagine? It's something I regret very much now.[60]

And Yara Nseir, a Christian from Damascus:

> There was such a positive atmosphere. It sounds incredible, but suddenly everyone had good ethics. People stood together. Their slogans were very beautiful. Remember this is a people who'd been brainwashed and kept apart for decades, the victims of a failed education system, a failed social system. In this context, what the people did was amazing. I went to Meydan to protest. It's a conservative Muslim neighbourhood, and I was wearing a skimpy top. One young man asked me, politely enough, to dress more appropriately when I came next, but his friend said, 'No, sister, you wear whatever you like; we're here for our freedom, after all.' We really were ready to transform into an open society. We had great momentum.[61]

Syrians were discovering themselves, and their country, anew. They were learning the names of towns and villages they'd never previously heard of – places like Kafranbel, which produced such witty banners, slogans and cartoons each week – and seeing familiar places in fresh ways. Homs (though it is ancient Emessa) used to be a nondescript city beside an oil refinery, and the butt of a thousand jokes; now it was the capital of the revolution, a noble city to be praised and emulated. Competition and resentment between cities and regions was the old normality; suddenly people in one place were chanting their solidarity with others. 'O Homs,' they sang (or Deraa, or Banyas, or Deir al-Zor), 'We're With You Until Death.' And Arabs learned the Kurdish word for 'freedom' – *azadi*.

In an endless spiral, protests were met by gunfire which led to funerals, which led to larger protests, which led to more funerals. Everybody on the streets now called for revolution, not reform. Protestors were seen raising their right hands to swear to continue the struggle until the regime was toppled, no matter what befell them. By attending protests and speaking out, hundreds of thousands had burned their bridges with a regime brooking no dissent. By principle, and for reasons of survival, millions were committed to the system's destruction, by peaceful means if possible. What remained was to build an alternative.

4

The Grassroots

It is true that ... [the revolution] includes various factions representing the diversity of the street ... but mostly the initiators are young and not influenced by ideology. They have no dogmatic concept of freedom but rather a realistic view which implies that the totalitarianism of the regime is the only obstacle to freedom.

Mazen Km al-Maz[1]

We knew nothing about self-organised civil society. We had to learn.

Marcell Shehwaro[2]

Revolutions die with the death of the civil resistance. Those who forget how the revolution started will not know how it ends.

Message on a banner held by an activist from the Selemmiyeh coordination committee[3]

The Syrian revolution wasn't led by a vanguard party and wasn't subject to centralised control. It didn't splinter, because it was never a monolith. It originated in the streets among people from all backgrounds. The plethora of initiatives that emerged organically to sustain the revolutionary movement were all the more astonishing given the absence of civil and political organisation before 2011.

In the revolution's first weeks, coordination committees or *tanseeqiyat* sprang up in neighbourhoods, villages and towns across the country.[4] This was the first form of revolutionary organisation and would remain the nucleus of the civil resistance. 'The *tanseeqiyat* were trust networks', says AbdulRahman Jalloud. 'Just five or seven full-time revolutionaries in each neighbourhood, working in total secrecy, but linked up to other networks throughout the city.'[5] They were usually formed by young men and women from the working and middle classes. Many quit their jobs or studies to devote themselves to the struggle.

Their mission was to organise resistance in their local communities. They focussed on street action, preparing slogans and banners for demonstrations, barricading areas to protect protestors, and documenting events which they uploaded on social media. Over time their focus would turn to setting up makeshift field hospitals and collecting and distributing food and medical supplies to besieged and bombarded communities.

Yara Nseir describes the networked cells in Damascus as an 'underground parliament'. Leadership in her committee rotated every month. 'It was a beautiful experience of discipline and mutual respect', she says:

> Decisions were taken collectively and by vote, and this was completely new for us. We included educated and uneducated people, secularists and moderate Islamists ... We started with a core, and then brought more people in. It was dangerous to do so but we had no other option. We worked in relief, setting up field hospitals, in media work. We didn't know what we were doing, but the experience made us think, discuss and learn. We worked hard to coordinate the slogans of the revolution across the country.[6]

* * *

As the uprising spread, the need for coordination among communities grew. Razan Zaitouneh and others founded the LCCs to link up small revolutionary units, to synchronise their political vision, to document the regime's abuses and to convey information to the media. Their model of collective action and non-violent civil disobedience greatly influenced the revolutionary movement as a whole.

Assaad al-Achi describes how

> at first we focussed entirely on organising protests. In mid-April, because of Razan's international credibility, we established the media office. For a while, unintentionally, we monopolised the media. This allowed other Syrians to hear of us, and attracted them to join ...

> There was no template. Each used whatever social tools they had, but each organised horizontally. Every decision was taken by vote. This ensured that everybody was aligned and on board, but it made decision making very difficult.
>
> As the committees spread we started dealing with people we only knew online. Revolutionaries from Deraa approached us – a young man called Alaa from Dael heard of Razan and started sending videos of what was happening there. Next, committees sprouted in Dael, in Tafas, in Deraa city. The same process took place all over the country. This meant that we didn't know everyone involved; we couldn't check them or trust them absolutely. This is why our political activity remained more centralised than we'd have liked.
>
> On 12 June we were the first revolutionary movement to issue a political declaration to clarify the demands of the uprising ... It emphasised that the revolution's first goal was regime change, and called for a national conference for transition to a democratic and pluralistic state within six months.[7]

While the LCCs were not politically aligned, they worked to encourage unity and dialogue among the traditional opposition, the Damascus Declaration and other civil society initiatives; later they would participate in (ultimately failed) attempts to represent the Syrian street internationally, first through the Syrian National Council, then the Coalition.[8]

The LCCs promoted non-violent resistance and rejected sectarianism and foreign military intervention.[9] Their civil disobedience attracted wide and diverse participation. In October 2011, for example, they joined, among others, the Syrian Non-Violence Movement, Nabd (Pulse), and the Syrian People Know their Way, to establish the Freedom Days collective which, in December, called for a 'Dignity Strike'. Students, workers and small business owners participated. The LCCs documented more than 600 striking locations across ten governorates.[10] In Damascus and Aleppo there were strikes at the universities and in the suburbs, but businesses and government offices in the city centre stayed open.

Another of the LCCs' key activities was documenting and recording footage of protests and repression, aiming to counter the regime's narrative to both domestic and foreign audiences. (It wasn't easy to reach the wider Arab world. The main pan-Arab channels, Al Jazeera and Al Arabiya – aligned to the Qatari and Saudi regimes respectively – rarely took statements from the LCCs, instead giving air time to religious or elite figures.) Activists travelled the country offering training in webcam-use, social media and Internet security. This improved the quality of uploaded footage. 'Citizen journalists joined us', says Assaad al-Achi. 'Nobody was paid a penny for his work, but we did supply cameras, laptops, camcorders, satellite internet, and so on. I was the shopper. I bought most of the stuff from Dubai, in my own name and with my own money.'

By July 2012, battles were raging in Damascus and Aleppo:

> In this period we started feeling the enormity of the humanitarian catastrophe ... We moved into aid work – in my opinion this was the biggest mistake we made. We took on more than we were capable of – in terms of planning, funds and distribution ... International aid organisations wouldn't deal with us, because we were 'rebels' and not a sovereign state. But some states found in us the cheapest way to deliver inside the country, and the most efficient. Razan [Zaitouneh] is a factor in everything we do. If Razan hadn't had relationships with the European Union, they wouldn't have trusted us, but we used the goodwill she'd built around her name in everything we did. France, America and the EU provided some aid.[11] Later we sought funding of two sorts – money for the full-time members of the LCCs to live on, and money for advocacy campaigns – for detainees, for example, or the right to education.[12]

The LCCs weren't the only group networking between coordinating committees. Another was the Syrian Revolution Coordinators Union (SRCU), founded by Amer al-Sadeq. It promoted peaceful resistance while supporting people's right to armed resistance, and organised such campaigns as a boycott of regime-supporting businesses.[13] But over time tensions appeared within the SRCU between secularists and moderate Islamists. According to Yara Nseir, 'the real damage was done by the security situation. We needed money to survive, and here was a problem. Those with money – the Muslim Brotherhood and other Syrians outside – also had agendas.'[14] Possibly the largest grassroots coalition was the Syrian Revolution General Commission (SRGC), founded by Suhair al-Atassi. It coordinated with the political opposition and the Free Army, aiming to unite the internal and external opposition.

Many activists remained sceptical of any group claiming to represent them.

* * *

Students played a key role in the struggle. From the outset, and with the collaboration of university authorities, they were savagely repressed. So they organised in secret, forming the Union of Free Syrian Students in September 2011.[15] Revolutionaries from both public and private universities joined. Aleppo university in particular became a centre of resistance, earning itself the title 'the university of the revolution'. It organised demonstrations, founded a magazine called 'Voice of the Free' and campaigned for the release of student detainees. In Hama, students plastered stickers of the revolutionary flag around their university building; in Damascus they poured red paint in the streets in solidarity with students in Aleppo. All around the country students posted videos of themselves online, their faces covered with balaclavas, reading their demands and calling on others to join the struggle.[16] They contributed to many nationwide campaigns, such as one in solidarity with female hunger-striking detainees in Adra prison.

While the civil resistance had a large youth component, one of its weaknesses was the lack of an organised workers movement. Syria did not experience the mass industrial strikes which were key to toppling the dictatorships in Tunisia and Egypt. There were no major factory occupations or experiments in workers' self-management.

There are a number of reasons for this. The first is the structure of the Syrian economy. Only around 16 per cent of the labour force was employed in industries like manufacturing, mining, construction and oil.[17] Most workplaces in Damascus and Aleppo were family enterprises employing fewer than 14 people.[18] Many workers were traditional artisans, proprietors of their own workshops or small traders. Many more worked in the informal sector. These factors inhibited the development of a class consciousness which could have been a powerful cross-sect unifying factor.

The labour movement had been destroyed by the Baathist regime and no independent unions existed. The Syrian left, through the co-opted Stalinist parties, were regime apologists and thus thoroughly discredited. 'Normally communist and leftist leaders,' wrote Syrian anarchist Mazen Km al-Maz, 'through their ideological discourses and their actions, are supposed to study the bases of revolution and identify ways to prepare for social revolution, cause it to break out and triumph over the ruling class. Alas, on the contrary, we can see how these leaders do quite the opposite ... they justify totalitarianism and maintain the dominance of the exploiting class.'[19]

The LCCs did call for general strikes on a number of occasions, and in cities such as Deir al-Zor and Homs, the Chambers of Commerce participated. The regime's response was predictable – mass arrests and burned businesses. During the Dignity Strike, over a hundred shops were damaged in Deraa alone.[20] A factory in Aleppo was burned to the ground. One story says it was set alight by security forces. Another says the factory owner dismissed all the striking workers, and they did it in retaliation. In the two months following the strike the regime closed 187 factories and laid off more than 85,000 workers (according to official figures).[21] In the two economic centres, strikes occurred most frequently in revolutionary neighbourhoods, such as in Aleppo's Salahudeen district in July 2012.[22]

Although their membership remained small and they received little outside support, independent leftist groups did participate in the revolution, advocating class struggle. One such was the Revolutionary Left Current, which even established an armed brigade in March 2014; another was the Syrian Leftist Coalition. Many radical left activists remained non-party aligned or participated in the revolution as individuals.

The Syrian Revolutionary Youth (SRY) – a group working to bring a more radical vision to the street – was founded in May 2012 in Damascus's Rukn al-Din neighbourhood, and later spread to Homs. The SRY wanted to move beyond political demands to address the socio-economic factors which were mobilising the most impoverished communities. They called for free education and health care, gender equality, the liberation of the occupied Golan Heights and Palestine, and they raised Kurdish flags at demonstrations. They organised many daring protests, setting up flaming barricades to protect themselves from *shabeeha*. They were emphatically opposed to foreign intervention and continually stressed the need for cross-sect unity. They remained self-funded, refusing to be pacified by NGOs or co-opted into external agendas. Maybe because of this, they had limited reach. By the end of 2013, most of their activists had fled the country or were languishing in jail. At least six were tortured to death.[23]

* * *

Tartous is a regime-controlled coastal city where Sunnis are a minority and Alawis the majority. The first committee established in the city had an almost exclusively Sunni composition, because its activists feared Alawi members might be *mukhabarat* plants, and also because it emphasised Sunni identity. At the same time, another, Alawi-majority (but largely secular) revolutionary committee was set up, called Ahbab Saleh al-Ali (the Lovers of Saleh al-Ali – referring to an anti-colonial Alawi leader).

The activist and rapper Abo Hajar was trusted by both sides. He describes himself as 'neither Sunni nor Alawi', but perhaps it's better to say he's both. He's the son of a Sunni father, and most of his friends were from the Alawi neighbourhood where he grew up.

When the revolution began, Abo Hajar was a member of the Qassiyoun faction, one of the largest Communist trends co-opted into the state's National Progressive Front. Disgusted like many young members by the party's silence on regime repression, he left when the uprising opened new political horizons.[24] He and his friend Nawar Qassem, a leftist of Alawi origin, marvelled at their previous naivety. 'Just think, not long ago you were part of that ridiculous group!' taunted Nawar. 'Who are you to talk? You had a picture of Stalin on your phone!' replied Abo Hajar. Now Nawar is an anarchist. Abo Hajar is 'somewhere to the left of Marxism'.

When the Coalition sent a representative to Tartous who was widely considered corrupt, the two committees agreed to work together to have him removed. Out of this experience, Ahrar Tartous (the Free

People of Tartous) was formed as an umbrella for both groups, the Sunni and the secular. Soon it included cross-sect committees in nearby towns like Banyas and Safita.

Ahrar Tartous activists were able to organise demonstrations, but their most important work was creating social links between Sunni and Alawi revolutionaries. Abo Hajar took Alawi friends to Damascus to meet revolutionaries at protests, and succeeded in persuading them to join the struggle. Many kept their politics hidden in public for security reasons, but made themselves known to like-minded people in Ahrar Tartous. The organisation was planning for what Abo Hajar calls 'the day after'. 'Many in Tartous see the revolution as a threat coming from the east,' he says, 'as Sunnis coming to kill them. When the regime falls, there could be a lot of blood in the city. The Alawi majority may react badly, just to protect itself, so the best way is to show them that they can protect themselves by talking to these figures who are pro-revolutionary Alawis. It's very important that there are figures from both sects, already known to revolutionaries, who can act as mediators.'

Abo Hajar was imprisoned from March to May 2012. 'It was so tough for me', he says. 'I didn't want to leave Syria, but I didn't want to die in prison. If I'd gone back to prison I'd have died there, I know.' One morning in July he was drinking maté in his garden (the Argentinian drink very popular on the Syrian coast) when security came to the door. He jumped over the garden wall and fled. On the same day Nawar Qassem was abducted by security, shot twice, and thrown from their car into the forest, given up for dead. Somebody found him, he survived, and was able to flee.

'After 2012,' Abo Hajar continues, 'most of the male activists had fled or been detained, so women were the backbone of continuing activity. And women tended to find it easier than men to work with people of other sects.' Since then activism has died away in Tartous, and in Damascus too, as a result of repression. So many people have fled or been killed or detained. But Abo Hajar believes it will return when the regime falls:

> You can see it in the liberated areas. The activism never stopped. Life is continuing, and that's because of activism. Who else is working

> there but activists? The only limitation on activism in Tartous is the dictatorship. It reached the point where I couldn't move. When the regime falls, we will return. There will be no state. We will squat, as they did in Germany after the war. The activism will resume.
>
> As for sectarian tensions in Tartous, well, every day I hear someone else has left. But still the mediating figures are there, and they are sometimes prominent people, in art, in music, even religious figures. Now I believe in society much more than in the state. It won't be easy, but we'll move forward. But we need to prepare and train for preserving civil peace.[25]

* * *

People were working elsewhere too, to counter the regime's attempts to sectarianise the conflict. The LCCs organised countrywide protests under the banner 'Freedom is My Sect'.[26] In Aleppo demonstrations brought together Arabs and Kurds, and Christians and Muslims holding the cross and crescent aloft.[27] Marcell Shehwaro, an activist from the city, brought a group of Muslim protestors to the church to explain their aims, specifically to defuse tension over the Allahu Akbar (God is Greater) slogan. And a group called Nabd (Pulse) was formed in June 2011 by Yamen Hussein, an Alawi from Homs, both to promote sectarian coexistence and to organise against the regime. It operated primarily in secular strongholds and mixed communities.

One community where Nabd was active was Selemmiyeh, a city east of Hama with a large Ismaili population. It is also home to Sunnis, Twelver Shia and Alawis, and has long been a model of sectarian coexistence. Its secularism has been real – a genuine popular tolerance for difference, not the debased, propagandistic 'secularism' of the regime.

Selemmiyeh, famous for its motorcycle 'freedom rides', quickly became a centre of resistance. Its people welcomed those fleeing the crackdown in nearby areas; its activists smuggled food and medical supplies into besieged Homs (it was often easier for minorities to cross regime checkpoints). The women established their own coordination committee and initially participated in demonstrations. Later, following the arrests of female revolutionaries, they posted photos and videos online of 'domestic sit-ins'. 'No one can fool us with this lie of protecting minorities', one said. 'The Syrian revolution is one for all Syrians.'[28]

Organising in Christian majority areas was particularly perilous. Yara Nseir was detained on 1 August 2011:

> I was arrested early in the morning while distributing flyers. The flyers were aimed at the Syrian army, calling for their neutrality, as the army had remained neutral in Egypt. It was a civilised call to the conscience of the soldiers – a paper, not a tank. I made the mistake of working in my own area, where my face was known. What hurt me most is that it was the people of the neighbourhood who called the police. It's a Christian neighbourhood. I suppose you can say most Christians are against the revolution, because the regime has played with them for years, and because there's an alliance between church and state.
>
> Of course, not all Christians were pro-regime. There was a priest in our group; we were all Christians from the Qusar neighbourhood – we went into the suburbs to work; we did a microfinance project in Douma, and psycho-social support for traumatised civilians. When the church participated in pro-regime celebrations, we wrote a letter asking the clerics to refrain from politics.

Yara spent 18 days in prison:

> It wasn't too bad. It helped that I'm a Christian. They didn't want to provoke the community. But I and other activists from the 'minorities' were followed after our release – this intimidation resulted from the regime's desire to show that only Sunnis were against them. The *mukhabarat* came frequently to my home and threatened my mother. In the end she sent me to Beirut. But I shouldn't have left. Getting rid of civil activists like me was a deliberate strategy. We were savagely repressed. Most were killed.[29]

* * *

Women played, and continue to play, a key role in the civil resistance, with the two largest grassroots coalitions founded by women. Sometimes women were the only ones who could protest. In Bayda, for instance, where most men had been detained, women demonstrated alone.[30] In Zabadani, women regularly organised demonstrations, veiling their faces to avoid recognition by security, and worked in medical and humanitarian assistance.[31] In Aleppo, women founded the first independent radio station (Radio Naseem); it promoted activism and gender equality. In several communities, female-only coordination committees were established to focus on issues specific to women.

The revolution was challenging traditional and patriarchal gender roles. 'Civil resistance led to a real recognition of women's roles in society', says Yara Nseir. 'In conservative neighbourhoods women went out to protest in the streets. Men depended on women to carry supplies through the checkpoints. Now women like these will call to inform their husbands they're spending the night outside because, for example, they have to deliver aid. This was unthinkable before.'[32]

But it wasn't always easy, especially in more rural or conservative areas. Razan Ghazzawi, a leftist blogger and activist detained twice by the regime and forced to flee the country, temporarily moved back to a village in liberated territory in 2013. 'I am the only outsider (as in Syrian but not from the village), non-veiled, living-in-a-house-alone female in this village who's working among male revolutionaries', she wrote. 'It's hard to be an outsider all the time: an outsider as an active woman occupying man's spaces.' Although people found her lifestyle and political views strange, she felt welcomed by the local community. 'I am satisfied to see what kind of woman I have become, due to this revolution and its space, due to revolutionaries who are mostly patriarchal, but willing to work, respect and love me as I am.'[33]

As the revolution militarised, women's roles would be marginalised in many ways, though in others they became even more important. Many provided logistical support to the Free Syrian Army (FSA), and some formed female battalions to fight the regime.

* * *

Omar Aziz came up with the idea of the local councils as a form of local governance and to decentralise the Syrian state completely. Their main job was to provide administrative services to the community. Omar was an anarchist, God rest his soul – he was martyred under torture.

Assaad al-Achi[34]

Omar Aziz (fondly known to friends as Abu Kamel) was born in Damascus. An economist, anarchist, husband and father, he returned from exile in 2011 at the age of 63 and committed himself to the revolution. Working with locals to distribute humanitarian aid to suburbs under regime attack, he was inspired by the diverse actions he came across – the various forms of protest as well as the solidarity and mutual aid within and between communities, including voluntary provision of emergency medical and legal support, turning homes into field hospitals, and food collection. He saw in such acts 'the spirit of the Syrian people's resistance to the brutality of the system, the systematic killing and destruction of community'.[35]

Aziz believed that protests alone were insufficient to bring about a radical transformation, and that a new society had to be built from the bottom up to challenge authoritarian structures and transform value systems. He produced a paper in the revolution's eighth month, when the movement was still largely peaceful and before land was liberated, in which he advocated the establishment of local councils.[36] These were envisaged as horizontally organised grassroots forums in which people could work together to achieve three primary goals: to manage their lives independently of the state; to collaborate collectively; and to initiate a social revolution, locally, regionally and nationally. He proposed that councils network to foster solidarity and mutual aid, and to share experience. Aziz helped establish the first local council in Zabadani, and then others in Barzeh, Daraya and Douma.

One of those attracted by Aziz's vision was long-time dissident Faiek al-Meer (known as Abu Ali), imprisoned for ten years from 1989 for activities in the unauthorised Syrian Communist Party (Political Bureau), and then again for activities in the Damascus Spring. As well as assisting in council formation, he regularly attended protests and would later organise relief for civilians trapped in the besieged and bombarded eastern Ghouta. He was arrested on 7 October 2013 and imprisoned on charges of 'undermining national feeling and security'. In court, al-Meer responded to the charges like this: 'My aim is to maintain Syria's sovereignty, liberate the occupied Golan, end tyranny, and create a democratic country.'[37]

Omar Aziz didn't live to witness the extent of the challenges that would beset Syria's revolutionaries, or the successes and failures of their experiments in self-organisation. He was arrested at his home on 20 November 2012. Shortly beforehand, he said, 'We are no less than the Paris Commune workers – they resisted for 70 days and we are still going on for a year and a half.'[38] He was detained with 85 others in a cell of four metres by four. This contributed to the deterioration of his already weak health. He was later transferred to Adra prison, where he died in February 2013, a day before his 64th birthday.[39]

But his vision had a huge impact. Local councils (sometimes known as revolutionary councils) sprouted up in 2012, especially and by necessity in the north as the regime withdrew. With the regime's retreat came the withdrawal of government services.[40] Local councils ensured the provision of humanitarian aid and the fulfilment of basic needs including water, electricity, education and waste disposal. They coordinated on security with armed resistance groups.

The councils follow no single model, and each has a different size and capacity; members are civil activists, family and tribal leaders, and people selected for their technical or professional skills. In general they implement a form of representative democracy, and free local elections have been held in some areas – the first free elections in Syria in over four decades.

Yabroud, located in the Qalamoun Mountains 80 kilometres north of Damascus, is home to Syria's oldest church and a long-standing, comfortably coexistent Christian and Sunni community.[41] The town was liberated in late 2011, the security forces expelled. Then it managed to run its own affairs for over two years.[42] The local council, elected by democratic ballot, was responsible for the town's administration. Schools and hospitals continued to function. A council security patrol directed traffic. With new pride in their community, young people planted flowers and decorated public squares in the revolutionary colours. 'For us,' one activist said, 'revolution is about culture and new ways of thinking ... we are not terrorists as the regime claimed.'[43] The town refused to fall into sectarian division, and worked to promote tolerance. A sign in the town declared: 'I don't care if you are a loyalist or a dissident, respect yourself by respecting me'.[44]

Although it remained under regime control, Selemmiyeh, also established a local council. Aziz Asaad (whose previous imprisonment was described in Chapter 2) participated:

> It was difficult for us – particularly in the middle of a revolution calling for pluralism and democracy – to select revolutionary representatives by democratic process ... It was made worse by the fact that we were in a regime-controlled area and so constantly feared arrest. When we formed the local council in Selemmiyeh we adopted what you could call 'the democracy of the revolutionary elite'. In secret we chose eleven people from about 55 ... Then I and other activists set up the media office for Selemmiyeh city and countryside in order to present more reliable news and to combat the informational chaos in which stories and videos were floating unedited and disordered. In this capacity I accompanied several Free Army brigades to their battles, to witness and record.[45]

* * *

The experience of Manbij highlights some of the successes and challenges of self-management in liberated areas.[46] Located in the Aleppo governorate, it's a socially conservative city serving a large agricultural hinterland. In 2011, Monzer al-Sallal and his friends

> did nothing but work on protests and strikes. We focussed on civil resistance from the beginning to the liberation ... We set up a revolutionary council, at the start in secret. We had twelve offices – one in charge of protests, a legal office, a media office, a security office, and so on. We were preparing so we could run our city when the regime fell, and for any other eventuality. And when Manbij was liberated on 19 July 2012, we were able to do that. All the civil servants stayed at work, the hospital continued to operate, even the bank continued paying salaries – it was the only bank in the

> liberated areas which was able to do so ... In the secret stage, voting wasn't possible. Everyone in the council was wanted for execution by the regime. But after the liberation we held elections for council positions.[47]

Syrian-American academic Yasser Munif visited Manbij in 2013, when Islamist groups were raising their profile in the city:

> The town is managed by a revolutionary council, with a sharia court and a police force. The revolutionary council is made of 20 persons and acts as the executive body. Then you have the Revolutionary Trustee Council that is made of some 600 people [including from the tribes and Kurdish community but no women] and acts as a sort of legislative house. The Trustee Council meets on a weekly basis. There was originally a revolutionary court, which was a positive experience with seculars and liberals part of it, but they had no funding and no police to implement decisions and to keep order. However, five months ago, a police force was established with around 60 members, which is improving security conditions. Meanwhile, a sharia court replaced the revolutionary court. So unfortunately, it's a more religious form of law that is applied, but at least the court is now better funded and with the presence of a police force its decisions are being implemented. The city also has several newspapers and it has what is, to my knowledge, the first and only trade union established in the liberated areas. The union is already campaigning for a rise in wages.[48]

* * *

Some councils have been plagued by power struggles; some proved unable to cast off the authoritarian structures inherited from the regime. Tensions often arose between younger revolutionaries and traditional leaders. Women faced exclusion from council positions despite campaigns by activists calling for their representation. While most councils are neither party aligned nor ideological, the Muslim Brotherhood, for instance, tried to dominate Aleppo's provincial council. Many councils, particularly in rural or depopulated areas, failed to find the necessary technical and professional expertise.

At the start, most were funded by donations from local or expatriate Syrians as well as by levying taxes. As their needs increased they became reliant on alternative sources, often from NGOs or foreign governments. In March 2013, the external opposition's Coalition created a Local Administrative Council Support Unit in order to institutionalise the local councils and provide them with support. Some of this funding came from the Western powers which tepidly backed the Coalition. (The political trajectory of the Coalition will be examined in Chapter 9.) AbdulRahman Jalloud refers to this when he complains that 'the local councils set up in 2013 took influence and funds from the West. Therefore they weren't so grass-roots'.[49] Yet most remained chronically underfunded. Speaking from the eastern Ghouta in September 2013, Razan Zaitouneh warned that without assistance to the council, people would be 'forced to be dependent on the battalions that volunteer to provide such services in return ... [for] loyalty and power'.[50] In some areas militant Islamist groups stopped the work of the local councils, or set up parallel sharia commissions.

Self-criticism provoked adaptation and improvement. In 2013, Assaad al-Achi worked within the LCCs to counteract the effects of the regime's siege on Douma:

> Gradually we realised that aid was turning the people into consumers, so we focussed more on development and trying to restart the economy – even in these conditions. Our pilot project in Douma was the Local Development and Small Project Support Office. Our main goal was to support the nascent administrative structures in the liberated areas. In Douma, these were the local administrative council, the eastern Ghouta Unified Services Office, the Unified Relief Office, the traffic police, and so on. We funded, monitored and evaluated performance. We supported such projects as a cleaning campaign, road maintenance and extracting methane from waste to produce renewable energy. On a big scale that becomes too dangerous, but on a small scale it worked.[51]

In Deir al-Zor, meanwhile, activists campaigned for people to participate in monitoring the performance of the local councils.[52]

* * *

An inspiring social revolution was also underway in the Kurdish regions, where new and sometimes radical alternatives to totalitarianism were being developed. Following the apparently coordinated withdrawal of Assad's forces and the transfer of control of most security and administrative bodies to the PYD in July 2012, an Autonomous Region was set up in the Kurdish-majority areas of Afrin, Jazeera (around Qamishli) and Kobani – also known as Rojava, or Western Kurdistan.[53] The PYD is closely linked to the Kurdistan Workers' Party (Partiya Karkerên Kurdistanê, or PKK) in Turkey, and is the only Syrian-Kurdish group in control of (or allowed to control) an armed force – the People's Protection Units. The PKK, originally a Marxist-Leninist party, had in recent years adopted the concept of 'democratic confederalism', inspired by anarchist thinker Murray Bookchin. So too had the PYD.[54]

In November 2013, a transitional government was established by the PYD and smaller allied groups. A Social Contract acts as a kind of constitution for Rojava, setting out the principles and structures for democratic autonomy and local self-governance within the existing state.[55] It stresses the desire to 'build a society free from authoritarianism, militarism, centralism and the intervention of religious authority in public affairs'. The contract promotes unity and coexistence among the region's diverse ethnic and religious groups, a respect for human rights, and an end to gender discrimination; it also affirms the right to self-determination and the principle of self-government for the cantons.

In each canton, councils and public institutions have been established through direct elections. These include the administrative structures dealing with security, service provision and justice. All are linked up in a decentralised confederation. Through local communes, people also self-manage areas such as health, education, environmental protection and food supply, discuss community problems, and mediate to resolve disputes before they go to court. Workers' cooperatives have also been set up. The region's minority ethnicities – Arabs, Yezidis and Assyrians – are included in these grassroots forums, and 40 per cent of commune and council members are women.

A representative of Tev-dem (the Movement for a Democratic Society), which coordinates between grassroots structures and the parliament, gives an overview:

> Our system rests on the communes, made up of neighborhoods of 300 people. The communes have co-presidents, and there are co-presidents at all levels, from commune to canton administration. In each commune there are five or six different committees. Communes work in two ways. First, they resolve problems quickly and early – for example, a technical problem or a social one. Some jobs can be done in five minutes, but if you send it to the state, it gets caught in a bureaucracy. So we can solve issues quickly. The second way is political. If we speak about true democracy, decisions can't be made from the top and go to the bottom, they have to be made at the bottom and then go up in degrees. There are also district councils and city councils, up to the canton. The principle is 'few problems, many resolutions'.[56]

But there's a worm in the apple. In the Kurdish regions, the revolutionary process was more top-down and party-led than elsewhere. Despite its supposed libertarian turn, the PYD remains a highly centralised and authoritarian party, and it exercises ultimate control over the canton-level councils. It has been accused of suppressing political opposition and peaceful protest, closing down independent radio stations, and assassinating, imprisoning and torturing opponents.[57] It has implemented compulsory conscription and (like all armed forces in the country) includes child soldiers in its ranks. PYD leader Salih Muslim has also called for the expulsion of Arabs from the region – this comes in the context of Baathist Arabisation policies, but still hints at worrying chauvinist trends.[58]

Noor Bakeer, a teacher from a village near Afrin, describes his disappointment: 'It was splendid when Afrin came out en masse chanting for freedom and for the KNC. I can't describe my feelings; I felt strong and enthusiastic; I felt our life was finally beginning. But the following

Friday when people gathered to demonstrate, masked thugs from the PYD dispersed them by force. Lots of young people were wounded.'[59]

The KNC to which Noor refers is the Kurdistan National Council, a grouping of 15 Syrian-Kurdish parties founded in October 2011. The KNC was supported by the Kurdistan Regional Government in Iraq, and it later joined the Coalition. It was easily marginalised by the PYD, for the simple reason that the PYD was armed. Noor continues:

> As a Kurd I know all about the criminal practices of the Assad regime. Even before the revolution, hundreds of Kurdish activists were arrested and too many of them died in prison. We were surrounded by corruption and our living standards were low. But nothing much changed when the regime withdrew from Afrin and the PYD took over. The terror and repression continued as the PYD imposed themselves by force. They stopped other political parties from operating and tried to rule alone. PYD double standards and the fact they collaborated with the regime made [Arab] opposition forces consider Afrin an enemy of the revolution. This led to their punitive actions against Afrin, such as imposing an unjust siege on the city which doubled the citizens' suffering. As a result, many people, especially the educated, decided to leave.

Noor was working with a humanitarian organisation called Bihar:[60]

> We distributed aid in secret because the PYD banned us. They harassed us constantly, confiscating the aid, arresting our workers and accusing them of being agents for Turkey or the FSA. The real reason for this treatment is that we refused to obey their orders. Later they did sign an agreement permitting us to work freely in Afrin. This is because they needed us. After the huge exodus from Aleppo, they found themselves unable to meet the needs of the displaced.

In Rojava, revolutionary energies are channelled, controlled and sometimes repressed by an authoritarian party. Yet on a Kurdish national level, the experiment so far has been an undoubted success.

Kurds established their own police and courts; Kurdish became the language of instruction in schools.

It's to be hoped that the gap between the progressive and more retrograde aspects of the PYD programme will be narrowed in the future. The vestiges of PYD authoritarianism may in the end be dissolved by the ideas spread under its name.

* * *

The regime's response to non-violent struggle was unfailingly brutal. In central Damascus, four women marched through Medhat Basha market in late 2012, dressed in white wedding gowns. These 'Brides of Peace' held signs calling for an end to violence.[61] All were imprisoned, later released. Clearly they were less of a threat than Ghaith Matar, a 26-year-old member of Daraya's coordinating committee and a well-known advocate of peaceful resistance. Under his influence protestors offered flowers and bottles of water to the soldiers sent to shoot them. Ghaith was arrested in September 2011. A few days later his tortured corpse was returned to his family. In another example, activist and film-maker Bassel Shehadeh was arrested for protesting in the Meydan area of Damascus. Released, he moved to Homs to document the repression and to train activists in video production and editing. He died under shelling on 28 May 2012.[62] Tens of thousands of civil revolutionaries were disappearing into Assad's dungeons.

As the revolution militarised, the vibrant popular movement gradually lost its prominence. Civil revolutionaries adapted and continued their work, trying to keep their ideals alive, but necessarily focussing first on personal and community survival. Still, what they have achieved, and continue to achieve, in the most difficult of circumstances, is as worthy of celebration as it is absent from media accounts. Pressed on all sides, these are people who've truly made history, enough to compete with and for a moment drown the savage history made by states.

5

Militarisation and Liberation

The strategies of nonviolence cannot defeat the state – they tend to reflect a lack of understanding of the very nature of the state. The power of the state is self-perpetuating; it will defeat liberation movements with any means at its disposal. If attempts to overthrow such a power structure survive the first stages of repression, the elite will turn the conflict into a military one, and people using nonviolent tactics cannot defeat a military. Pacifism cannot defend itself against uncompromising extermination.

Peter Gelderloos[1]

The idea of liberating land was wrong. Weapons began to kill the revolution, and so did the regional interventions. But worst of all was the regime's constantly escalating violence. We must criticise the revolution, but we must also remember the first cause of all this.

Yara Nseir[2]

On 29 August 2011, the LCCs issued the following statement:

> In an unprecedented move over the past several days, Syrians in Syria and abroad have been calling for Syrians to take up arms, or for international military intervention. This call comes [after] five and a half months of the Syrian regime's systematic abuse of the Syrian people, whereby tens of thousands of peaceful protesters have been detained and tortured, and more than 2,500 killed. The regime has given every indication that it will continue its brutal approach, while the majority of Syrians feel they are unprotected in their own homeland in the face of the regime's crimes.
>
> While we understand the motivation to take up arms or call for military intervention, we specifically reject this position as we find it unacceptable politically, nationally, and ethically.

Controlling the big guns and fielding the best-trained fighters, the LCCs argued, the regime would emerge victorious from any pitched battle. Oppositional violence, moreover, would alienate those constituencies the uprising was working so hard to win over – the upper-middle class, religious minorities, the stability-firsters – and 'would minimise popular participation in the revolution'. It would serve Assadist propaganda, pushing the uprising off the moral high ground and thereby relieving international pressure against the regime. Furthermore, it would poison the future:

> We believe that the overthrow of the regime is the initial goal of the Revolution, but it is not an end in itself. The end goal is freedom for Syria and all Syrians. The method by which the regime is overthrown is an indication of what Syria will be like post-regime. If we maintain our peaceful demonstrations, which include our cities, towns, and villages; and our men, women, and children, the possibility of democracy in our country is much greater. If an armed confrontation or international military intervention becomes a reality, it will be virtually impossible to establish a legitimate foundation for a proud future Syria.[3]

This call was posted to social media and forwarded using email by religious and working class as well as secular and bourgeois Syrians. The 'selmiyyeh' imperative still resounded on Syrian streets. Yet by the spring of 2012 the armed struggle had come to dominate. In June 2012, UN Head of Peacekeeping Herve Ladsous referred to the Syrian situation as a civil war, and in July the Red Cross formally declared it to be so. Activists responded angrily to the designation on the grounds that the conflict remained essentially a one-sided regime assault against a civilian population only occasionally defended by poorly armed and uncoordinated militias. But nobody could deny that a cycle of mutual violence had taken root.

In the months and years that followed, everything the LCCs statement had feared came to pass. Militarisation – more specifically the scramble for weapons and funds – transformed the revolution from a leaderless movement into a cacophony of a thousand competing leaders, from horizontalism to a jostle of hierarchies. The horizontally organised committees and councils continued to work, and their work, increasingly focussed on basic community survival, became even more crucial in the absence not only of the state but sometimes of any infrastructure whatsoever. Furthermore, women's role in the revolution was increasingly marginalised. Although women, particularly Kurds, did sometimes take up arms, they were largely excluded from the military struggle – a male hegemonic domain – and the civil struggle became much less visible, although no less important.[4] As indiscipline and opportunist criminality tainted the resistance, and later as jihadism flourished, the regime found an excuse for its already steadily escalating violence, and gradually persuaded many at home and abroad that its survival was the least worst option for Syria and the region.

Still, abstract criticisms of the revolution's militarisation miss the point. Syria's revolutionaries didn't make a formal collective decision to pick up arms – quite the opposite; rather, a million individual decisions were made under fire. Yassin Swehat puts it like this: 'It wasn't a choice. Look at Homs. When thousands are praying in a square, peaceful, unarmed, and they are shot at, murdered – what do you expect to happen next?'[5]

Violence has its own inevitable momentum. When residential areas are subjected to military attack, when neighbourhoods experience the horror of children tortured to death, when young men are randomly rounded up and beaten, soon they will respond. Before moving on to media work, Ziad Homsi, a thin man with an intellectual demeanour, fought in Douma, in the Damascus suburbs: 'It was a matter of self-defence. Everyone defended his own home, his own alley. Brigades were formed by the residents of one neighbourhood, or by a group of men who worked together. It was a spontaneous process.'[6]

According to Assaad al-Achi, the threat of sexual violence in particular pushed people towards arms. 'Syria is very much a conservative, traditional society. Rape is something that will outrage the people. It is very emotional for them ... By December 2011 rape had become a standard practice not only in prisons but by the army as well. When it went into towns, the first thing [soldiers] did was go into homes and start raping women in front of their fathers, brothers and husbands.'[7]

But perhaps the greatest of all motivators for the armed struggle were traumatisation and the thirst for vengeance. When AbdulRahman Jalloud left prison he continued to pursue civil revolutionary activities, but he puts this down to his prior political awareness and contacts. Those young men without such a background responded to their torments in a more concrete manner: '90 per cent of detainees picked up arms as soon as they were released. They had very personal reasons. The fighters I know, their houses were burned, their relatives killed, they were on the run.'[8]

In this sense, the militarisation was inevitable, and once it had become an undeniable reality, most civil revolutionaries sought to adapt. Some, in the face of the regime's persistence, rethought their non-violent principles.[9] One was Basel al-Junaidi, living in Aleppo:

> We all expected death. I was scared to shower naked in case a bomb dropped. I saw massacres myself. For example, I saw the aftermath of a barrel bomb. I saw human remains scattered in the street; I heard the screaming. I'm trained as a doctor, but I was unable to act. I just stood there, petrified. The West thinks we're used to this, but we aren't of course. We're like anyone else – we use computers and cars, not camels and tents. Look, I'm a secularist, an atheist. ... A religious person who saw this would want to blow himself up. Even me, if a close family member had been murdered like this, I'd certainly have taken up arms. At the start I was totally against militarisation. Now I support it. I realise the regime can't be toppled by peaceful means.[10]

In other words, militarisation was not solely a natural human response to regime brutality; it also grew from the logical realisation that civil resistance was not enough, that the regime would only go if forced. For after months of struggle, not only had sections of the populace failed to mobilise against the regime, some – most of the Alawi community, and the professional/sectarian core of the army – were prepared actively to support it, even to fight and die for it, no matter what atrocities it committed.

Marcell Shehwaro reports:

> The violence was more than the people could bear. We couldn't answer the question how civil resistance would bring down the regime. 'OK', they said, 'we can stick to the Dignity Strikes, but Bashaar's being funded from outside. We can't bring down the Iranian and Russian economies!' We were offering them nice stories from Egypt while they were burying their dead. They asked, 'Do you stick to selmiyyeh tactics because they'll bring us victory, or for the sake of the selmiyyeh tactics?' We could tell them that the West would see us in a brighter way if we were peaceful, but we couldn't tell them this would bring victory. We couldn't tell them, for instance, how civil resistance would free the detainees. Our stand, therefore, didn't succeed. Every day people died, every single day. So the people armed themselves; they became used to weapons as they'd become used to civil resistance before.[11]

This popular recognition of the limits of civil disobedience is repeated in the analysis of Lebanese Marxist Gilbert Achcar, who distinguishes between 'neo-patrimonial' regimes such as Egypt's or Tunisia's – in which the military-industrial complex is 'more devoted to its own interests than the chief of state's' and is therefore capable of removing its Mubarak or Ben Ali to placate the people, a case of cutting off the head to save the body – and fully patrimonial regimes such as Syria's, in which head and body cannot be separated:

> The allegiance to the state leader displayed by the ... military-sectarian complex of the kind found in Syria is such that they are willing to go to war against the majority of their country's populace ... In sum, a mass uprising, however big, stands little chance of peacefully overturning a patrimonial regime that is protected by a praetorian guard with tribal, sectarian or regional loyalties. To overthrow such a government, an armed confrontation is required.[12]

* * *

So the first – and seldom mentioned – component of the armed resistance was civilian. Every adult Syrian male had undergone compulsory military training; it wasn't difficult, therefore, for terrorised 'farmers and dentists' (as US President Barack Obama would call them) to organise defensive militias.

Alongside these volunteers – although volunteer is not the word – army defectors formed the core of the growing anti-Assad force. Very often they acted as the civilians did – they returned to their home towns, where they organised with their neighbours. These soldiers had been ordered to shoot protestors, and very often did, lest they themselves were shot by the intelligence officers at their rear.[13] A combination of guilt, horror and fury propelled many to escape when they could, but perhaps most were killed in the attempt or hunted down in the following days. Usually they took only one weapon with them; sometimes they managed to break weapons out of stores. In every case they had to be prepared to fight to resist capture. Those who sheltered them had to face the fury too. Zaid Muhammad, a Palestinian-Syrian photographer from Aleppo, expresses the existential urgency of the situation: 'Soldiers were ordered to kill their compatriots or be killed themselves. It was natural that those who were able to would defect, and the defectors had a right to defend themselves. Should the people have turned these men over to the regime? Of course not. That means the people had to prepare for battle.'[14]

Defections mounted as steadily as the regime's repression, worst in Homs, where the Clock Square Massacre – as Joly described it, 'a terrifying, terrible and a transformative moment' – had tolled an early bell for the death of peaceful protest as a realistic strategy.

That was 18 April 2011. The violence continued to mount. On 25 April there was a second assault on Deraa. The following months saw major operations in Homs and Lattakia. By June, Sunni residents, especially Palestinians from the Raml camp, were fleeing Lattakia for Sunni-majority areas further inland, or to Turkey. Down the coast at Banyas and its Bayda suburb, where nine regime soldiers had been killed in early April (perhaps in violence instigated by out-of-favour Baathist Abdul Halim Khaddam), another cleansing took place in May. Tel Kalakh, a town in Homs province, was attacked in the same month, its inhabitants forced to flee. Such mass expulsions reinforced the need for self-defence; collective punishment meant it was no longer possible to avoid repression by keeping out of politics.

Then came a watershed moment for loyalists and defectors alike: the early June 2011 rebellion in Jisr al-Shughour, in the northern Idlib province, and the regime's response.[15] The town had been tense since the regime's slaughter of 15 workers on 20 May. Then on 4 June, security forces positioned on the roof of the central post office opened fire on a funeral. In response, mourners burned the building, killing eight officers inside, then seized weapons from a police station. In the ensuing violence, intelligence officers executed soldiers who refused to fire on civilians, provoking a mass defection. A military convoy was ambushed shortly afterwards. More died when the security building was overrun. It was the revolution's first large-scale attack on Assadist forces.

The army returned with helicopter gunships and tanks, chasing the defectors in the next fortnight from Jisr al-Shughour to the nearby town of Bdama and a newly sprouted refugee camp at Khirbet al-Jouz. A total of 120 soldiers lost their lives; it's a matter of dispute how many were killed by revolutionaries and how many by their own officers. An unknown number of civilians were killed too, and at least 10,000 fled across the border to Turkey – the first wave of around two million in total.

These events hardened positions on both sides. Regime supporters saw them as proof that the civil protests were a mere cover for armed insurrection, and called for an even harsher 'security' response. Revolutionaries were outraged at the regime's open war on civilians, and were inspired by the mass defection, hoping it would be the first of many.

The defection of Lieutenant Colonel Hussein Harmoush was not the first, but was the most widely noticed and influential of all, introducing a new vocabulary of resistance, specifically the FSA label. On 9 June 2011, in what became a paradigm for a thousand similar videos, Harmoush held his ID card towards the screen and declared his defection from the regime's army to the 'ranks of Syrian youth, alongside a number of the Free Syrian Arab Army'. He gave as the new army's purpose 'the protection of the unarmed protestors demanding freedom and democracy', and condemned the mass killing of civilians, 'particularly the massacre at Jisr al-Shughour'. After reminding Assad's soldiers that 'We have sworn in the army to point weapons only at the enemy, and not at our people,' he appealed 'to all the free people of the world: the people of Syria intend to board the boat of freedom and democracy with bare chests and olive branches, so help them achieve this.' He ended his statement by repeating the anti-sectarian slogan 'One, One, One, the Syrian People are One'.[16]

Harmoush's rebellion was short-lived. By September, tricked by intelligence agents into recrossing the border from Turkey, he appeared on state television, a much thinner, much older man, to make contradictory condemnations of the 'armed gangs' which killed civilians and the 'external opposition' which had made him false promises of support. Terrible reprisals were taken against Harmoush's family. His wife was shot in the leg before being abducted. Two brothers, two cousins, a nephew and a son-in-law were also taken. The tortured corpses of one brother, the two cousins and the son-in-law were returned to the family. A third brother was shot, but managed to escape. The rest are still unaccounted for.[17]

Despite this exemplary punishment, six months into the protests tens of thousands of conscripts and lower-ranking soldiers had deserted. Many congregated in rural Idlib, a neglected province between Aleppo and Lattakia reaching the Turkish borders, and specifically in the Jabal az-Zawiya, a mountainous area which, according to Assaad al-Achi, 'was liberated without violence. Locals – civilians and unarmed defectors – removed the regime checkpoints and kicked out regime officials themselves.'[18] Ideologically more than militarily, the roads between the towns in the north were slipping beyond regime control. Men and children jeered and threw rocks at the military convoys that passed.

Defectors also gathered in the towns and villages of the Homs countryside, demonstrating the extent of the collapse of the old Baathist cross-sect alliance, for this was a rural Sunni constituency which in an earlier generation had been loyal to Baathism, and was still a traditional military recruiting ground, perhaps the country's primary source of Sunni officers. The town of Rastan, for instance, is home to Hafez al-Assad's co-conspirator General Mustafa Tlass, and his sons the tycoon Firas and the Republican Guard general Manaf.

All three had left Syria by 2012, the latter making a public defection, but it was Manaf's cousin Lieutenant Abdul Razaq Tlass who led the Farouq Brigade against Assadist forces.[19]

From Homs southwards, defectors gravitated towards the Lebanese border, through the Qalamoun mountain villages to Zabadani. (In January 2012, Zabadani would become the first town to be liberated by force of arms.) The poorer Damascus suburbs housed many on-the-run soldiers, as did the villages-turned-towns of the Ghouta which had made such trouble for the French.

Sometimes the new militias held off regime incursions with rocket-propelled grenades and small arms fire; sometimes they laid roadside bombs. Their most constant work at this stage, however, was to encourage and assist further defections, staging raids which aimed to kill commanders and allow conscripts to flee, and smuggling the families of officers abroad so the officers could then 'safely' switch. Revolutionary soldiers also remained inside Assad's army in order to send intelligence to their comrades outside.

In the cities, the Free Army's job was to defend protests, providing a warning system when the *shabeeha* arrived and covering fire while the revolutionaries scattered.

* * *

The 'Free Syrian Army', of course, was an umbrella term. It was never an army but a collection of militias, some mobile, most local and defensive – all signed up to the twin aims of destroying the regime and establishing a democratic state. An International Committee of the Red Cross index of armed groups listed a thousand operating by late 2012, half associated with the FSA. The term 'army', therefore, was unhelpful. As Zaid Muhammad says, 'It looked to the world like one army was fighting another, but all we had was a resistance, not an army. Nobody was in charge.'[20]

This was not a centrally recruited and trained organisation. Crucially, it was never centrally armed or funded, at least not sufficiently, efficiently or continuously. One result was that it was unable to impose an enforceable code of conduct on its troops. Perhaps the best-known example of an FSA atrocity – and a gift to Assadist propagandists – was the 'heart-eating' incident, when a commander named Abu Sakkar himself filmed cutting into the torso of a dead soldier, removing flesh and biting into it. The deranged fighter later justified his action by saying his relatives and neighbours had been killed by regime forces, and that there were rape videos on the dead soldier's phone.[21] More revealing was the response of senior FSA official Salim Idrees: 'We condemn what he did. But why do our friends in the West focus on this when thousands are dying? We are a revolution, not a structured army. If we were, we would have expelled Abu Sakkar. But he commands his own battalion, which he raised with his own money. Is the West asking me now to fight Abu Sakkar and force him out of the revolution? I beg for some understanding here.'

Another consequence of the lack of central funding was an unrelenting process of regionalisation, whereby different militias dominated their own areas – Liwa al-Tawheed in Aleppo, the Syrian Revolutionaries Front in Idlib, Jaysh al-Islam in Douma, the Farouq and Khaled ibn al-Waleed Brigades in Homs, and so on. Leadership was local, and perhaps its first qualification was a funding source. He who could provide food, weapons and ammunition to his men was able to keep their loyalty.

Syrians – regime supporters and the apolitical as much as anyone else – had been furiously buying smuggled weapons since the crisis began.[22] These were ubiquitous in the Lebanese, Turkish and Iraqi border areas where the black market thrived and the armed conflict burned earliest. Networks of businessmen and expatriate Syrians provided the money. Other weapons were captured from regime checkpoints and stores or bought from corrupt officers. Still more were manufactured in amateur workshops; the tragi-comic sight of gas-bottle missiles and grenades launched by catapult soon became common.[23]

An inconsistent and uncoordinated supply of mainly light weaponry also came from regional states, particularly Saudi Arabia and Qatar. The ebb and flow of outside commitment was directly reflected on the battlefield. For example, there was some progress in the south until autumn 2012, when Jordanian assistance dried up. A stalemate then prevailed until the winter, when Saudi Arabia sent Croatian anti-tank weaponry, which translated into immediate territorial gains.

When regional states turned the taps off, fighters even went hungry. Ahmad, a teacher from Banyas who'd survived the May 2011 massacre by hiding in a cupboard, later fought with an FSA militia in the Jebel al-Akrad in northern Lattakia. 'First we ran out of ammunition. We stayed on the mountain, being shot at and bombed, unable to fire back, waiting for ammunition to arrive. It never came. Then we ran out of food. The villagers were feeding us, but they didn't have enough to eat themselves. At that time I left for Turkey. What was the point?'[24]

For these reasons the top leadership of the FSA was never very relevant on the ground. It was in any case beset by rivalries. Early lower-ranked defectors like Colonel Riad al-Asaad, the first FSA commander, were challenged by generals such as Mustafa al-Shaikh. Later on the most damaging conflicts were between Qatari- and Saudi-funded officers. Serious efforts were nevertheless made to unify decision making. In the spring of 2012, regional military councils were established in each province. Unable to solidify their authority by consistent weapons distribution, these were often ignored, especially by the factions which would later form the Islamic Front, but the Deraa council, in the south, was a reasonable success. In December 2012, the Supreme Military Council was set up under the leadership of Salim Idrees. It was directly linked to the external Coalition, and its founding meeting was held under Turkish auspices in the presence of Western and Gulf intelligence agents. Hopes were soon dashed that this show of state approval would translate into stepped-up foreign support.

* * *

The FSA engaged in hit-and-run guerrilla attacks and set roadside bombs. It launched attacks on border posts and laid siege to airfields. Gradually it took the countryside, and increasingly the regime withdrew from the areas it found too expensive to control. The withdrawal looked like liberation, but in some cases it may also have been a deliberate counter-revolutionary strategy. Bombs continued to fall on the liberated areas, their depopulation sped up, ensuring that no successful alternative would flourish.

AbdulRahman Jalloud complains: 'I don't know if any area in Syria has been liberated. The regime withdraws. Then it transforms its crimes against humanity to crimes of war, and the world believes there are two equal sides.'[25] Zaid Muhammad points out that in Aleppo strategy as well as necessity determined the extent of the regime's redeployment: 'The regime tried to keep the wealthy areas and left the poor neighbourhoods to us.'[26] This heightened class conflict and saddled the revolution with the problems of areas already neglected before their destruction by barrel bombs. And Ziad Homsi describes the inevitable squabbling that developed in the neighbourhoods abandoned by the regime:

> At the start we all worked together, and for free of course. The regime withdrew in the hope that we'd fight each other and compete for power. He who rules an alley is not like he who rules a state. And indeed, factionalism and regionalisation crept in more and more. We were hungry and surrounded by bombs. Our so-called liberated area was a huge prison.[27]

One regime redeployment which was certainly strategic was from the three Kurdish-majority enclaves along the northern border collectively known (to Kurds) as Rojava. Serdar Ahmad, a Kurdish resident of Aleppo whose family originates from Afrin, was there to witness what he calls 'the theatre of liberation – a few bullets fired in the air, that was all. Everything was arranged between them.'[28]

By 'them', he means on the one hand Assad, and on the other the PYD and its armed wing the People's Protection Unit, to which Assad handed over power and weaponry. The PYD is closely linked to the PKK, which led an insurgency against the Turkish state in the 1990s. Hafez al-Assad had arranged training for PKK militants in Lebanon, and sheltered PKK leader Abdullah Ocalan until 1999, when Turkey threatened war. In return for support against Turkey, the PYD cooperated with the regime inside Syria. Rather than demanding rights at home, militant Syrian Kurds were urged to join the struggle to the north, and in 2005, according to Serdar, 'it was the PYD which stopped our Kurdish revolution, just as in 2011 it was the PYD that acted as Assad's *shabeeha* in the Kurdish areas, beating protestors with sticks.'[29]

It's going too far to paint the PYD as a regime agent, and not only because it has sometimes clashed with Assad's forces. It practices, rather, a ruthless pragmatism. Working with the regime saved the Kurdish areas from bombardment and allowed them to build an alternative. The PYD's suspicion of the Arab opposition, and of Turkey's influence upon it, is justified so long as the opposition is unable or unwilling to offer guarantees of future Kurdish autonomy. Later the Kurds would clash with Islamist forces, most spectacularly with ISIS at Kobani.

* * *

Unlike Rojava, the 'liberated' Arab areas were subjected to continuous war. Homs, the country's third largest city, was the first. Here, after the Clock Square Massacre in April 2011 and the military assault in May, the FSA was defending its own densely populated urban areas. The zones between revolutionary control and regime checkpoints resembled Palestine during intifada. Young men darted from the shelter of doorways to taunt the soldiers, and back again to dodge the bullets. Civilian protests were still large and frequent. Joly describes them thus:

> I attended students' protests, women's protests and normal protests for everyone, and these were all protected by the Free Army. In fact, before the Free Army as such, these were just men from the neighbourhood, or from nearby areas. Insha'at, for example, was a wealthier area and its men didn't carry weapons, but men came from Baba Amr to defend the protests there. They guarded the entrances to the area so they could warn us if the security or *shabeeha* were coming, and so they could confront them and give us time to escape.

This was the period when celebrities such as goalkeeper Abdul Baset al-Sarout and (Alawi) actress Fadwa Suleiman led demonstrations characterised by humour and resilience, and punctuated by wild singing and dancing. Despite the danger, there was a tremendous sense of optimism and solidarity. 'In the first months,' Joly says, 'social relationships were really excellent. Everybody asked after everybody else, everybody wanted to help each other.'

Afterwards, when people were driven from their homes, this atmosphere faded. 'There were constant complaints and disputes amongst families, particularly the displaced. They lived in schools, which were like camps with roofs. There was an extended family in each classroom, and they had to share the toilets.'

By now Joly was working for the Red Crescent, providing psychological support to displaced women and children. 'The children were very affected. When I asked them to draw, the first thing they drew was the home they'd left, and they were sad. They told stories you don't expect to hear from children, unbelievable stories of dismembered, headless bodies. But these were things they'd seen.'[30]

The regime's loss of control in Homs was certainly not a deliberate strategy. The city was part of 'useful Syria' (in French colonial terminology), home to a major oil refinery and acting as a bridge between the capital and the coast. It also contained a large Alawi population. From September 2011, the cross-sect efforts of revolutionaries and community elders to guard against sectarian violence increasingly failed. A spate of mutual murders and kidnappings for ransom, and the separation of quarters by checkpoint, sharpened the city's divisions. Alawi families moved away from Sunni-majority areas, and vice versa.

Through the autumn and winter of 2011, the regime laid siege to defectors and thousands of civilians in the working class quarter of Baba Amr. Back and forth street fighting was followed by intense bombardment throughout February 2012[31] – witnessed from al-Wa'er by Joly: 'We could see Baba Amr from our balcony. I saw it with my own eyes, day after day – helicopters dropping bombs, artillery explosions, missiles flying over our heads to hit the people there.' A ground assault in March finally brought the area back under Assadist control.

The tide had turned against the uprising in Homs. First, at the Clock Square, the angel of non-violent revolution was riddled with bullets. Then the armed alternative was defeated in Baba Amr. The resistance came up against two persistent and unavoidable facts: the regime had far more and better weapons; and to achieve its aims, it was prepared to slaughter civilians and destroy urban infrastructure on a grand scale.

By now only about 20 per cent of the city was free. As more neighbourhoods were gradually clawed back from the FSA, Joly felt the net tightening:

> It became more and more difficult to work. Before I joined the Red Crescent, and after my studies were stopped, I'd ended up staying at home. The checkpoints had got much worse for girls. They started searching us too, and insulting us. And now, when I was in my work clothes, the soldiers accused the Red Crescent of smuggling weapons to the fighters, and called us 'the Brotherhood Crescent' [after the Muslim Brotherhood]. Once a soldier demanded, 'Why are you laughing at me?' Of course I wasn't laughing or even smiling, but he kept on saying it. The boys I was with distracted him until he calmed down.[32]

The city's fate was determined by the crucial battle in May 2013 at al-Qusayr, in the countryside beyond Homs towards the Lebanese border. Hundreds of Lebanese Hizbullah fighters participated in the attack on the liberated town, making explicit the fact that Iran's Republican Guard was playing an increasing role in reorganising Assad's fightback, and that its regional clients – Hizbullah first among them – were fighting on the front lines. Hardened by battle with Israel, and at the time widely considered the region's best fighters, it nevertheless took three weeks for the Shia militia – attacking now rather than defending – to conquer and clear the area. Once it succeeded, it and conventional Syrian forces were able to concentrate on Homs itself.

By July 2013 the crumpled Khaldiyeh quarter was back in regime hands, and in May 2014 the last fighters departed the city centre for still-liberated parts of the countryside. They left behind a blasted landscape, a Stalingrad for the twenty-first century. Joly hears from those at home how the city feels now: 'There's a false stability based on fear, but there's still no electricity or heating fuel. There are checkpoints everywhere and continuous arrest campaigns, so almost all the young men have left. Of course there are no protests, not even any coordinating committees.'[33]

At the time of writing the suburb of al-Wa'er, its population doubled by the displaced, still held out under daily bombardment. Joly was no longer there. She'd left Syria after the January 2013 massacre at Haswiya, a village outside Homs where FSA fighters had been sheltering. Some of her relatives were among the revolutionaries murdered there; she feared the regime, now it knew their identity, would take reprisals against her immediate family. In any case, she'd already had too many close encounters with death. Gozdikas (Russian-made artillery) had hit her home twice, and once she'd missed a car bomb at her local petrol station by only a few seconds. Her 30-year-old neighbour was killed in that blast.

* * *

At the cost of depopulating and almost razing the city, the regime had won the battle of Homs. This of course is no surprise – it commanded a centralised army, fielded tanks, planes and artillery, and enjoyed solid support from international allies. The opposition enjoyed growing recruitment and substantial popular support, but was comprehensively outgunned.

Yet the armed uprising had grown significantly in strength and geographical reach. The regime's loyal troops were overstretched – exhausted by the endless game of whack-a-mole as the Homs challenge was replicated in other cities. Sunni conscripts of doubtful allegiance were often locked down in barracks or otherwise kept away from the front line lest they defected at the first opportunity. With Iranian help, the regime began to organise new state and substate militias, and to welcome foreign fighters, but still it could only focus on one city at a time.

Meanwhile in Douma, in the eastern Ghouta suburbs of Damascus, the founding core of the LCCs was struggling to adapt to the new reality. Assaad al-Achi describes the process:

> By early 2012 the militarisation was no longer confined to Jabal az-Zawiya, Jisr al-Shughour and Homs. Weapons were spread all

> over the country, and liberated areas started to appear. We had to decide whether to support or oppose the militarisation, and this debate brought us almost to breaking point. In a horizontal system, and on such a crucial issue, a 50/50 vote was unacceptable. We debated for three weeks in January 2012, seeking an internal consensus. Eventually we decided to oppose militarisation, not to become involved with the armed uprising, but at the same time to build relationships with whatever armed groups appeared. In that domain, the first thing we worked on was a code of conduct for the Free Army. Razan [Zaitouneh], as a lawyer, worked on it, and she sought help from international legal experts. From spring to summer 2012 we offered a three-day training to fighters, and won the approval of 60 armed groups for the code. Then in August 2012 we started documenting violations by all sides – the regime, the Free Army, and [the al-Qaida-linked] Jabhat al-Nusra.[34]

Meanwhile some of the LCCs turned to military activity: 'Either we turned a blind eye or, in some cases, kicked them out'.[35]

By now a strip along the Turkish border was almost entirely liberated, including the towns north of Aleppo. The regime was losing territory too in the deserts and mismanaged agricultural plains of the east, particularly in Deir al-Zor, a province rich in cotton, wheat and oil. The region's tribal population is closely linked to tribes across the border in Iraq's Anbar province, and the rural areas had always been armed, even with heavy weapons since the 2003 Iraq war. Marginalised by Hafez al-Assad, made restive by the sufferings of their Iraqi neighbours, Deir al-Zor's residents quickly organised against Bashaar's assault. The city neighbourhood of Muhassen – a key source of Sunni officers for the army, like Rastan in Homs – became a defectors' hub. Muhassen had always had a strong socialist as well as military tradition. Even Deir al-Zor's Baathists were historically closer to Saddam Hussain's Iraqi branch.

On 2 August 2011, regime forces occupied Deir al-Zor city, which remained contested between them and the FSA until June 2014, and between them and ISIS thereafter. Beyond this, Assad's fortified strongholds – a few urban corners and bases and airfields in the desert

– formed a steadily shrinking archipelago. By April 2012 all of the Deir al-Zor countryside was liberated.

Ahmad al-Agyl, a teacher and poet, describes what happened next:

> The Free Army in Deir consisted of local militias. Most, like the one in my village, were formed by local defectors. After the liberation, some brigades stayed to defend their own areas; others went to Qusayr to fight Hizbullah, or to Damascus or Homs or Hasakeh – but wherever they went they fought in areas inhabited by Deiri people, they supported their relatives. For example, in Damascus they fought in Tadamon, which has a Deiri community. What this means is that the revolution turned into a regional more than a sectarian war.[36]

Ahmad witnessed the looting of factories by opportunist gangsters who he insists were 'not the Free Army', as well as tribal rivalries among the resistance which he blames on the regional Military Council, staffed entirely by defected officers from the Muhassen neighbourhood.

* * *

Aleppo, briefly, was the armed resistance's greatest success. And it suffered the worst destruction of all.

On the night of 19 July 2012, as battle erupted in the Salahuddeen neighbourhood, thousands of fighters poured into the city from the northern and eastern countryside. Videos of the convoy filled distant revolutionaries with enthusiasm to echo that of the men on the backs of trucks or bulging from car windows, brandishing Kalashnikovs and freedom flags. 'To Aleppo!' they cried, as if the word were synonymous with victory. Historic Aleppo: the country's largest city and economic powerhouse. The armed revolution's momentum suddenly seemed unstoppable.

Aleppo more than anywhere else had benefitted from the Bashaar decade's neo-liberal reforms and from intensified trade with Turkey. Partly as a result, the city centre, like central Damascus, had remained largely calm in the revolution's early months, though protests had grown steadily throughout 2012. The poorer people of the outer suburbs and nearby towns felt a certain resentment towards those overcomfortable Aleppans who'd sat on the sidelines, although according to Serdar Ahmed, 'The distance between rich and poor was not as large as some think. Many big merchants donated money to the revolution, but they did so anonymously.'[37] In any case, the liberation of Aleppo had a definite class dimension – armed farmers and workers of the rural hinterland were welcomed by militants in the city's working class zones. Many wealthier residents left the liberated area; sometimes their abandoned homes were transformed to rebel barracks.

Other Aleppans travelled in the contrary direction, like Basel al-Junaidi:

> When the armed resistance took half of Aleppo in July 2012 – and these were the poorer areas which the regime had never cared about – we moved there from our homes in the regime-held side, which was more middle class. Bustan al-Qasr was the passage between the two halves of the city; at first we could cross back and forth, but then the regime's snipers closed it. Living next to them, we got to know the revolutionary fighters. We had good relationships with them; at that point they were all locals, the sons of the neighbourhood or the suburbs nearby, and they were very open towards others. They helped us find a house; they had no problem that we were unrelated men and women living together, even if we were in a conservative area. They were pleased we were there working with them. It really felt like freedom. Posters of Bashaar were laid on the ground at the doors of houses so you had to wipe your feet on him.[38]

Serdar Ahmad reports that 'three quarters of activists in Aleppo in 2011 were secularists. The rest were moderate Islamists. They were people who wanted freedom, and when the Free Army came, they wanted it too.'[39]

This was liberated Aleppo before the grinding work of barrel bombs, before the advent of black banners and beheadings, when fighters could be spotted dancing *debkeh* or playing guitars in breaks between the fighting. In their committees and councils, and through their group projects, revolutionaries did their best to manage the war-struck city.

Most of Aleppo's fighters were affiliated with the Tawheed, or Unification Brigade – originally a merger of the revolutionary militias formed in the northern countryside. The name is redolent of Islam – the 'unity' of God is the religion's central tenet – but also of the national unity envisioned by the slogans of 2011. Yet Tawheed ultimately presided over a cantonisation rather than a collective rebirth. In August 2012 the rebel advance stalled when the ammunition supply ran out. The liberated Sunni-majority areas were cut off from the Christian and wealthier quarters, and under the pressure of regime bombardment and enforced deprivation, began to depopulate. Over the next years there would be advances and counter-advances, but the general condition was an agonising paralysis.

Hungry for bullets and food, rebel commanders squabbled over resources. By December, looting and gangsterism were common. Aleppo's factories were stripped and sold off – sometimes to feed the fighters, sometimes to buy villas in Turkey. Some, posing as FSA militants, became full-time highwaymen.

In Serdar Ahmad's words: 'At first the Free Army was great, really wonderful. Then as time dragged on, opportunists joined for their own criminal reasons. For profit. Those rich people who'd chosen to stay became kidnapping targets.'[40] In the eyes of many, criminal elements tarnished the resistance as a whole. This was one of the open doors the more 'clean-handed' jihadists would later step through.

Indiscipline led to such self-defeating acts as the filmed execution of several members of the 5,000-strong Berri clan, including clan leader Zaino Berri, earning the determined enmity of the rest. A Tawheed commander justified the killings as the result of a 'field trial'. The Berris had certainly served as regime *shabeeha*, and were accused of torture and rape. The ugliness of such 'revolutionary justice', however, did nothing to reassure bourgeois Aleppans and handed another gift to pro-regime propagandists.[41]

Civil revolutionaries worked with the fighters to minimise abuses, but in impossible circumstances. As Basel al-Junaidi describes:

> We set up a legal committee to observe the treatment of prisoners in FSA prisons. They cooperated, but in the end we stopped doing it. Jaysh al-Mujahideen, for instance, are moderates, good people, the cleanest militia in Aleppo, but they committed violations. Sometimes they killed their prisoners – either for revenge or simply because they didn't have food for themselves, let alone to feed prisoners. But if there were two or three violations in FSA prisons, there were hundreds in regime prisons. So should we damage the revolution's reputation and help Assad? We couldn't see violations and not report them – so we stopped looking. We saw the media was attacking the revolution in any case, using any excuse. Of course, if we'd felt we had friends in the world, we would have acted differently.[42]

Aleppo's considerable Kurdish population, meanwhile, had risen in concert with – and also parallel to – their Arab neighbours. The Kurds of the Salahudeen Brigade fought the regime under the Tawheed umbrella, but before long the PYD had seized control of the city's Kurdish quarters. As in Rojava, the organisation was hostile to both the regime and the FSA.

The Armenian community, their politics coloured by memories of the 1915 Turkish genocide, saw Turkish agendas behind the revolution, and in general opposed it. They and other Christians formed self-protection militias which often served the regime. At the same time, some Christians fought with the Free Army, and Muslim rebels were generally good neighbours to the Christians of the liberated area.[43] Later of course, as the rebellion hardened its sectarian tone, the divides between Christians and Muslims, and between Kurds (Muslims, but usually suspicious of Islamism) and Arabs, widened.[44]

The FSA boasted many principled, disciplined and forward-looking leaders – men who worked against national fragmentation – but many of the best were killed or, as time passed, eclipsed by fiercer figures. In particular, Aleppo produced two field commanders who won a wide following far beyond the field – one a civilian turned fighter, one a defected officer.

The civilian is Abdul Qader al-Saleh, formerly a seed merchant and part-time preacher from Marea in the Aleppo countryside. Saleh organised protests before setting up a brigade in his hometown, finally becoming leader of the Tawheed Brigade. A member of the Supreme Military Council command structure, he called simultaneously for sharia law, democratic elections and a pluralist society. A figure seemingly capable of containing the uprising's contradictions, many secular supporters of the revolution made his portrait their social media profile picture upon his death in a regime airstrike in November 2013.[45]

The defector is Yusef al-Jader, or Abu Furat, who commanded one of Assad's tank brigades until ordered to shell a revolutionary village in Lattakia. Had the regime fallen sooner, communities loyal to it would have found an eminently reasonable interlocutor in men like Abu Furat. One of many films uploaded online shows him receiving an Alawi visitor, prompting a rhetorical complaint against Bashaar:

> Why did you plunge your own sect into a battle for your sake and try to make them hate Sunnis? Why? Don't you ask how we're going to live together in the future? Well, we'll live together despite you. I know the Alawis are generous and good people. Many of them are poor too. And you use these people to achieve your own malicious goals. These are the children of villages. Bread probably takes a year to make its way to their villages. They're poor, they don't have enough food, they don't have bread; if one of them is sick, he dies for lack of medicine.
>
> But I want to ask you, my Alawi brothers – and you know me, I've sat and drunk maté with you. Be aware! We're not your enemies; we're your brothers. We're joint participants in the nation, and we've lived together. Saleh al-Ali [the anti-colonial Alawi leader] refused to work under the French flag; he refused to separate into an Alawi state, and his sons and grandsons will also refuse. The plans have been exposed, and our Alawi brothers will return to us, for we are the same.[46]

Before attacking Aleppo's Infantry School in December 2012, Abu Furat appealed on film for those inside to defect or desert, providing phone numbers so arrangements could be made, promising that cadets of all backgrounds would be protected, and hundreds did manage to leave before the assault. Once the complex had been taken, Abu Furat was interviewed again. Rather than taking a triumphant tone after the victory, he seemed sad. His battlefield humanity comes across clearly in his words:

> I am bothered because these tanks are our tanks. The ammunition is our ammunition. Those fighters are our brothers. I swear to God, every time I see a person killed, from our side or from theirs, I feel sad. Because if that bastard had resigned, Syria would have been the best country in the world. But you clung to your throne, you bastard! Why? You started killing people when we were telling you we were peaceful, and you were saying it was all armed gangs. And we officers sat on our beds watching, while you were calling people terrorists. Honestly, we are not terrorists. You are the one who wants us to become terrorists.[47]

Regime fire killed Abu Furat a few minutes later.

* * *

According to defected diplomat Bassam Barabandi, 'Assad learned from the Libyan case that a hasty resort to large massacres, or the threat thereof, could draw intervention from NATO forces. A slower increase in violence against opponents, however, would likely go unchecked.'[48]

The military escalation was slow but certain. From February 2012, heavy artillery regularly beat down on Homs, very often on civilian neighbourhoods containing no military targets. By June 2012, helicopters routinely fired missiles and machine gun rounds on rebel-controlled quarters. The jet bombing of Aleppo was underway by August. Later in 2012 came the cluster bombs and ballistic missiles. In December the first scud missiles were fired at the Shaikh Suleiman base in Aleppo. A month later they were being directed at densely packed civilian zones in Aleppo and Damascus. And the worst escalations would soon starve the capital's suburbs.

In July 2012, as the Tawheed Brigade prepared for the push into Aleppo, the FSA advanced into inner Damascus for the first time.

Gun battles raged in the city centre. In response, regime tanks and helicopter gunships struck the neighbourhoods of Meydan, Tadamon, Hajr al-Aswad, Kafr Souseh and Barzeh. The heavy artillery dug into the mountain above the city rained fury on the suburbs below. For AbdulRahman Jalloud – on the run in the Damascus suburbs – it was a turning point:

> I used to say, if 100,000 die every day, we still shouldn't militarise. I changed my mind during the first battle of Damascus, July 2012. The first shelling in the capital was on Tadamon, on the 19th. It was a shock. It outraged everybody. Even some regime supporters were protesting. We burned fires in every street in Damascus, and for a while the regime was frightened enough to stop the shelling. The police hid in their stations and the security in their branches. They took down some checkpoints so it became easy to move around, even during the battle.[49]

In part, the regime was responding to the 18 July bombing of the military crisis unit in Damascus, the single most grievous blow directed at its heart. Three key officials were killed: Defense Minister Daoud Rajha, Presidential Security Adviser Hassan Turkmani, and Deputy Defense Minister (and Assad's brother-in-law) Assef Shawkat. Intelligence Chief Hisham Bekhtiyar was seriously wounded, and there were unconfirmed reports that the president's brother Maher lost a leg.[50]

The FSA's Damascus offensive was beaten back, and through the latter half of 2012 regime forces were increasingly reinforced by Hizbullah and Iraqi Shia militias such as Asa'ib Ahl al-Haqq and the Abu Fadl al-Abbas Brigade. By the spring of 2013, all the revolutionary suburbs of the western and eastern Ghouta were under siege.

The Palestinian-Syrian citizen journalist Qusai Zakarya experienced the impact in Moadamiya, in the western Ghouta:

> I saw the full impact of Assad's 'starve or surrender' weapon myself. In October 2012, Assad's forces commenced a total siege on Moadamiya, blocking all food, medicine, and humanitarian supplies from entering the town. While we initially found sustenance from

> a bumper crop of olives, food began to run out as winter set in, and residents were reduced to eating weeds and stray animals ... I consoled parents on the deaths of their young children – such as my friend Abu Bilal, who was a grocer before the siege but could not even save his own daughter during it. Another friend of mine was desperate to get medicine for his dying daughter, but was caught by regime intelligence. We found him with his throat slashed and the skin peeled off his entire body.[51]

Lubna al-Kanawati was based in Harasta, in the eastern Ghouta, where the blockade was equally tight:

> In June 2013, on the first day of Eid, the regime imposed a total siege on the eastern Ghouta. Snipers were essential to this – now it became impossible to smuggle food in through the back routes. Every day the Ghouta suffered mortars like rain. MiGs were in the sky from dawn to dusk. They used everything against us – elephant missiles, scuds, barrel bombs. It got worse and worse until the winter, which was terrible. People were eating leaves and animal fodder. The water supply didn't work because the electricity needed to pump it was switched off, so people were digging wells in the streets. There was no medicine whatsoever, no sanitary towels, no Internet or mobile or landline. At one point the regime and the FSA made a deal and food came in, but at incredible prices. Eighty dollars for a kilo of tea, for example.

Speaking in southern Turkey in December 2014, Lubna complained she was still unable to control her eating, that she never felt full: 'Hunger is the most effective weapon of all. A hungry person is an angry person who inevitably acts impetuously. Hungry people are incapable of helping each other. If you can't help yourself, you can't think of others. In the end people fought in the streets over food.'[52]

* * *

Another area where people starved to death was south Damascus's Yarmouk camp, housing the largest Palestinian population in Syria, though Syrians live there too. In the late 1940s and early 1950s, the camp looked similar to those housing Syrian refugees today. People driven from northern Palestine, particularly the Safad area, lived in tents separated by muddy paths. Then shacks were built, which grew in the next decades into densely packed residential blocks.

Protests broke out in Palestinian camps in Lattakia and Deraa in 2011, and in Yarmouk too, though on a smaller scale than in neighbouring areas. Yarmouk's restraint resulted from two factors: the prominence in the camp of the Popular Front for the Liberation of Palestine-General Command (PFLP-GC), which acted as Assad's *shabeeha*, and a genuine desire for neutrality in the struggle for Syria's destiny.[53] This stance allowed the camp to offer refuge to Syrians displaced by repression elsewhere. During 2011, Yarmouk's population exploded from around 200,000 to around 900,000. Throughout 2012 the neighbouring suburbs Hajr al-Aswad and Tadamon were subjected to repeated assault, as witnessed by Salim Salamah, who works with the Palestinian League for Human Rights – Syria: 'I used to sit on my terrace in Yarmouk and watch Tadamon being brutally bombed, rockets passing over my head, and I could smell the burning meat.'[54] Activists and protestors from the camp were detained, often tortured to death, and shells and sniper fire rattled its perimeters, but still its neutrality was preserved – until 16 December 2012, when regime jets targeted a mosque, a school and a hospital, killing at least 40 people. The camp responded with furious protest; resistance fighters arrived from neighbouring areas the following day. From then on the camp was rebel territory; as such, it qualified for the full force of Assad's collective punishment.[55]

Immediately a partial siege was imposed, with the PFLP-GC blocking the camp's entrances and prohibiting the passage of goods. Hundreds of thousands of civilians were able to leave to become refugees once more, though the young men passing the checkpoints risked detention and murder. But tens of thousands remained, immobilised by illness or age, or wishing to stay with their property, or having nowhere at all to go.

On 8 July 2013 the siege became total. The Palestinian League for Human Rights reports on the results:

> Some of the opposition armed factions began to steal from and seize warehouses containing relief supplies, failing to help the inhabitants endure the siege. The regime forbade the entrance of food and medical supplies, except occasionally a very small quantity of baby milk and one single delivery of polio vaccines ... More than 170 died of various siege-related causes including starvation to the end of February 2014. After this especially harsh period, international humanitarian organizations and UNRWA [United Nations Relief and Works Agency] began to distribute aid supplies to the camp's besieged residents, in the form of deliveries of parcels containing some foodstuffs. Despite the regime agreement and promises that civilians would be unmolested during food deliveries, dozens were arrested by regime forces present in the delivery area at the camp's entrance, and dozens more were killed during delivery operations, either by snipers or in clashes between regime and opposition forces, both indifferent to the presence of civilians.[56]

The siege was reinforced shortly afterwards. By now Yarmouk's emaciated residents were chewing boot leather and leaves; a cleric even issued an edict permitting the camp's Muslims to eat stray cats and dogs. In June 2014 the water supply was cut off too.

* * *

By the summer of 2013, better-armed and organised opposition offensives had brought the Damascus front line to the edge of the city centre and only five miles from the presidential palace. For the regime this represented a greater challenge than the brief offensive of the previous summer; besieged in the Ghouta suburbs, rebels had nevertheless established and kept a bridgehead as far as Jobar and Abbassiyeen Square from which they might launch future strikes on the capital's key installations. Repeated regime offensives had failed to dislodge them. Did this cause desperation in Assad's inner circle? It certainly resulted in the most dramatic escalation yet.

At 4.45 in the morning of 21 August, Qusai Zakarya was preparing for bed after a sleepless night in the besieged western suburb of Moadamiya. Suddenly he felt 'a knife made of fire' tearing his chest.

Recognising a gas attack, Qusai called for the men nearby to get into the open air. Outside in the dark street his neighbour screamed that her three children were unconscious. Qusai helped to heave them into a pick-up before he lost consciousness himself. He was given up for dead when his heart stopped, but came round half an hour later vomiting white foam.[57]

Between 2.00 and 5.00 am similar scenes unfolded across the city to the east, in the rebel-held and fiercely revolutionary suburbs of Ain Tarma, Zamalka, Irbin, Saqba, Kafr Batna – distraught, panicked civilians screaming for their loved ones; men and women foaming at the mouth and nose; children convulsing; then rows and rows of white-shrouded bodies lined on pavements, hospital hallways, in mass graves.

Razan Zaitouneh witnessed it:

> At the beginning, we thought that it's like the previous times, that there will be only dozens of injured cases and number of murders, but we were surprised by the great numbers which the medical points received during only the first half of hour following the shelling. Things started to become clearer after that. Hours later, we started to visit the medical points in Ghouta to where injured were removed, and we couldn't believe our eyes. I haven't seen such death in my whole life. People were lying on the ground in hallways, on roadsides, in hundreds.
>
> There haven't been enough medical staff to treat them. There is not enough medications for more serious cases. They were just to choose to whom they will give the medication, because there is no medication for everybody. Even doctors were crying because they couldn't help the injured people, because the lack of the medication and oxygen. The paramedics were telling us how they were breaking in doors and houses in Zamalka and Ain Tarma, where the shelling took place, and get inside and find whole families dead in their beds. Most of the children didn't make it.
>
> In cemeteries which we visited, victims were buried in mass graves, 15 or 20 dead bodies in every grave because the large number of injured people. People were – also there was hysterical between the people. Families are searching for their children. People

> were searching for their children in every town in Ghouta. Children in the medical points were crying and asking for their parents. It wasn't believable.[58]

It was the deadliest use of chemical weapons since the Iran–Iraq war, the greatest single poisoning of civilians since Saddam Hussain's slaughter of the Kurds at Halabja. Estimates of the dead reach 1,729 – so many because people were sheltering from the artillery barrage in their basements, the worst place to be, where the gas sank and thickened.

Even as spokesmen made official denials to the foreign audience, regime-associated webpages were celebrating the attack.[59] According to a defected general, 'It happened for internal reasons. For weeks, the rebels have threatened Assad's home province of Lattakia, where they have captured several villages ... But many of the irregular fighters, which the government has used instead of the army, are Alawites from the region. Now they're going back to protect their villages.' So the attack fulfilled the twin aims of 'holding the thinned out front around Damascus and strengthening the morale of the fanatics in their ranks'.[60]

There may be truth to this version, but the attacks served a still greater function. The regime clearly believed – perhaps had been advised by Russia's Vladimir Putin – that Obama's threat to intervene if the chemical weapons 'red line' was crossed was empty. In this, as events soon showed, the regime was absolutely correct. Not only was no punitive action taken against it, the very possibility of action was removed from the table; implicitly, the chemical decommissioning deal that arose in the aftermath handed the Syria file to Assad's Russian sponsor. So the message of the sarin heard by resistant Syrians was this: no one's coming to save you, not in any circumstances.

Lubna al-Kanawati, who'd been injured by mustard gas a week before the sarin strikes, observed the mood: 'After Obama's failure to act over sarin, a profound sense of depression and isolation afflicted the people. They knew they'd die hungry and in silence, ignored by the world.'[61]

* * *

The safest place to live is near the front line. In the civilian areas away from the battle – this is where the barrel bombs drop, where the artillery strikes. For the regime, the battle against the civil and political alternative is more important than the military battle.

Ziad Hamoud.[62]

The regime pursued a scorched earth strategy. It was all very deliberate and self-declared. The *shabeeha* scrawled it on the walls: 'Either Assad or We'll Burn the Country'. In the countryside they killed livestock and burned crops. In the towns the army shelled bakeries, schools, hospitals and market places. Hundreds of barrel bombs dismantled Aleppo – more bombed than any city since World War II – and Deir al-Zor, Homs, Deraa and suburban Damascus.[63] Women feared the roads lest they were raped by *shabeeha* at checkpoints; men feared detention or forced conscription. The most obvious consequence of this terror was the mass expulsion of the population from the liberated areas, creating another World War II comparison – the greatest refugee crisis in seven decades.

Even as it destroys the old system, a successful revolutionary movement must create alternatives. When Syria (necessarily) became a battlefield, the voices of the civil organisers who'd made the revolution were increasingly drowned out by the thunder of bombs; and power – which in 2011 had been brought to community level – was increasingly claimed by authoritarian militia leaders competing for funds and local dominance. Syrian elites, such as the Coalition, were unable to establish a presence on the burning ground. If the FSA had been seriously supported from outside, if Assad had not been so generously armed and funded by Russia and Iran (these international factors will be examined in Chapter 9), then the armed struggle might have lasted months rather than years, and civil activism might have quickly regained its role. But the war stretched on, and the liberated areas became death zones. This was the vacuum in which jihadism would thrive.

In June 2013, Ra'ed Fares, director of the media centre at Kafranbel and one of the symbols of the revolutionary movement, was asked if he'd have joined the protest movement in 2011 had he known what would happen next. He answered matter-of-factly:

'No. The price was too high. Just in Kafranbel we've had 150 martyrs. As many as that are missing; they're probably dead too. As for me, I can't cry anymore. I don't feel properly. I've taken pictures of too many battles. I've photographed the martyrs.'

Hands on the wheel of his battered car, he shrugged his shoulders.

'But it's too late now. There's no going back. We have to finish what we started.'[64]

6

Scorched Earth: The Rise of the Islamisms

The regime relied on an implicit sectarian discourse from its first moment, but before the revolution it had always forbidden its public expression; many revolutionaries, on the other hand, slipped into sectarian speech – although their sectarian acts were much less than the regime's ... The conflict became sectarian gradually, because the majority of Alawis sided with Assad, and when the regime's sectarianism became blatant, and because of the support offered to revolutionary brigades on the condition that they would raise certain [Islamic] banners and slogans. This ultimately meant that the opposition failed to present a national discourse that could persuade the minorities as a whole to stand with the revolution.

Aziz Asaad[1]

In 2012 I talked to FSA leaders in Idlib who were convinced that Alawis shouldn't be targeted, even though they knew the pilots bombing them were Alawis. But through that year I began to hear people describe the revolution as a Sunni intifada. I spoke to my friends on Skype – men who'd worked for the Dignity strike, or made posters – and I saw them slowly changing.

Yara Nseir[2]

We used to laugh at the regime propaganda about Salafist gangs and Islamic emirates. Then the regime created the conditions to make it happen.

Monzer al-Sallal[3]

Tormented, bereaved and dispossessed, the Syrian people turned more intensely to religion. This doesn't mean they became advocates of public beheadings and compulsory veiling; almost all were horrified by the appearance of these phenomena and most still expressed the desire for a civil rather than an Islamic state. A minority, disgusted by the uses to which religion had been put, questioned it more intensely than before. But in general religious emotions were enflamed, and religious references were reinforced.

The first cause was the same one which powered militarisation – the brute fact of extreme violence. In most cultures the proximity of death will focus minds on the transcendent – there are no atheists in foxholes, as the saying goes – and more so in an already religious society like Syria's. Faith is intensified by death and the threat of death, and by the pain and humiliation of torture. And when the nation is splintering, subnational identities are reinforced. In death's presence, people want to feel like we, not like I, because I is small and easily erased.

The sung slogan 'Ya Allah Malna Ghairak Ya Allah' (O God We Have Nothing But You) became ubiquitous among protestors facing bullets. An intense relationship with God became a survival framework for the detained.[4] Religious slogans became cosmic rallying calls for the fighters. In the Syrian context, radicalisation is better named traumatisation.

Islamism – in both moderate and extreme forms – flourished. The trend was more pronounced among the fighting formations than among the people in their committees, liberated towns and villages, and refugee camps – and there were concrete reasons for this to do with arms supply, funding and discipline. The most serious consequence for the course of the revolution was the hardening of divisions between the Sunni Arab majority and the rest, and foremost among them the Alawis. By 2014, battlefield events (and certainly media reports) were often dominated by the acts of the most extreme Sunni Islamist militias – either the al-Qaida-linked Jabhat al-Nusra or the even more extreme ISIS. But at first these organisations were by no means the most important Islamist actors.

The persistence of sectarian resentment in secular, even unbelieving countries such as Ireland or Scotland reinforces an obvious point – these conflicts aren't about theology but concern group fears and resentments, and their exploitation by power. Communal tensions, in other words, are the result not of ancient enmities but of contemporary political machinations. Communities engaged at one moment in seemingly unforgettable strife are, at another, busily engaging in intermarriage or political alliance. In Lebanon, for instance, the main civil war cleavage was Christian–Muslim, but now tends to divide Sunni–Shia, with Christian groups allied to both sides. And in Iraq, before the 2003 invasion, a third of marriages were cross-sect Sunni–Shia.

There was nothing fated about the sectarian breakdown in Syria. It was deliberately provoked and manipulated, by a host of secondary actors but primarily by the regime. Why would the regime provoke first armed resistance and then a fierce sectarian backlash? Because Assadist policy under father and son, at home and abroad, is to present itself as the essential solution to problems it has itself manufactured – a case of the arsonist dressing up as a fireman.[5] The double aim of the counter-revolutionary strategy was to frighten secularists and religious minorities into loyalty, and the West into tolerance of the dictatorship's violence. The first goal has been partially achieved, the second – at the time of writing – more so.

How did the regime undertake its project? To start with, it targeted Sunni areas for collective punishment and sectarian provocation, as Marcell Shehwaro saw:

> The sensation of Sunni identity is based on something real – I can't pretend that the regime isn't sectarian, that there haven't been sectarian massacres. Look, there were stages on the way. When they started killing Sunni civilians randomly as opposed to just those protesting – this increased it. People asked 'Why are they killing my children when none were carrying arms, and while they're sending provisions to the nearby Shia village?' When they played Shia songs at the checkpoints in all-Sunni neighbourhoods. Then my atheist friends began asserting their Sunnism, which is now more of a social than a religious identity.[6]

Add to this a symbolic assault against Sunni sacred sites. Regime forces fired anti-aircraft guns at minarets until they crumbled.[7] The Umawi Mosque in Aleppo burned, its thousand-year-old minaret fallen, and the minaret of Deraa's Omari Mosque, erected in the seventh century by Caliph Omar ibn al-Khattab. The Khalid ibn al-Waleed Mosque in Homs, built around the mausoleum of the famous Muslim general and companion of the Prophet, was shelled and burned. In the regime's cells, meanwhile, in a parody of the Muslim profession of faith, detainees were forced to swear that there was no god but Bashaar. Writer Samar Yazbek describes the provocation:

> When the uprising began, they attacked or destroyed symbols of the Sunni religion. In Kafranbel in August 2013, every day for 20 days, when people broke their fast during Ramadan, the Assad forces used to shell them at that moment, when they were about to eat, when they were saying their prayers. They used to hear the people in the planes on the telephones saying to each other, 'We want to make them eat death. We want to make them break their fast with death'. And they did. This is where extremism comes from – from violence and brutality. I am sorry, but anybody who has had ten of their children die is going to become an extremist.[8]

Then the drowning tyranny threw its arms around the neck of the Alawi community, advertising its complicity in its crimes and making it a potential target for revenge. The Zahra neighbourhood of Homs, for instance, was a visible affront to the besieged and shelled areas surrounding it. An Alawi community brimming now with soldiers, with rocket launchers set up in the square, the whole area was lit up while the rest of the city was dark. There were goods in Zahra's shops, and very cheap furniture, clothes and electronics on sale in the 'Sunni market' – all looted from opposition homes. Alawi women too were encouraged to join in the repression of their neighbours – eliciting a predictable response. 'They come into people's houses and take money if they find more than a little', complained one Sunni woman. 'They steal mobile phones. They kick and punch. And what have we done to deserve this? Is it because we're Muslims? Because we say there is no god but God? Is that why we lost our youth and our homes?'[9]

Collective punishment for Sunnis; the collective tarring of Alawis. The most crucial of all mass-implications, and another bloody turning point in the conflict, was the series of state-directed sectarian massacres on the central plain between Homs and Hama through summer 2012. On 25 May, 108 people were murdered at Houleh, a Sunni population surrounded by Alawi and Shia villages. The victims – almost half of them children – had their throats cut, their skulls split open and were riddled with bullets. On 6 June, between 78 and 100 people were similarly murdered at al-Qubeir, again a Sunni farming area surrounded by Alawi villages. On 10 July, between 68 and 150 people – both civilians and rebel fighters – were killed at Tremseh.[10]

In these and many smaller incidents, it was the *shabeeha* accompanying the army who did most of the killing. In Aleppo and Damascus the *shabeeha* militias are manned by thugs of all backgrounds, but in the Homs, Hama and Lattakia regions they are exclusively Alawi and Shia. Using locally recruited gangs as death squads transforms neighbouring communities into bitter enemies. The strategy is coldly intelligent; it incites the victim community with a generalised thirst for revenge, while exploiting the spectre of this revenge to frighten even dissenting members of the 'perpetrator community' into redoubled allegiance.

Next, the entry of Lebanon's Hizbullah and other Iranian-backed militias gave the conflict a Sunni–Shia flavour and fitted it into a regional struggle which had flared since the American occupation of Iraq. The Shia were by no means a natural target for Syrian Sunni enmity – they constituted only 1 per cent of the population, and before the revolution were not particularly associated with the regime.[11] When Hizbullah was perceived as an anti-Zionist resistance force, it was wildly popular among Syrians, Sunnis as much as everyone else, and in 2006, when hundreds of thousands of southern Lebanese – most of them Shia – fled Israeli bombs for Syria, they were housed in private homes. Several thousand were welcomed in the border town of Qusayr.

In any case, orthodox Shia like orthodox Sunnis tend to consider the Alawis heretics. The alliance between Assadist Syria and Shia-theocratic Iran is political, not religious – but that's not the way it felt on the ground. By word and action, Iran and its clients seemed to confirm the discourse of the wildest anti-Shia propagandists. Hizbullah's role in Assad's recapture of Qusayr was followed by the regime burning the Homs land registry, and then reports that Alawi families were being invited to take over Sunni homes. Sunnis feared an agenda linking Alawi tyranny and ethnic cleansing to Shia regional expansionism. The results soon began to emerge. Hizbullah secured Qusayr on 5 June 2013; and on 11 June there was a savagely sectarian response at Hatla in Deir al-Zor, where 60 Shia – some *shabeeha* but at least 30 civilians – were murdered.[12]

* * *

> *The ideal citizen was the citizen closest to the military-security system. Amongst the Alawis as among the other communities the idea of citizenship diminished little by little to be replaced by loyalty to sect, family, clan or class. The mass Syrian national identity itself crumbled into sub-national fragments, each in apparent rivalry with the other to seize what opportunities it could. For the Alawis, if the sect provided both identity and privileges, then it became the homeland; an attack on the sect became an attack against the homeland; defence of the sect was defence of the homeland; sacrifice for the sect was sacrifice for the homeland's sake.*
>
> Rasha Omran[13]

> *As far as we were concerned this was a Syrian revolution, not the rebellion of any sect. Sunnis didn't really identify as Sunnis – the Sunnis of Aleppo were different from those of Damascus; the Sunnis of the countryside weren't like those of the city. But sectarianism grew when people saw 90 per cent of Alawis stayed loyal.*
>
> Basel al-Junaidi[14]

If 90 per cent of Alawis stayed loyal, 10 per cent sided unambiguously with the revolution. High profile artists and intellectuals spoke out for freedom and against regime repression.[15] Alawi actress Fadwa Suleiman lived under bombs, addressed the streets, and went on hunger strike for the revolution's sake.[16] In October 2012, Zubaida al-Meeki, an Alawi general, became the first female officer to defect. (She went on to train FSA fighters.)[17] Around the country, Alawi revolutionaries worked in committees and councils, organising protests and smuggling aid to the besieged.[18] Most had to keep their activities hidden from their families; if found out they risked social ostracism as well as torture and imprisonment.

Still, the great majority of Alawis did remain loyal to the regime even as it waged war on Syria's people and infrastructure. How can this be explained? Historically, the syncretic and esoteric Alawi faith – a mix of Shiism, Sufism and Neoplatonism – was an almost constant target of orthodox denunciation.[19] The infamous *fatwa* of thirteenth-century theologian (and intellectual ancestor of Wahhabism) Ibn Taymiyya, declaring Alawis heretics, was sometimes used as justification for spilling their blood. Under the Ottoman Empire, Alawis – unlike Shia Muslims, Christians or Jews – were not considered 'People of the Book', and were therefore stripped of legal and civil rights. Until the 1920s, they tended to keep to their mountain villages overlooking the coast. When they came to the cities in the decades after that, the main marker of their difference was their poverty.

During these years, Alawis alongside rural Syrians of all sectarian backgrounds migrated to the cities to work and study, but – because of their poverty as well as the regime's sectarianism – they also rose disproportionately through the Baath Party and army, particularly after the 1963 Baath coup, and then Hafez al-Assad's 1970 'corrective movement'.

The community is riven by significant regional and tribal divisions, and these are exploited by Assadism; some villages are favoured while others are not (the Alawi families of Jableh, in general, profited from Hafez al-Assad's rise, while those of Tartous didn't). And by 2011, Sunnis and Alawis were used to working together in mixed urban areas, sometimes intermarrying.[20] Yet almost every Alawi family has a son, cousin or uncle in the army or security services. Those who live in the Alawi enclaves built by the regime on the strategic approaches to the main cities are overwhelmingly employed by the military and security services, and are therefore entirely dependent on the state. Mezzeh 86, a suburb of Damascus near the presidential palace and today a target of opposition mortars and car bombs, is one example.

The officers of the Republican Guard, the special forces and the security agencies – the real powers running the country – are almost exclusively Alawi. This 'empowerment' of the community after 1970 arguably reversed its growing acceptance by the Sunni majority.

Once despised, Alawis were now feared and resented. It was also the reason why the regime found it necessary to reduce Alawi identity to its Baathist, or more properly Assadist, component. Because the regime depended on Alawi soldiers for its survival, it was potentially at their mercy. Therefore it needed to ensure that no alternative source of authority existed within the community. Leftist and dissenting-Baathist Alawis were ruthlessly repressed.[21] Independent Alawi religious leaders were likewise imprisoned, exiled or intimidated into silence. Hafez al-Assad's brother Jameel, unqualified to say the least, attempted to make himself a spiritual leader in their place. Religious education in schools centred on Sunni tenets and rituals (Christian students had their own classes). The president prayed Sunni-style in public, and Alawis were encouraged to give up their religious difference, to build mosques and go on Haj like the Sunnis.

As a result, the Sunni slander that 'they have no religion' is a lot more true today than it was in 1970. Most Alawis are not religious and most know very little about their own tradition. When they do turn to religion, they often practice Sunni or mainstream Shia Islam. (This may be changing; under the strain of war Alawism is experiencing a revival in parallel with its Sunni competitor.) Today, Alawi group identification is not primarily religious but as a historically oppressed community whose fortunes are inextricably tied up with the repressive mechanisms of state, and with the Assad family itself. Even as it sought to reduce Alawi religious difference, regime policy has made the community's social difference still more distinct and politically salient. For those Alawis who have no alternative ideology or self-identification, the fall of Baathism is unthinkable.

When the revolution erupted – long before the rise of jihadist extremists – state propaganda played on the community's carefully nurtured fears. Rasha Omran describes how

> the regime mobilised to counter the challenge by besieging the revolution in specific areas and alienating it from others – stock divide-and-rule methods. At a time of peaceful protest, state media spoke of armed takfiri gangs killing soldiers and security agents (those honourable patriots), and of their goal of sectarian war in Syria. Then it launched false-flag operations and spread rumours

amongst the Alawis, reminding them with increased intensity of the narrative of historical persecution. The regime also sacrificed some Alawis in areas of sectarian friction in order to frighten the rest into believing that those who claimed to stand for revolution were actually sectarian killers intent on revenge for Hama. Simply put, the regime let loose the monster of fear which had been latent in Alawi minds, and reinforced once again the link between homeland and sect.[22]

* * *

In the 1960s it seemed much of the Arab world was set on a secular trajectory similar to Europe's. Political discourse referenced socialism and nationalism more than religion, and such visible signs of piety as the headscarf were rapidly diminishing in Cairo, Baghdad and Damascus.

Then came the catastrophic defeat by Israel in 1967 and the collapse of nationalist dreams. By the 1979 Revolution in Iran, Islam was at the top of the political agenda. In the following decades a region-wide religious revival saw a dramatic increase in actual and symbolic religious observance.[23] More than before, religion was exploited by power, and also served as a site of resistance to power.

Any serious attempt to understand the phenomenon must move beyond the false binary of 'secular' dictatorships versus Islamism, for the return to religion came in the age of the security states, and was in large part a consequence of them. The corruption of education systems, the chaining of free expression, and the generalised pollution of public space, gave back to the mosque an importance it had been losing. In Yassin Swehat's formulation: 'The source of morals in a corrupt and lawless country is religion.'[24]

The elimination or co-optation of the left removed one of religion's natural competitors. Religion answered to popular dissatisfaction with an economic, cultural and social reality (wrongly) perceived as 'secular', and filled welfare gaps for the poor abandoned by regimes in their neo-liberal stages. Religious fervour mourned a supposedly more authentic and ethical past, cashing in on the nostalgia and unease captured by Libyan novelist Ahmad al-Faqih when he wrote, 'A time has passed and another time is not coming.'

In the Assadist 'secular' state, atheism was forbidden. The constitution determined that the president must be Muslim. One sect was over-represented in the state-security nexus. There was no civil code for personal law – marriage, divorce and inheritance were governed by sharia for Muslims and church law for Christians. Where it existed, the regime's 'active' secularism was top-down, like the Baathist revolution itself, and often aggressively sectarian. During the 1980s repression of the Muslim Brotherhood, for instance, Rifaat al-Assad's 'Daughters of the Revolution' militia used to rip the headscarves from (Sunni) women on public transport. Meanwhile the discussion or even acknowledgement of sectarian differences was made taboo. The specificities of the Alawi, Ismaili and Druze faiths were mentioned neither in school nor on television – and so remained unknown to Sunnis, except through colourful rumours. Silencing the issue made it more salient. What Syria needed was a national conversation about historical fears and resentments aiming towards greater mutual understanding; instead people discussed the other sect in bitter secret whispers, and only among their own.

On social matters, the regime frequently conceded to the conservative social demands of the Sunni clergy, or *ulema*, so long as they failed to call for, or openly opposed, democratic reform. In the Bashaar years, for example, the state pacified the clerics by removing the book *Down With the Veil!* from shops, quadrupling sharia high schools between 2005 and 2008, and awarding a 50 per cent salary rise for mosque personnel.[25]

The *ulema* – recruited in the post-Ottoman period from the ranks of 'petty and middle class craftsmen-merchants, and – though to a lesser extent – rural immigrants and foreigners'[26] – are the guardians of tradition and 'managers of the goods of salvation'.[27] Through evening classes, and radio and Internet broadcasts, they've met an increasing public demand for religious education, and under Bashaar's neo-liberal dispensation they emerged as 'the actors most capable of raising funds from the private sector in order to develop private welfare in a context of growing inequality'.[28] This made them potentially influential social actors, and it was important for the regime to co-opt those it could. The female-led, upper class and highly secretive Qubaysiyyat movement for instance, which had set up schools and encouraged many young women to wear the headscarf, remained loyal through the uprising – though this caused splits and desertions from the organisation. And state-appointed Grand Mufti Ahmed Hassoun, a man smaller than his title, at first seemed to veer towards solidarity with the revolution, calling it a 'revolution of dignity' at a funeral in Deraa – but was later whipped back into line. In October 2011, this liberal cleric, who'd campaigned against honour killing and called for interfaith dialogue, threatened Europe with an army of suicide bombers should there be intervention against Assad.[29]

A much weightier figure in religious circles was the revered scholar Shaikh Ramadan Bouti. Of Kurdish origin, this long-time loyalist had supported the regime's brutal response to earlier Kurdish protests, declaring: 'I put my Kurdishness under my feet'. And now Bouti rehearsed regime propaganda that the nationwide uprising was a foreign conspiracy, wittered about 'Israeli war against Syria' while the regime shelled Homs, and emphasised the traditional Sunni teaching that the *wali al-amr* (or ruler) should be obeyed even when he's unjust. Bouti was killed while delivering a mosque lesson on 21 March 2013.[30]

Like their Christian counterparts, most *ulema* of the big cities either remained loyal to Assad or were cowed into irrelevance by state repression and the failure of their traditional bourgeois base to mobilise. According to Thomas Pierret, 'by September 2011, all of the oppositional ulema of the capital had retreated into silence, a posture that badly damaged the image of the whole clergy among opposition activists'.[31] By summer 2012, every rebellious Damascene cleric was in exile.

The Sunni religio-political alternative to the *ulema*, which is in many ways more progressive, is Islamism in its various forms. Unlike the *ulema*, Islamists prioritise 'structural changes in the political system: their aim is to modify the central principles of the monopoly on legitimate violence, changing those controlling this monopoly, the rules governing to whom the power may be devolved, and the general limits of its application – in the case of Syria, for instance, they demand free elections, respect for human rights, and the end of the single-party system'.[32]

It's too easy to see Islamism from outside as a monolith of reaction. People educated in secular schools are usually more receptive to Islamist thought than traditional seminary students; it is natural that such people would want to examine issues of state and social organisation through the prism of their own cultural references. Though Islamism generally tends to the right, there are leftist, even feminist versions too. Many of the old anti-imperialist and nationalist themes are subsumed into the discourse. Islamism can be liberation theology, or bourgeois democracy, or dictatorship, or apocalyptic nihilism.

In Syria the Islamist umbrella covers liberals such as Jawdat Sa'id, a preacher of non-violence, human rights activists like the lawyer Haytham al-Maleh, and independents like Muaz al-Khatib, briefly head of the Coalition. The traditional motor and focus of Islamist activity, however, was the Muslim Brotherhood; but the organisation was almost totally eliminated inside the country by 2011, and was anyway tainted in popular perception by memories of the armed wing's 1980s adventurism. Therefore it had no ground presence in the revolution's first months, though its exiled members in Europe and the Gulf scrabbled to dominate the external opposition, while sending aid to civilians and funds to some military formations inside.

Unlike the tame *shaikhs* of the big cities, the provincial *ulema* stood firmly with the revolution. Nevertheless, the failure of Bouti-style quietist Islam in the face of such savage repression greatly benefitted political Islamism in general, and – in the absence of the Muslim Brotherhood – the activist Salafist trend in particular. The most powerful of the Islamist militias to emerge during the armed struggle would be led by Salafists.

Salafism is a puritanical version of Sunni Islam which seeks, either by force or persuasion, to return society to the presumed way of life of the first Muslims. A key factor behind its regional and international spread has been the projection of Wahhabism, its Saudi variant, by Saudi-owned media and imam training schemes, or through migrant workers' contacts with the Saudi kingdom. But this by itself doesn't explain the phenomenon. Salafism has a literal rather than a mystical or superstitious tone, and so appeals to urbanising, 'modernising', populations. At the same time, its millenarian political vision offers symbolic solace to those suffering oppression or alienation. And as a seeming challenge to power, the obsession of its activist trend with capturing and reshaping the state fits well with the paradigms established by previous oppositional movements, whether nationalist or socialist.

In Syria the movement had been both savagely repressed and cleverly exploited. Sometimes the regime used its image theatrically; in February 2006, for example, an apparently spontaneous but certainly staged gathering of Muslims infuriated by the *Jyllands-Posten* cartoons burned down the Danish and Norwegian embassies in Damascus. In this way the regime sent a message to the still gung-ho Americans next door in Iraq: 'Remove us too, and you'll have to deal with these lunatics.' Inside Iraq, they sent a still clearer message. In this period, the regime allowed Salafist networks to operate unimpeded in Syria, even facilitating their passage across the border to fight the Americans and the Shia government (and to help precipitate the civil war). When these fighters returned to Syria, they were arrested and imprisoned.[33]

By 2013, activist Salafism was in the air regionally and locally. It provided a ready vocabulary for previously apolitical men suddenly finding themselves having to fight, alienated by the weakness of traditional religious discourse and searching for an ideology within which to frame their dramatic new experience. So conspiracies aren't needed to explain the phenomenon. Nevertheless, once again, the regime did its utmost to encourage the rise of the Salafists.

From March to October 2011, at the same time that it was targeting thousands of non-violent, non-sectarian revolutionaries for death-by-torture, the regime released up to 1,500 of the most well-connected Salafist activists from its prisons. These were the same men who'd unwittingly served the regime's interests in Iraq; now they became useful again. According to a defected intelligence officer, 'The regime did not just open the door to the prisons and let these extremists out, it facilitated them in their work, in their creation of armed brigades ... The regime wanted to tell the world it was fighting al-Qaida but the revolution was peaceful in the beginning so it had to build an armed Islamic revolt. It was a specific, deliberate plan and it was easy to carry out.'[34] Many leaders of key Islamist militias – Zahran Alloush of the Army of Islam, for instance, or Hassan Aboud of Ahrar al-Sham, as well as founding members of Jabhat al-Nusra, and Abu Athir al-Absi and Awad al-Makhlaf, important figures in ISIS – were beneficiaries of Assad's 'amnesty'.

* * *

In response to the regime's violence and sectarianism, there was undoubtedly an intensification not only of religiosity but of Sunni identity and sectarian resentment. But still this shouldn't be over-exaggerated. When Islamic vocabulary first overwashed the armed resistance, it didn't necessarily signify an Islamist political agenda. In the words of Ziad Homsi, who fought in Douma: 'We used the word martyr for our dead. People wanted to die as martyrs if they had to die, but they weren't fighting to raise the black flag [of the jihadist groups].'[35]

And Yassin Swehat warns against Islamophobic overgeneralisations:

> The Islamic names reflect the country's culture. For example, there was a brigade in Raqqa named Ammar bin Yasser [a companion of the Prophet] – and there's a high school in Raqqa of the same name. They're referencing their neighbourhoods. And it's more communitarian than religious. If the Shia hate a particular companion of the Prophet, people will choose that name. They're angry Muslims rather than Islamists. And as for the Islamists, they're not all the same. In the Islamic Front, Ahrar al-Sham or Alloush's Jaysh al-Islam, for instance, are pursuing political projects, whereas Liwa al-Tawheed just represents the conservative culture of rural Aleppo.[36]

Even in circumstances of war, most Syrians are not Islamists. In a 2014 opinion poll conducted among refugees, only 30 per cent expressed the desire for a religious-based state – a remarkably low proportion given the anger current in the hearts of the displaced, and considering that in the ears of many Syrians the phrase 'Islamic state' doesn't connote corporal punishment or enforced gender segregation, but rather 'just government' or 'a clean social space'.[37]

Yet the fighters on the battlefield were visibly Islamising. Three obvious factors animated the process. The first was funding. With the FSA hierarchy unable to establish a consistent weapons supply, the fighting brigades had to organise their own networks of support. The most easily tapped sources were Salafist fundraisers and businessmen in the Gulf. In their nomenclature and (filmed) symbology, therefore, resistance militias increasingly appealed to this audience.

Lubna al-Kanawati saw the shift in Harasta: 'When they saw they might receive money, they changed their names, their appearance, their symbols and speech.' And Ziad Hamoud supports her by example: 'A militia called "Guevara" doesn't win funds. In the Ghouta there was a brigade called "the Martyr Meshaal Temmo." It changed its name to "the Mujahid Osama bin Laden".'[38]

As for state donors, Saudi Arabia funded militias led by men with tribal or personal connections to the Kingdom, and some of these were Islamist (though the Sauds usually funded secular groups like the Syrian Revolutionaries Front). Qatar, in tune with its regional pro-Muslim Brotherhood policy, armed Muslim Brotherhood-linked as well as Salafist groups. In addition, the airtime given by Gulf TV channels to Islamist and Salafist anti-Assad activists may have been as influential on the ground as Gulf money.[39]

The second factor was the air of corruption and disorganisation hanging over the FSA label, and the Islamists' contrasting reputation for order. Yassin Swehat speaks of the fighters as 'men living in post-apocalyptic conditions, who need discipline and a strong ideology so they can withstand these conditions.'[40] By their enthusiasm and willingness to die, and sometimes because of their previous experience in Iraq, Islamists proved most effective on the battlefield. And Islamists were often able to provide services to civilians where secular or non-ideological brigades had failed.

The third factor in the military Islamisation was the lack of an international response to Assad's massacres and ethnic cleansings – particularly after the August 2013 sarin attacks in Damascus, when the external opposition's hopes of significant Western support were finally buried. The 3 July military coup in Egypt, meanwhile, and the slaughter of Muslim Brotherhood supporters that followed, seemed to prove the supremacy of violence over electoral politics.

* * *

On 22 November 2013, following a summer of meetings, the Islamic Front declared its existence. Five of the seven brigades contained in this new alliance – Jaysh al-Islam (prominent in the Ghouta suburbs of Damascus), Liwa al-Tawheed (Aleppo's most important formation), Suqour al-Sham, Liwa al-Haqq and the Kurdish Islamic Front – had previously fought for the FSA and would still fight alongside it, but were now emphasising their independence as well as their Islamic identity.

Some Syrians saw the Islamic Front's formation as a necessary move to deny the jihadists of Nusra and ISIS a monopoly over the vocabulary of armed Islam.[41] These two groups – which will be discussed later in this chapter – were making their presence intensely felt. Other Syrians worried over the Islamic Front's confusing position on democracy. On the one hand its spokesmen called unambiguously for a sharia state, rejecting the concept of popular sovereignty as expressed through democratic elections. (In conversation, Islamic Front associates sometimes substitute democracy with the medieval concept of *ahl al-hal wal-aqd*, or 'those who loose and bind' – an assembly of clerics, merchants and experts who would elect and guide a caliph. This may or may not be an advance on Assadist totalitarianism; it's certainly not a model likely to long satisfy the popular urges unleashed by the revolutionary process.[42]) On the other hand, the Islamic Front promised not to impose its programme on the Syrian people. Its role was simply to bring down the regime.

On the possibility of sectarian coexistence, the Islamic Front's proclamations were no less contradictory. Jaysh al-Islam leader Zahran Alloush promised protection for minorities (which implies no automatic equality of citizenship), while also vowing to 'cleanse Syria of Shia filth'.[43] This threat may well have been a political response to Iran's role in propping up the regime, but was naturally read by pro-regime communities as an omen of ethnic cleansing – specifically of driving the Alawis back to their mountains.

In May 2014, after revolutionary criticism, and seeking to distinguish itself from ISIS – with whom it was now at war – and Jabhat al-Nusra, the Islamic Front (alongside other 'moderate Islamist' brigades) signed a Code of Honour which rejected 'extremism' and promised 'the Syrian revolution is a revolution of morals and values, aiming to achieve freedom, justice and security for Syrian society and its diverse social fabric, made up of all racial and sectarian elements'. Significantly, the Code did not call for a sharia state.

Ahrar al-Sham, the largest and most extreme organisation in the Front (along with Ansar al-Sham, it had never been part of the FSA structure) was implicated by Human Rights Watch, alongside Jabhat al-Nusra and ISIS, in the August 2013 slaughter and abduction of Alawi civilians in Lattakia province – the first documented large-scale sectarian attack by Sunnis, and a strategic blow against the revolution and national unity.[44] Ahrar al-Sham denied involvement. On 9 September 2014, Ahrar's leader Hassan Aboud and 27 other senior commanders were killed by a suicide bomb. ISIS was probably responsible.

The nature of Islamic Front rule is best judged by examining Douma and elsewhere in the eastern Ghouta, where the Islamic Front's Jaysh al-Islam is the dominant armed force. Zahran Alloush frequently appears in the area to deliver sermons and shake hands (a politician in the Western sense, he's also often presented advising his men on the front line, cool-headed under fire).

Jaysh al-Islam enjoys a degree of genuine popularity among the hungry residents (Douma was always split between Islamist and Nasserist tendencies), primarily because of its courage and military prowess. Ziad Homsi, who moved from fighting to media work as the conflict Islamised, explains: 'By the summer of 2012, all of Douma was liberated, but sometimes Assad's army re-entered town and then the Free Army brigades fled. But Alloush's men didn't leave when the others did.'[45]

Neither did they persecute the few Alawis still in the Ghouta. These were supporters of the revolution or they would have left the area, and they were left alone. Secularists and minorities were nevertheless compelled to live according to Alloush's social standards. Lubna al-Kanawati, for instance, was told to wear the hijab in the street (but permitted to remove it when meeting people indoors). Under these constraints (and under the regime siege and bombardment) she was able to survive in the Ghouta until ISIS established a presence, and threatened her. Then she left for Turkey.

Jaysh al-Islam won plaudits for pushing ISIS out of the area in 2014. But by then residents were accusing the militia of stockpiling food, and they protested against it. Lubna describes the mood: 'The people know they're pursuing their own interests, not religion. They say, solve the food crisis first, then think about your Islamic state. In the Ghouta, people still want freedom and human rights, but increasingly they're too scared to speak. It's a new form of dictatorship.'[46]

The most blatant sign of new dictatorship was Jaysh al-Islam's likely abduction and perhaps murder of 'the Douma Four' on 9 December 2013.[47] Three of these revolutionaries – Razan Zaitouneh, her husband Wael Hamada and Nazem Hamadi – were part of the founding core of the LCCs. The fourth was Samira Khalil, wife of prominent leftist Yassin al-Haj Saleh, described as 'a motherly figure who loves everybody, who tries to keep everyone happy, who's very generous in helping others.'[48] Samira had stayed on in Douma after her husband left to continue setting up women's centres – the first centre in Douma is called Women Now; another was established in Mesraba, and still another is planned for Harasta. It's unclear whether this work marked her for Alloush's displeasure, or whether she was simply in the wrong place at the wrong time – in the company of Razan.

Razan and her husband Wael had moved to Douma, where Wael's family lived, in April 2013. This was a boon to revolutionaries around the country. Previously they'd been on the run and therefore very difficult to get hold of. Now they were based in liberated territory – where they were ultimately no safer. Assaad al-Achi describes the damage done by the abduction, and its possible causes:

> The abduction of Razan, Wael and Nazem was a terrible blow. They were the backbone of the LCCs. We've survived since then, but I can't say we're living. What upset Zahran Alloush? First, Razan [through the Violations Documentation Centre] was documenting the violations committed by his Army of Islam; second, the LCCs were competing with Alloush's Mujahideen Consultative Council. He was very angry when we supported the local council in Douma. He wanted all support for civilians to go through his organisation. Beyond that, he was offended by Razan's personality. She never dissembled or hid her identity. She's a liberal woman who will never veil, who won't allow anyone to dictate how she behaves. In her opinion, if Bashaar al-Assad was unable to impose upon her, no

> other dog would do so either. Those are her words. For a Salafist, such a free spirit is dangerous.[49]

In Aleppo too, new forms of authoritarianism were constricting revolutionary space. Zaid Muhammad was detained for three days by the city's sharia court for expressing secularist ideas. As his freedom had been taken by 'moderate Islamists' rather than extremists, by Syrians rather than foreign ideologues, popular pressure (from Islamist as well as secular revolutionaries) was enough to release him.

Marcell Shehwaro, who had once brought protesting Muslims to meet members of her local church, was also starting to feel less comfortable in her surroundings: 'Slowly, with the growth of wounded Sunni identity, I felt attitudes towards me change. At first everyone was very positive, very pleased that I was there, as a Christian, living the revolution with them. Later some were more likely to ask why the other Christians hadn't come with me. As far as Daesh were concerned, when they were there, I was part of the West, nothing else.'[50]

* * *

The first major jihadist organisation to arrive on the battlefield was Jabhat al-Nusra, or the Victory Front. Nusra is the Syrian branch of al-Qaida, though unlike the global organisation it focuses its fight solely against the Syrian regime rather than Western targets. Its core membership consists of Syrians who fought with Abu Musaab al-Zarqawi's al-Qaida franchise in Iraq. The US added the group to its terrorist list in December 2012.[51]

At first Nusra remained a fringe group, although it was widely blamed for a string of suicide bombings against civilian targets in 2011 and 2012.[52] Then time and trauma played their roles. Beyond this, Nusra's rise was powered by the same non-ideological factors which favoured Islamist formations in general. Its existing arsenal (acquired from Iraq and from private donors in the Gulf) wedded to its cadres' fearless fighting skills (developed on Afghan and Iraqi battlefields), allowed it to capture a string of military installations in the east, and thus to procure more weaponry, including heavy guns. Then it took on new and bigger targets, such as the Taftanaz airfield in Idlib province, and in the process won more weapon-hungry recruits.

It was careful, meanwhile, not to repeat the al-Qaida experience in Iraq, where the oppressive application of 'Islamic' punishments had caused the population to push it out. In Syria, Nusra presented itself as a lighter version of al-Qaida – good for defeating the regime, but not so scary that it would cause a post-regime problem.

In Aleppo, regime bombing of bakeries, poor supply lines, and the looting and indiscipline of the FSA militias, sparked a bread crisis in the winter of 2012/13. Jabhat al-Nusra stepped into the breach, set up the Islamic Services Committee to provide bread and water, and won plaudits from locals as it safeguarded and fairly distributed grain supplies. Zaid Muhammad concedes: 'On the political level, they're a catastrophe, but in terms of services provision, they've often been successful.'[53]

Basel al-Junaidi points to Nusra's organisational skills as the key reason for their acceptance:

> There were two or three hundred Nusra fighters in Aleppo – out of tens of thousands – from the first days of liberation. They weren't liked because of their extremism – stopping people playing songs, for instance, this was strange for our culture. At the same time, they were respected for their organisation and discipline – this was when the Free Army fighters were still wearing slippers. They were respected as strong, well-trained soldiers, so people – including secularists like us – decided to tolerate them until the regime had gone. We had faith that Syrian society would never accept their rule. Now we can see this was a mistake.[54]

However extreme the ideology of Nusra's leadership, it should be remembered that its large popular base consists mainly of Syrians who joined up for pragmatic reasons and, at least at first, did not necessarily support the Salafist state-building project. Research conducted by the Voices of Syria project in early 2012, showed that the Islamist fighters interviewed were surprisingly supportive of democracy: 60 per cent of fighters from Ahrar al-Sham and Jabhat al-Nusra agreed that 'democracy is preferable to any other form of governance'; 78

per cent also strongly agreed that 'it is essential for Syria to remain a unified state'.[55] Though the terrors of the intervening years have likely hardened attitudes, it is probable that many of these men will leave the jihadist ranks once Assad falls.

The foreign fighters are a different matter. If the regime's first self-fulfilling prophecy was 'armed gangs', the next was 'infiltrators'. Some foreigners – including many who'd participated in bringing down the Tunisian and Libyan dictators – were not Salafists at all, but democrats, and they joined FSA brigades as well as working in medical and material aid.[56] But as the state broke down and jihadist networks exercised their logistical skills, disgruntled Islamists flocked to Syria from Chechnya, all corners of the Arab world, and Europe.[57] Most were funnelled towards Jabhat al-Nusra, though some ended up in smaller jihadist groups such as the Chechen-led Jaysh al-Muhajireen wal-Ansar.

'We were desperate enough to welcome Chechens and others to fight the regime', says Ziad Hamoud. 'We didn't ask them to come, but they came, and at first we said "he's willing to stand with me, to protect me from those killing me"'.[58] With Assad's bombs falling, and the FSA confronting the regime everywhere, a few thousand bizarre foreigners seemed more a source of amusement than a danger. In June 2013, foreigners were occupying the village of Atmeh in Idlib province, just across the Turkish border. Inhabitants of the nearby refugee camp complained these people weren't fighting the regime but sitting around instead eating peculiar food. They called them 'the spicy crew', and said it would take 'two minutes' to get rid of them once the regime had fallen.[59] Six months later the foreigners were flying ISIS's black banner, and Free Army fighters, civil activists and foreign journalists didn't dare pass through Atmeh.

* * *

'There's a price for every defeat, and al-Qaida was defeated in Iraq', says Yassin Swehat, referring to the 2007 rout of al-Qaida franchise the Islamic State in Iraq (ISI) by the tribal-based and American-backed Sahwa militias. 'Daesh is the revolution within al-Qaida.'[60]

Perhaps Yassin oversimplifies. It might be more accurate to say that the Iraqi version of al-Qaida was already a revolution against Bin Laden and Zawahiri's parent organisation. Led by Abu Musaab al-Zarqawi, ISI had pledged allegiance to the al-Qaida label despite significant ideological differences. The original al-Qaida, for instance, believed that spectacular attacks on civilians should only be applied in Western, non-Muslim settings, whereas the Iraqi incarnation of the organisation believed that Iraq's Shia Muslim civilians were also fair game. Its anti-Shia terrorism was a major cause of Iraq's sectarian civil war of 2006 and 2007, and one reason why the Iraqi Sunni populace eventually turned against it.

In April 2013, Abu Bakr al-Baghdadi announced that ISI had birthed Jabhat al-Nusra in Syria, and that the two organisations would now merge, under his leadership, into the Islamic State of Iraq and Sham (the old name for greater Syria) – ISIS, or Daesh by its Arabic acronym.[61] Nusra leader Abu Muhammad al-Jawlani, however, backed up by al-Qaida's Ayman al-Zawahiri, refused the merger. Baghdadi pushed ahead nevertheless, and Nusra split – the foreign fighters in particular left to join ISIS. In February 2014 al-Zawahiri rejected all connection to Baghdadi's new formation. ISIS, in other words, is too extreme for al-Qaida.[62]

Its fighters arrived in Syria as they'd once arrived in Iraq, gently at first, exploiting the people's torments at the hands of a well-armed occupier – in Iraq the Americans, in Syria the delegitimised regime. In the town of Saraqeb, in Idlib province, for example, at first only ten representatives came, and they brought with them large amounts of medicine and food, as well as money, with which they recruited local fighters. Then reinforcements arrived – 'Libyans, Algerians, a lot of Iraqis, some Afghans and Turks, one white Belgian and one white American' – enough to frighten thieves into good behaviour, which at first increased the organisation's popularity.[63] But in May 2013, just after the split with Nusra, they whipped two men in a public square for an infringement of Islamic family law. In June they took absolute control, forbade drinking and smoking, and made public prayer compulsory. Then they closed the printing press used by local revolutionaries to produce the children's magazine *Zeitoun wa Zeitouna* (a second press still ran at a secret location). Yasser Barish, brother of

Saraqeb's coordination committee founder Manhal, was detained and beaten for 'taking photographs of women' (the 'women' in question were girls under the age of thirteen participating in a *Zeitoun wa Zeitouna* workshop). In July 2013, ISIS attacked Saraqeb's media centre and abducted Polish journalist Martin Soder.[64]

In March 2013, revolutionaries took control of Raqqa, a city between Aleppo and the Iraqi border and the first provincial capital to be entirely liberated. Media activist Bashaar Abu Hadi is cynical: 'The regime withdrew from Raqqa like the Israelis withdrew from Gaza – they wanted a bad example'. Jabhat al-Nusra was there in force, setting up its own sharia court. Like-minded jihadists, more interested in establishing their own power base than toppling the regime, flocked to the city from Idlib and Aleppo. From April, ISIS increasingly dominated Raqqa, attacking shrines and churches and causing the city's substantial Christian population to flee.[65]

ISIS's most prominent Christian victim was Father Paolo Dall'Oglio, a Jesuit priest of Italian origin who'd revived and run the desert monastery at Deir Mar Mousa for three decades. Paolo – who spoke perfect Syrian Arabic and had long lost his 'foreigner' status – worked tirelessly for greater understanding between Christians and Muslims; the monastery was open to visitors of all faiths. When the revolution erupted, he spoke out against regime violence and for a transition to democracy, and delivered the funeral oration for film-maker Bassel Shehadeh, killed by regime shelling in Homs. As a result the regime exiled him in June 2012. He worked from Italy for a while, encouraging greater Christian solidarity with the revolution, but soon returned to Syria to meet (and pray with) FSA commanders.[66] Then he travelled to Raqqa to urge ISIS to release prisoners. On 29 July 2013, he was kidnapped by ISIS militants – the very people he'd hoped to reach out to. An unconfirmed but seemingly credible report claims he was murdered shortly afterwards.[67]

Conditions in ISIS prisons were not unlike those in the regime's, as Ziad Homsi can testify. Following his rapid shifts from student to detainee to militia fighter, Ziad had met and befriended the respected revolutionary intellectual Yassin al-Haj Saleh, who was living with his wife, activist Samira Khalil, in besieged but liberated Douma. Later Ziad accompanied Yassin on a perilous journey across the desert to

Raqqa, Yassin's home town now fallen from Assad to ISIS – or in Yassin's language, from neck-tie to long-beard fascism.[68] Yassin was as wanted by ISIS as he was by Assad; ISIS had already abducted one of his brothers. Eventually he crossed the border to Turkey. But Ziad wanted to get back to Douma, where his parents were, and so he set off with an FSA convoy carrying aid and weapons to the besieged Ghouta suburbs. ISIS stopped the convoy just outside Raqqa. Ziad was imprisoned for 39 days:

> They put us in a group cell and asked us questions about religion. There were foreign journalists too, but in a different place. Daesh kept telling me that Zahran Alloush was a foreign agent. For them, if he receives Gulf funding, he's an agent of the West. There was less torture than in a regime prison, but still Kurds and Free Army fighters were badly tortured. They say the Free Army is fighting for democracy, and that democracy is unbelief. Their definitions of Muslim and unbeliever are very different to ours.[69]

Like the regime, ISIS specialised in exemplary barbarity, proudly boasting about its violence (the regime, unlike ISIS, played a different tune in international arenas). Its territories witnessed not only public floggings, but stonings, crucifixions and the hurling of presumed gay men from towers. Its rule presaged a totalitarian year zero; libraries and shrines were destroyed, schools were turned into propaganda and recruitment centres, and the reign of terror targeted FSA, Islamic Front and Nusra fighters, civil activists and media workers, as well as foreign journalists and aid workers. Syrians who were in any way 'different' – those who'd lived abroad, for example, even those with light features – risked death at ISIS checkpoints. From southern Turkey, Bashaar Abu Hadi complains, 'We are all wanted by both the regime and Daesh. Daesh killed the elite of the revolution.'[70]

ISIS had undoubtedly become a third force in the conflict, and an enemy of the revolution before Assad. Indeed, the regime pursued an undeclared non-aggression pact with ISIS for months, bombing Raqqa's schools, hospitals and market places but not the large and obvious ISIS headquarters. It also bought oil from the jihadists. This strategy aimed to achieve the usual twin goals – to scare minorities, secularists and in this case the religious but non-extremist population into loyalty, and to convince Western powers that the dictatorship, despite the savagery of its counter-revolution, was the lesser threat. Depressingly, several Western columnists and government officials took the bait, calling for cooperation with Assad against ISIS, ignoring the context – Assad's even worse atrocities – which created the chaos in which ISIS grew.[71]

The people in the liberated areas, meanwhile, proved they could take on ISIS without seeking the aid of their chief tormentor. During the winter of 2013/14, popular protests against *al-dowlatain* – the two states, the Assadist and the 'Islamic' – spread across the north. ISIS's murder of Abu Rayyan, a doctor and fighter affiliated with Ahrar al-Sham, brought tensions to a head. On 3 January 2014, dubbed 'Friday of the Martyr Abu Rayyan, the Victim of Betrayal', countrywide protests demanded action.[72] The FSA, the Islamic Front and Nusra all responded, driving ISIS from its border strongholds in Idlib and Aleppo, where it had controlled the passage of men, goods and weapons. ISIS was also pushed out of Aleppo city – 300 journalists, activists and fighters were freed from its prison there – and greatly weakened in Deir al-Zor and Raqqa.

ISIS seemed to be on the way out. A few weeks of rebel operations, backed by popular support, had done what Assad had refused to do. Strangely, however, this turnaround was only very lightly covered by the Western media. In contradiction of the evidence, columnists continued to lament that there were no Syrians on the ground who could take the fight to ISIS. 'The opposition fought Daesh without any support,' says Basel al-Junaidi, 'by its own initiative, without anybody's permission. This was a popular intifada against Daesh, but nobody wanted to see it. The West ignored it.'[73]

Then in June 2014, events in Iraq brought ISIS back from the brink in Syria. Iraq had also been touched by the Arab Spring, though the protests there, coming in a post-Saddam, post-civil war context, had a sectarian flavour from the start.

A 'Day of Anger' across the country's Sunni Arab areas on 25 February 2011 had developed on Fridays thereafter into protests of tens of thousands, involving a range of civil society groups, women's organisations and trades unionists. The movement was not predominantly Islamist, but was certainly an expression of Sunni revanchism and a response to the sectarian oppression of the post-occupation Iraqi state – its army, police and associated Shia militias.

The democracy brought to Iraq by American tanks was based on a sectarian electoral system which undercut the possibility of cross-sect alliances and naturally favoured identitarian representatives of the country's Shia majority. The Shia political forces which assumed power – primarily the Iranian-backed Dawa party – embodied a backlash to Saddam Hussain's Sunni sectarianism. The government's supposedly 'anti-Baathist' and 'anti-terrorist' legislation was used to disenfranchise Sunnis, who suffered increasingly at the hands of the security forces. The government refused to incorporate into the national army the Sahwa militias which had driven al-Qaida out of Sunni areas in 2007 and 2008. And after 2011 it permitted and even facilitated the work of the Iranian-backed substate Shia militias fighting on Assad's behalf against the Sunni Arabs across the border. The enormous Iranian influence on Iraq in general – military and political as well as economic and cultural – was another key factor alienating Sunnis (and Kurds too).

Iraq's March 2010 elections seemed to present an opportunity to move beyond sectarian politics. With both Sunni and Shia support, the nationalist Iraqiya bloc won two seats more than the divisive and unpopular Nuri Maliki and his State of Law coalition. But Maliki manoeuvred to stay on as prime minister, despite an opinion poll showing only 14 per cent of Iraqis thought he should.[74] Iran lobbied hard to preserve Maliki, and President Barack Obama, via US ambassador Chris Hill, acquiesced.

The 2011 protests in Iraq's Sunni Arab areas were repressed, but erupted again in 2013. This time the widespread demonstrations and sit-ins looked like a full-blown intifada. Protestors managed to block the highway linking Iraq with Syria and Jordan. In April, government forces stormed a protest camp in Hawija, killing 56 and provoking gun battles across nearby areas. From then on, civil protests, met increasingly by mass detentions, torture and live ammunition, dwindled, and violence rose.

In December, in response to the kidnapping of Sunni MP Ahmed al-Alwani, tribal forces joined by defected Sunni policemen took over the major towns of Fallujah and Ramadi. Sensing an opportunity even as it reeled from defeats in Syria, ISIS increased its presence in Iraq's Sunni-majority areas through the spring of 2014. By June, although it fielded a minority of fighters, it was leading a Sunni coalition including Baathists (of the Iraqi wing), tribal forces, Naqshibandi Sufis, and many non-aligned men. It was careful to recruit officers from the pre-occupation Iraqi army – some of whom were now allied with the jihadist agenda, but many of whom joined for pragmatic reasons.

This means that ISIS's composition in Iraq is somewhat different to that in Syria, where a majority of its commanders are foreigners. As coalition leader rather than a latecomer exploiting an originally non-sectarian popular revolution, its support base in Iraq is much more solid than in Syria.[75] Those Iraqi Shia, Christian and Yazidi civilians unlucky enough to live in the ISIS-controlled area were forced to either flee or suffer mass execution, enslavement or forced conversion to Islam. Many Iraqi Sunnis, however, were prepared to tolerate the jihadists at first, so alienated were they from Iraq's government. (And many others weren't. Hundreds of thousands of Iraqi Sunnis have since fled ISIS rule, many to Iraqi Kurdistan.)

In June 2014, ISIS led an offensive which took huge swathes of northern and western Iraq out of government hands. Most significantly, the city of Mosul, Iraq's second largest, fell to ISIS on 10 June after only four days of battle. General Mahdi al-Gharawi – a proven torturer who had run secret prisons but was nevertheless appointed by Prime Minister Maliki as governor of Nineveh province – fled, and his troops, who greatly outnumbered the ISIS attackers, deserted.[76] This meant that the US-allied Iraqi army, on which the US had spent billions of dollars, was less able to take on ISIS than Syria's 'farmers and dentists'. Many Syrians saw a conspiracy in the Iraqi collapse, a play by Malki to win still more weapons from America, and by Iran to increase its regional importance as a counterbalance to Sunni jihadism. It's more likely that the fall of Mosul was an inevitable result of the Iraqi state's sectarian dysfunction. Shia soldiers felt themselves to be in foreign territory, and weren't prepared to die in other people's disputes. Many Sunni soldiers defected to ISIS.[77]

ISIS's control of the Iraq–Syria border, and especially of Mosul, was a game changer. The organisation collected the arms left behind by the Iraqi army, much of it high-quality weaponry inherited from the American occupation. Perhaps more importantly, it cleaned out Mosul's banks. Then it returned to Syria in force, using the new weapons to beat back the starved FSA and the new money to buy loyalties.

The FSA and Islamic Front in Deir al-Zor, besieged by both Assad and ISIS for months, begged the United States for ammunition, warning the city was about to fall. Their plea was ignored, and the revolutionary forces (plus Jabhat al-Nusra) pulled out in July, leaving the province's oil fields, and the Iraqi border area, in ISIS's hands.[78] ISIS reinforced itself in Raqqa and surged back into the Aleppo countryside and the central desert. Suddenly it dominated a third of Iraq and a third of Syria. In a tragic parody of the old Arab nationalist dream, it made good propaganda of erasing the Sykes–Picot border; in a tragic parody of Islamic history, it declared itself a Caliphate at the end of June.

Immediately it met a new form of resistance. In the absence of the FSA, locals self-organised, took up what weapons they could find, and managed to liberate a number of villages. The mysterious 'White Shroud' group emerged, launching small-scale guerrilla attacks and assassinations of ISIS militants.[79] Rattled, ISIS took savage reprisals against the Shaitat tribe which formed the backbone of Deir al-Zor's fightback. Over 900 of the tribe's members – mostly civilians – were murdered. Thousands more fled to Turkey.

ISIS's precipitous expansion meant that the undeclared non-aggression pact with Assad was finally at an end. It now took on regime forces in the east, most dramatically at the Tabqa airbase in August, where its execution of 220 surrendered conscripts shocked revolutionary as well as pro-regime constituencies. And Assad responded, for two reasons – ISIS was now a real threat to his regime, no longer simply a burden on the revolution; and now that the inattentive West was suddenly watching more closely, he had to demonstrate himself as a useful ally. Still, however, his war with ISIS was limited to areas of regime influence. When the FSA and ISIS fought, Assad's planes bombed the FSA.[80]

* * *

Events in the city of Manbij, north-east of Aleppo and not far from the Euphrates, are worth examining because they exemplify ISIS's rise, fall, and further rise.

Illustrating the organic ties between civil and military activism in the revolution's early stages, Monzer al-Sallal is both an activist-organiser and a military commander. Manbij's revolutionary council set up an FSA brigade called Kateebat al-Karama (the Dignity Battalion), which later affiliated with Liwa al-Tawheed (which dominates Aleppo). 'Our aim,' says Monzer, 'was to protect the city, to keep the residential areas secure, and to defend army defectors who were sheltering there.'[81]

A clean-cut, cigarette-smoking Muslim, Monzer studied sharia in Egypt's al-Azhar university. His opposition to Salafism, and particularly to *takfir* – the practice of 'excommunicating' Muslims who follow different interpretations of Islam – is therefore theological as well as political. He insists on the importance of open debate and tolerance in Muslim society, and sees no contradiction with civil government: 'We're Muslims, but this doesn't mean we can't be democrats. We had Islamic laws under Assad; we didn't revolt against these laws but to have all the law applied properly and fairly.'

Ahrar al-Sham and Jabhat al-Nusra fighters arrived ten months after the city's liberation. In April 2013 these men would defect to join the newly declared ISIS. They were initially welcomed by sections of the population for their rough and rapid application of extreme punishments, a severity that brought an end to the spate of kidnapping which had been plaguing Manbij. In this period Monzer witnessed the birth of the Islamic Front – a response to the jihadists: 'The Front consists of old Free Army brigades who strengthened their Islamic vocabulary and image in order to compete with Nusra and Daesh.'[82]

ISIS, of course, considered the revolutionary council to be both secular and 'atheist'. For a while the two administrations jostled for influence, but ISIS won out in the end. The key struggle was over bread. Control of grain was important to feed the people – the city's pre-revolution population of 200,000 had swollen with the displaced to 400,000 – as well as to generate funds. 'We produced bread more cheaply than elsewhere,' reports Monzer, 'and raised a small tax on it. This paid for electricity and ammunition. A year after the liberation we had to buy the grain harvest from the peasants so we could feed the city for the following year. We searched for money, and eventually the ACU [the Coalition's Assistance Coordination Unit] paid us $100,000. But by then Daesh had grown, and they seized the grain silos. Solutions and aid always come too late.'[83]

Gradually, however, the revolutionary council rebuilt influence through its sharia court and police force. More significantly, Manbij's residents were increasingly angered by ISIS's foreign leaders, their mismanagement of the grain, and their intrusion into people's private business. Yasser Munif describes the growing resistance:

> During my second trip, the population was clearly and openly rejecting [ISIS] control over Manbij. You would see graffiti on the walls, for instance, such as '[ISIS] out' or the raising of a very large independence flag – a flag [ISIS] bans. A cultural club was also set up giving the opportunity to debate. Gradually, the [ISIS] people became more afraid and remained constrained to their barracks, very much like the regime did in rebellious regions. Therefore, when the revolt against [ISIS] began the city was ready. The police force was instrumental in the operation to kick them out as were many residents who are armed but do not belong to any brigade of the FSA.[84]

ISIS returned and established total control over the city after its June 2014 victories in Iraq. Monzer, now a member of the Aleppo regional council, risks death when he returns home. 'It's worse than Assad in the 80s,' he says. 'Today the father is scared of his own son. If he wants to smoke he has to hide in case his children inform on him.'[85] (The punishment for smoking is public flogging and three days imprisonment.)

* * *

Following its dramatic expansion, ISIS went on a recruitment drive, bringing thousands more Syrians and foreigners into its ranks. How does it attract these foot soldiers? There are separate answers – one for Syrians, one for foreigners.

It's important to re-emphasise that ISIS has little popular support in Syria – but it does have some, and it may be growing. The first reason, as ever, is trauma. The victims of Assad's scorched earth policy are enraged, and ISIS is a repository as well as a generator of rage.

Yasser Berro, a musician and owner of an ice cream business in Aleppo, illustrates one such case. As he tells the story he points to a photograph of a smiling young man in jeans and T-shirt:

> This is a friend who worked with us in aid distribution. He was a secularist; here you see him surrounded by unveiled women. One day a regime shell hit his house and his brother was killed. He came to me and said 'everything we're doing is useless – I'm going to fight'. Next I heard he'd joined Jabhat al-Nusra. Then he moved to Daesh. Once he was with them, their brainwashing turned him into someone unrecognisable. The last time I spoke to him on the phone, he told me he'd behead me himself if I ever came back to Syria. The whole process took six months.[86]

For some, the very extremity of its rule makes ISIS attractive; its violence seems to herald a completely new start, its repression removes crime as well as dissension from the public space. Some support it, therefore, for the sake of stability, and because it appears to be the strongest, most credible available option. As it parodies nationalism and Islamic history, so its nihilism parodies the anarchist ideal; in its territories the rich, the notable families, and all political parties are rendered irrelevant. Peasant boys and Bedouin can rise to command without education and without the traditional power structures behind them – so it seems. Necessarily – because its militants are not sufficiently numerous to govern the vast areas it controls – ISIS sometimes relies on local leadership. Co-opting sections of tribes or villages against others, its divide-and-rule strategies are as coldly intelligent as Assad's.

In this way ISIS's pretensions to statehood serve it well. Its militants compel the doctors and engineers under its sway to work for it, and seize control of oil fields and food reserves. This terror-discipline, and the money won from oil and hostage deals, allow it to provide services efficiently.

Beyond that, ignorance and propaganda play a role. Many young people have joined up in order to fight the regime which bombs them, and have been shocked to find themselves fighting Kurds or the FSA instead. All sides to the conflict have enlisted children as fighters, but none more than ISIS. In ISIS-controlled schools, children are taught that informing on insufficiently loyal friends and family members is an act which pleases God. In training camps, they are desensitised by violence.

Then there are the foreigners, on whom Zaid Muhammad makes the following comment: 'As for the foreigners – perhaps they aren't seriously Islamists but people who have a problem with their own societies. I don't know, but they appear to be insane.'[87]

Sham, or greater Syria, has great symbolic resonance for Muslims, sane as well as insane. The Prophet sought God's blessings on Sham and Yemen in particular, and several prophetic traditions predict that Sham will be the location of key end-of-days events. One, for example, states that the end will not come until soldiers of 'Rome' arrive in Dabiq. Today Dabiq is a small town in Aleppo province under ISIS control. Here ISIS militants filmed their murder of American aid worker Peter Kassig – a clear invitation to the new Romans to send an invasion force. ISIS also publishes an English-language magazine called *Dabiq*.

Moreover, Islamic discourse in the region (and further afield) is often so close to ISIS's that ISIS is able to present itself as the only true Muslim power, free of hypocrisy and unafraid to implement the law. The Saudi Arabian education system, for example, describes Christians and Jews as 'apes and pigs', and teaches that the death penalty is an appropriate punishment for Muslims who stop believing. With unintentional comedy, Egypt's al-Azhar university, the Arab world's supposed bastion of moderate Islam, condemned ISIS's brutality as un-Islamic and recommended the 'killing, crucifixion or chopping of the limbs' of its members.[88]

But that's not enough to explain the presence of jihad tourists on the battlefield. Zaid's comment goes further – these are people who have a problem with their own societies. Some – like the Chechens – are acting on impulses and neuroses developed on home battlegrounds. Others, especially those who come from Europe and America, have fallen headlong into the vacuum of identity politics. French novelist Karim Miské describes deracinated second-generation immigrant fundamentalists as 'craving the validation of others ... frequently tempted to reverse the feeling of stigma, to brand themselves proudly with the very religion which brought them such relentless contempt'.[89] Add to this the new phenomenon of gangster-Salafism. Because of the protective solidarity afforded by membership in a Muslim 'gang', and because of the media image of the Muslim as terrifying Other, violent Salafists are winning converts in British and French prisons, from all racial and religious backgrounds. Such people's discourse is drawn much more from hip-hop culture than Islamic texts. Here is one British convert's response to Bin Laden's 9/11 attacks: 'I was just thinking, oh my God, this man is a Gangster! This man's on top! I mean, this is one guy taking on the whole might of a country. That I can respect. Wallahi [by God], that's the kind of stuff that initially drew me to Islam.'[90]

But privileged young people as well as the marginalised have travelled to Syria to join ISIS.[91] The dream of the Caliphate, complete with swords and white horses, is a powerful lure. There are vague historical precedents to this which the Western jihadists would surely rather ignore. People have travelled before from the rich West to the poor East in order to impose their religious and political beliefs on natives perceived as barbarous.[92] It's one of postcolonialism's saddest ironies that some of the new colonists are the grandchildren of colonised people.

* * *

On 22 September 2014, America and its allies finally intervened openly in Syria – not in support of the popular revolution, and not to attack Assad, the prime cause of the country's collapse, but to attack ISIS, which is one of the symptoms of the collapse.

But not only ISIS. On the first day the Americans hit Jabhat al-Nusra, killing dozens of men and surrounding women and children too. They did so on the pretext that Nusra was sheltering a cell called 'Khorasan' which represented an imminent threat to the American 'homeland'. Later they also struck at Ahrar al-Sham. While these organisations are undoubtedly led by jihadist extremists who oppose the revolution's original democratic aims, both were at war with ISIS when attacked. More to the point, both were on the frontlines against Assad, and both might even have contained a majority of foot soldiers who do subscribe to democracy.[93]

Syrians in the liberated areas were astounded that the US, which had declined to bomb Assad when he slaughtered them with barrel bombs and sarin gas, was now bombing those who were defending them from Assad. Indeed, American and regime planes shared the sky; it was often difficult to tell whose plane had caused the slaughter on the ground. And the Americans were also bombing oil fields and grain silos. These funded ISIS, certainly, but they also provided civilian communities with fuel and food.

Monzer al-Sallal, the Free Army commander from Manbij, expresses the popular disgust:

> After Daesh killed Dr Abu Rayyan, we kicked them out of Idlib, Aleppo, Deir al-Zor, even part of Raqqa, and we were just small militias. We fought them without any help or orders from outside. The Americans destroyed Saddam's army in twenty days, and now they are talking about a war of many years to finish Daesh. What's this?
>
> Because there's no coordination with the Free Army, they don't know where Daesh is. They bomb far from the front lines where the Free Army could take advantage, and they bomb at night, when Daesh have left their positions and are sleeping in people's houses. Sometimes they hit the infrastructure.
>
> I'm against conspiracy theories, but really what can I think? We saw no serious pressure on the regime as it destroyed the country. They didn't even stop the foreign jihadists from coming. And for the last five months not one bullet has been delivered to [the FSA in] the north Aleppo countryside.[94]

The American raids provoked a series of protests across the north. Towns and villages which had previously opposed ISIS condemned the intervention and in some cases raised slogans suggesting that America had joined Iran and Assad in a war on Sunnis. America's action surely increased the terrorism threat against it in the medium and long term. In the short term, it exhausted what little influence the US wielded on the ground, and greatly increased the influence of jihadist groups.

In November 2014, Jabhat al-Nusra drove the Syrian Revolutionaries Front (SRF), a group tepidly backed by the US, out of Idlib province. They did so with a significant measure of popular support, because the SRF, already known for its indiscipline, was now perceived as an American agent.

Kobani was a happier story, although it took four months – from September 2014 to January 2015 – to repulse the ISIS invasion, by which time the Kurdish town was half destroyed. Here American bombs provided support to the PYD fighters on the ground. The men and women of the PYD fought valiantly (up to 40 per cent of PYD fighters are women), and were joined by Iraqi Peshmerga as well as the FSA. In February 2015, in what was hoped to be a breakthrough after the joint victory, the FSA and PYD signed an agreement to fight the regime together elsewhere in Aleppo province.[95] A contingent of international volunteers – some of them anarchists – also joined in Kobani's defence. Well-organised local ground forces acting in concert with international air power kept up the momentum through the spring. On 16 June 2015, the PYD backed by the FSA pushed ISIS out of Tell Abyad, cutting its last connection to the Turkish border and potentially threatening its 'capital' at Raqqa from the north. By mid-July the Kurds had surrounded ISIS in Hasakeh too.

Without coordinated air power, Syrian Arab rebels nevertheless won small battles against ISIS in Quneitra, the Qalamoun, and the Damascus suburbs. Yet on 1 April 2015 ISIS was able to infiltrate the Palestinian camp at Yarmouk in south Damascus. This led to intense fighting between ISIS and FSA-allied Palestinian militias, and ended with ISIS in control of much of the area. Activists in the camp blamed treacherous Nusra fighters for allowing ISIS in, and also the regime, which was besieging Yarmouk, stopping food from crossing but somehow missing the passage of armed ISIS cadres.[96]

Then on 20 May, ISIS captured Palmyra (called Tadmor in Arabic) from the regime. Palmyra's strategic importance – positioned in the central desert on roads leading to Homs and Damascus – is perhaps smaller than the symbolic significance of its ancient ruins. The surviving columns and halls of Queen Zenobia's city had now fallen into the hands of those who had already destroyed ancient Assyrian sites in Iraq. (At the time of writing ISIS has demolished some shrines at Palmyra, but has not launched the feared whole-scale assault on the ancient city.)

A few days before taking Palmyra from Assad, ISIS had captured Ramadi from the Iraqi government. Neither Assad nor Malki, and not the US-led airborne coalition, were able to stop the advance. Increasingly, pointed questions were asked of President Obama's floundering anti-ISIS policy. Syrian-American activist Mohammed Ghanem expressed the disquiet: 'We are mystified as to how ISIS columns with hundreds of fighters were able to traverse the Syrian desert and reach Palmyra without suffering a single air raid.'[97]

* * *

After the regime's failed Aleppo offensive of February 2015, the Islamic Front and FSA militias in the liberated areas of the city managed to push back the threat of encirclement. Progress in nearby Idlib province was even more marked. December 2014 had seen Nusra, the FSA and the Islamic Front cooperating in the newly formed Army of Conquest to take the regime's huge military complex at Wadi Deif. In late March 2015 the same groups liberated Idlib city – the second provincial capital to escape Assad's control. The Mastoumeh military base followed on 19 May, then Jisr al-Shughour (site of the June 2011 uprising) on 25 April.[98] Areeha fell in three hours on 28 May.

What – other than the continuing attrition to Assad's demographic base – explains this string of victories? Certainly Turkey, Qatar and Saudi Arabia under its new king Salman, set aside their differences (as well as their reservations concerning Jabhat al-Nusra) and coordinated an improved supply of anti-tank weapons. More important was the greatly increased cohesion of the rebels, who now managed to coordinate tens of thousands of fighters and heavy weaponry across long fronts.

In the southern Deraa province, meanwhile, revolutionary forces continued to make steady progress, liberating bases and hilltop positions, coming closer to shutting down key regime supply routes and potentially linking up with the besieged – but largely ISIS-free – Damascus suburbs. The effort was led by the Southern Front – a unified body of 57 FSA groups established on 18 February 2014. In early 2015, while Assad was crumbling in Idlib, the Southern Front was punishing him around Deraa. The historic town of Bosra al-Sham was liberated on 24 March, then the Naseeb border crossing on 1 April, cutting the regime off from Jordan. The enormous Brigade 52 base fell on 8 June.

The southern success is partly explained by proximity to the Jordanian border, and therefore to Gulf or Western supplies. But the south also benefits from its distance from the Turkish border, the main crossing point for foreign fighters. According to AbdulRahman Jalloud, 'Paradoxically, the regime's siege was good for the south. Until now the resistance there is more organised and much less infiltrated by Daesh.'[99] It is noteworthy that the Southern Front has refused to enter into coalition with Jabhat al-Nusra. Its symbology and rhetoric continue to echo the revolution's national and democratic aims. Many in Damascus are naturally hoping for a liberation from the south, by the FSA, rather than from the north, by Islamist forces.

The Syrian battlefield, however, remains inextricably interconnected; what happens in one region has an immediate effect on the others. On 11 June 2015, a Tunisian-led unit of Jabhat al-Nusra killed 23 Druze civilians in Idlib province. (All rebel forces, including Nusra, condemned the killings, and Nusra removed the Tunisian commander.) This crime – which apparently resulted from a dispute over property rather than sectarian hatred – led to various ramifications, including a halt to the Southern Front's attack on the Thalaa air base neighbouring the Druze-majority city of Sweida. Lebanese Druze leader Walid Jumblatt urged Syrian Druze in Sweida to ignore provocations and ally with the Sunnis of Deraa. Meanwhile, pro-Assad Druze civilians in the Israeli-occupied Golan Heights attacked an

Israeli ambulance carrying wounded Syrians, killing one. They were acting on the false assumption that the injured Syrians were Nusra fighters, a notion fed by the Assadist media conspiracy theories which imagine Israel and Nusra in alliance.[100] The episode shows how eagerly all sides will watch – and spin – the relationship between the Druze and the revolution. If the Druze were to open their gates to the Southern Front, Assad would lose all territory south of Damascus; conversely, Assad would gain an enormous advantage in the south if its Sunnis and Druze were to fight each other.

The regime, meanwhile, is facing a severe and worsening shortage of fighting men. Its hitherto loyal communities are increasingly better described as anti-revolution rather than pro-regime. Growing sections of the Druze community are resisting conscription, and more and more Alawis are fleeing the country – or joining local gangs – to avoid the draft. Economically, Assad's state is near collapse. It's been kept alive thus far by arms deliveries and credit lines from its allies, but these allies are now themselves squeezed by economic crisis, specifically by the dramatic fall in the oil price in the latter half of 2014. The 2015 nuclear deal between the United States and Iran may yet permit Iran another spending spree on its ailing client's behalf, but it will not reverse the steady dwindling of Assad's human and material resource base. For now it seems the regime is retrenching, shortening the fronts as it falls back to the bones of 'useful Syria' from Damascus through Homs to the coast. Assad admitted as much in a speech on 26 July: 'Sometimes, in some circumstances, we are forced to give up areas to move those forces to the areas that we want to hold on to. We must define the important regions that the armed forces hold on to so it doesn't allow the collapse of the rest of the areas.'[101]

As for ISIS, even with the continuation of current apocalyptic conditions, its project is unsustainable. If it continues its current war against almost everyone, it must finally be defeated; if for reasons of survival it chooses to moderate its discourse, it will lose its raison d'être, and most of its cannon fodder. And as soon as Jabhat al-Nusra imposes its rough version of sharia, it is met by protest and dissension. But both organisations feed on the desperation caused by Assad's counter-revolutionary war, and specifically on the regional sense of outraged Sunni identity, vulnerable to expanding Shia state and militia power. This means that so long as the regime survives and Iranian intervention persists, so too will violent Sunni reaction – under these or successor organisations. And still there is no real international appetite for bringing the regime to a hasty end, nor to work against ISIS with the oppositional Syrian Arab forces on the ground – and even less to curtail Iranian expansionism. The passage of time in some ways benefits ISIS, allowing it to expand recruitment and weed out dissent.

Assad is still likely to fall, perhaps suddenly when it happens, perhaps after several more years of struggle. In this sense at least, the revolution probably will enjoy its moment of celebration. Building a free and socially just society out of Syria's wreckage, however, will be an almost impossible task.

7

Dispossession and Exile

All the Syrian people are living a nightmare, they can't escape it. They had lives before and now they don't.

Maher, a Syrian refugee in Europe[1]

What does exile mean? No studies, no work, no return.

Ziad Homsi[2]

As the regime attempted to bomb, torture and starve the people into submission, a humanitarian crisis bloomed like a poisonous flower. By February 2015 more than 220,000 had lost their lives, and four times that number had been wounded.[3] In other words, at least 6 per cent of the Syrian population had been killed or injured since 2011.[4]

More than 150,000 have been incarcerated in Assad's dungeons. Many of them will never come out. In January 2014, 'Caesar', a defected military police photographer who recorded deaths in regime custody over a two-year period, released thousands of photos to human rights investigators. These provide evidence of the murder of 11,000 detainees, tortured or starved to death. The number accounts for those killed in only one region of the country.[5] One of the torture camps photographed was geo-located as being only 500 metres from the Presidential Palace in Damascus.[6]

War profiteers and criminal gangs proliferated as society stalled; kidnapping and extortion became rife. This drove the wealthy out – those who hadn't done so already fled the bombs. And when civil revolutionaries became targets of extremist jihadist militias as well as Assad, thousands more fled the once-liberated areas. Sectarian and revenge killings became increasingly common.

With the collapse of the economy and destruction of infrastructure, three million lost their jobs, pushing unemployment to 57.7 per cent.[7]

Four in every five Syrians were now living in poverty, and extreme poverty rose to 64.7 per cent.[8] Conditions were so desperate that 12.2 million people needed humanitarian assistance to survive, 4.8 million of them in areas that were difficult for humanitarian actors to reach.[9] More than 640,200 were besieged, facing starvation and illness, as the regime withheld food and water as a weapon of war, part of its 'surrender or starve' policy.[10] Qusai Zakarya describes the 'filthy truce offer' the regime offered the civilians of his neighbourhood:

> Assad has been starving the besieged people of Moadamiya for over a year, trying to make us desperate enough to resort to any means to feed our families and children. And so our local council has now approved an agreement to raise the regime flag high in our town, as a first step in a bigger deal. In return, the regime promises to deliver daily meals to the town. This tactic will keep incoming food under regime control. We will continue to be under their mercy for every meal on a daily basis.[11]

While the world turned a blind eye, the regime employed ballistic missiles, barrel bombs and chemical weapons against civilian areas with impunity, and in defiance of UN resolutions. Its war planes and helicopters wrought destruction on those below. In Aleppo alone, the Violations Documentation Centre reports 3,731 civilians killed by aerial attack in 2014.[12] Protestors' calls for a no-fly zone which could have protected civilians from regime bombardment went unanswered. People did what they could to survive. Activists informed people what to do in an attack – to run into the street or down into a basement to protect themselves from collapsing debris. Syrian-Kurdish activist and IT specialist Dishad Othman temporarily established an open source, citizen-run network called Aymta ('When'), sending alerts via phone, SMS and email to warn of a ballistic missile launch and its potential target area. The missiles generally take eight to twelve minutes to travel from launch site to destination. Usually they are fired from the environs of Damascus and filmed over Yabroud or Rankous. When they land, they can render whole neighbourhoods to dust.

The most damage of all has been wrought by the barrel bombs which rain down on markets and residential blocks in liberated, working class areas. These crude cylinders, cheaply produced, are filled with explosives, fuel and nails or ball bearings. They are by far the biggest killer of civilians in Syria today, and have maimed and traumatised countless more.

In the aftermath of the barrels, the unsung heroes of the White Helmets rush in to sift through the rubble. The over 2,000 volunteers of this civil defence brigade place their lives in danger every day to rescue survivors and transfer them to makeshift hospitals. They also work with local committees to train people in first aid. As of July 2015, 92 have been killed in the line of duty, mainly in secondary attacks – when the regime retargets an area once crowds have gathered to help the first round of victims.[13]

Sometimes the barrels are filled with chlorine, a substance not covered by the UN chemical weapons convention due to its potential for domestic use. On 6 March 2015 the UN Security Council passed Resolution 2209 in response, condemning the use of chlorine as a weapon and threatening Chapter VII action – authorising either sanctions or military operations – if it were used again. Undeterred as ever, the regime dropped chlorine on the town of Sarmeen in Idlib province on 16 March, killing at least 20 people – many from the same family – and wounding a hundred more, including many children.[14] 'The international community cannot turn a blind eye to such barbarism', raged US Secretary of State John Kerry. 'The Assad regime must be held accountable for such behaviour.' Syrians, tired of the rhetorical game, didn't hold their breath. Neither did Assad – on 24 March another chlorine barrel was dropped on Binnish, a town close to Sarmeen.

Cities became wastelands, villages, homes and livelihoods lay in ruins, communities were deserted as people fled in search of safety, shelter and food. A quarter of schools were inoperable – destroyed, damaged or providing shelter for the displaced, and over half of Syrian children weren't attending school. More than half of the country's hospitals were no longer functioning. Diseases such as leishmaniasis (known locally as 'Aleppo button' for its disfiguring sores), polio, hepatitis A and typhoid spread as water, sanitation and health systems collapsed. These figures, shocking though they are, can't convey the countless personal tragedies, the trauma and the sorrow.

* * *

In times of crisis, the most positive aspects of human nature are manifested alongside the most negative. Violence was often met by compassion, attempted coercion by solidarity and mutual aid. As the nation fractured, communities pulled together to survive. Activists in the committees and councils, often helped by local militias, distributed aid, secured shelter for the displaced, set up soup kitchens, carried out cleaning campaigns in bombed neighbourhoods, fixed damaged water pipes, and dug wells to make it easier for people to return to or remain in their homes. Doctors set up field hospitals, often in private homes, and teachers gathered local children for homeschooling. But even by January 2013, activists were struggling to respond to basic needs. 'We're gathering money and distributing food baskets, blankets and clothes for the displaced, and medical aid', reported Razan Zaitouneh. 'The fuel and electricity situation is very bad. There's no fuel left in Syria, but we can't do anything about that. We purchase small generators, but they are only enough to run laptops and mobile phones. All the cash money arriving is going to purchase weapons. Food and other materials need to come in instead and be distributed by recognised organisations and activists.'[15]

The aid was slow to arrive. The regime (and sometimes other armed groups) restricted access to international humanitarian organisations, and it took the UN until mid-2014 to authorise cross-border and cross-battle line aid without the consent of the state, finally allowing agencies to reach areas including Aleppo, Idlib and rural Damascus.[16] The situation in besieged areas was desperate. In February 2014, when the UN finally entered Yarmouk camp, there were apocalyptic scenes as thousands of emaciated civilians queued to receive food parcels among a shelled and crumpled urban desolation. In the same month, the first aid convoy in two years to reach starving residents trapped in the old city of Homs came under mortar attack.

* * *

Some attempted to establish self-sufficiency, turning rooftops, abandoned buildings and open space into family and community gardens. Sometimes local councils grew wheat, beans or spinach to feed the community. In areas under siege, this was an absolute necessity. The 15th Garden, a network of community gardeners and farmers in Syria and abroad, worked on sustainable seed exchange and supported the development of community gardens to grow 'free food for a free people' while building solidarity between Syrian farmers and farmers and peasants' resistance movements elsewhere.[17] 'People in Yarmouk approached us', says Zihni Zeytin, a German farmer involved in the project. 'They had started some urban gardening to counter the effect of the siege, but they were city people without experience so needed support ... within a year we spread to become the first Syrian food sovereignty network ... we have been smuggling seeds into both urban and rural areas, which have been donated by farmers in Europe, from Greece, Austria and Germany.' They met in workshops in countries neighbouring Syria to exchange skills and experience, also producing simple manuals to help those who hadn't gardened before. 'There is no one model ... it depends on each situation, such as the security situation where snipers may target those working even on a small garden. Some places distribute food for free, but in others it is very important for them to put the food on the market, at cheap prices, to push the prices down and challenge black market practices.' In rural areas the project helped farmers find a voice. 'Many farmers don't participate in local committees, which even in the small villages tend to involve the more educated people in society', says Zihni. 'So this is also a way in which farmers can be involved in community organising, to help defend food sovereignty. Many women are involved too.'

The 15th Garden's longer-term vision is to ensure that food can be produced independently of governments or corporations:

> We also do a lot of work about the dangers of hybrid seeds and GMO seeds and the dangers of international aid. We saw in Iraq how Monsanto took over local agriculture, GMO was implemented, the seed bank in Abu Ghraib was deliberately destroyed and the agriculture of Iraq was destroyed. The aid agencies play a part in this, bringing Monsanto into the country or other big international seed and chemical producers, once local food production systems have collapsed ... There are many state and company interests

> involved. When you are talking about USAID or other European donors, there is an obvious interest to take over the local market ... But of course, when people are starving they will take whatever help they can get. And under the Assad regime they already had decades of industrialised farming, it was very centralised, food production such as mills were in the hands of the state, all of the seeds were collected at the end of the season and then redistributed by the regime. So it was already a situation where people had no food sovereignty.[18]

When activists and communities could no longer self-fund their work, they had to look to external donors. This brought a new set of problems. 'To secure funding,' writes academic Nayla Mansour, 'the activist groups – first and foremost – struggle with the initial requirements of the donor. The organisational structures, processes, advance planning, strict contractual items, high-quality standards (often not adapted to the local context and the unstable security situation), all of these things give the impression that war and conflict are inevitable human destinies, not an emergency case calling for indignation, condemnation and spontaneous actions to stop the killing.'[19]

According to Yassin Swehat:

> It was a big mistake for the revolutionary councils to work in aid. Most people were clean, but still this opened the door to corruption. Some councils were built around political loyalties, and in some cases, aid was distributed to loyal constituencies first ... Worst of all were the NGOs, which depoliticised the councils as much as they could. Imagine a council in an area being bombed not daring to write the word 'revolution' in a proposal in case it upset the NGO audience.[20]

Abo Hajar echoes Yassin's displeasure: 'You donate money and you think it's going to the refugees and it's just going towards salaries or something ... Some people who were real activists before, now all they care about is money.'[21] Of course, many Syrians at home and abroad continued to devote themselves to raising funds to help those in need; many put their lives on hold to do so.

* * *

By July 2015 half the population was no longer living at home – four million had fled the country and 7.6 million were internally displaced. Many were displaced multiple times as the violence spread. Families were torn apart; communities fractured.

The rich at least had the funds to adapt. Much of Aleppo's business class, for instance, shifted operations to the Syrian coast, or to Lebanon or Turkey. Many middle class families were reduced to penury by renting but not working abroad. As the Damascene retiree Um Bassam describes it: 'There are people who go to live in Beirut. When they spend all their money they have to come home. When they arrive they find another family living in their house, or that the army's taken it, or that their furniture's gone. Then they wish they'd never left.'[22]

Those who remain live in friends' homes, in schools, in half-built or partially demolished structures, even under bushes. Unplanned camps cluster the border regions, not served by the UN or any organisation other than those run by Syrians themselves, locals or expatriates.

At the Bab al-Hawa crossing into Turkey, for instance, tightly packed plastic tents are pinned by rocks directly on to flat concrete. They flood in the rain and bubble under summer sun. A few kilometres away at Atmeh, a camp of 30,000 people hugs the border fence, the tents planted sometimes between olive trees, sometimes on churned-up open ground. In summer the hillside is cursed by an enervating, dust-laden wind, in winter by a bone-deep, dry, biting cold. Children's feet are protected from the snow only by flip flops. Some have frozen to death; others have burned in tent fires.

In one muddy quarter, all the tents are occupied by families from Kafranboudeh, an almost entirely pulverised town in Hama province. In such ways communities try to cohere, even in exile. The residents maintain their dignity, their smiles and a sense of hospitality, but, trapped in this limbo for year after year, they are also depressed and quick to anger. Many men in the camp are armed – fighters and smugglers. Battles between smugglers and Turkish police, or ISIS and opposition militias, or Arab forces and the PYD, have encroached on the camp's borders. Several camps have been raked by machine gun from regime helicopters.

Atmeh has an unpaved 'main street' of breeze-block and corrugated iron shacks. One is the kitchen, funded by Maram, an expatriate Syrian charity; this distributes one meal a day – lentil soup, typically – in buckets, to every section of the camp. One houses a dentist, paid by the Syrian American Medical Council. The others are shops, selling cola and falafel to those who can afford it. This is what the Palestinian camps looked like in the early 1950s, as permanence settled bitterly upon them.

A volunteer psychologist describes some of her cases. There's a child who refuses to leave his tent; when he still lived in a house he refused to look out of the window, having watched through a window his uncle being hacked to pieces. There are torture and rape victims washed up here, and those condemned to incestuous assault by enforced proximity to abusive relatives. Pre-existent psycho-social problems, the psychologist explains, are exacerbated in the camp by boredom, perceived impotence and the humiliation of endless waiting.[23]

It isn't easy to leave the country, and for many it isn't a realistic option. Abo Hajar crossed to Jordan and eventually made his way to Europe:

> I left Syria when I could because I had some money in my bank account. Not everyone could find a way. People who've fled the country are really financially able to flee; that's something not a lot of people will think about. To flee the country you need at least 1,000 or 2,000 US dollars. This money will soon run out and you'll need to work, but just to leave, you need to pay a smuggler, and that's not less than 1,000 dollars ... but I know a lot of people who would never think of saving more than 200, and these people are still there, they can't leave, so they're doing anything they can.[24]

Of the just over four million who managed to get beyond the border, as of early 2015, 35.1 per cent were in Turkey, 34.5 per cent in Lebanon, 18.7 per cent in Jordan, and 6.9 per cent in Iraq.[25] As of July 2015, by official United Nations numbers, 1,805,255 refugees were in Turkey, 1,172,753 were in Lebanon, 629,128 were in Jordan, and 241,499 were in Iraq.[26] The mass migration to these neighbouring countries placed a huge strain on their resources, stretched services to breaking point, and caused increasing insecurity. The host countries were largely left to carry the burden alone; wealthier states failed to provide sufficient assistance or to resettle significant numbers of refugees. Over time the neighbours imposed extra restrictions to try to stem the flow. Wherever they went, Palestinians tended to face the worst obstructions. Only 6 per cent of Syrians made it to Europe, the majority received by Germany and Sweden. By March 2015 the UK government had resettled a mere 187 Syrian refugees as part of its 'vulnerable person relocation scheme'. By June, an additional 4,000 Syrians had been granted asylum in the UK through the normal routes.[27]

* * *

The relief Syrians felt after making the arduous journey into Jordan was matched only by disappointment at their new conditions. Some arrived in their slippers, having walked for days, leaving the belongings they could no longer carry along the way. Sometimes regime snipers shot at fleeing civilians; many arrived with bullet wounds. Up to 4,000 crossed in a night, the majority from Deraa province, but others from Homs and elsewhere. Some were stranded on the border when Jordanian authorities restricted the numbers. Exhausted and shocked by the violence they'd witnessed, those without a Jordanian sponsor were huddled on to buses and taken to the Zaatari refugee camp, less than ten miles into the country.

Sprawling across two and a half miles of desert, at one point Zaatari was home to more than 150,000 refugees, making it the fourth largest city in Jordan. Now about 81,000 remain.[28] Zaatari is a hostile environment, with temperatures plummeting below zero in winter and rising into the forties in summer. Water is trucked in daily to this dry and dusty place.

In early 2013, those arriving were provided with a tent, a blanket and a weekly food box containing lentils, tuna, rice, sugar and tea. Bread was distributed for free. Later, food vouchers were introduced, allowing refugees more dignity and some choice. Residents cannot easily leave the camp and armed Jordanian Gendarmes patrol the perimeter. At times they have clashed violently with refugees protesting over food and living conditions.

Zaatari is a ramshackle maze of tents and metal containers called 'caravans'. People have hooked satellite TVs up to their tents, and water tanks are painted in the colours of the revolutionary flag. Aid agencies have brought in toilets, wash blocks and communal kitchens. Many are immediately dismantled by entrepreneurial Syrians, their materials used to construct shops along the main street – known, with fierce irony, as 'the Champs-Elysees'. The street boasts cafés, barbers, falafel and sweet shops. Some sell frozen chicken packed in refrigerators powered by rigging the street lamps (these only exist in the camp's older section). One business has wedding dresses for hire; another delivers pizza. Syrian farmers bring fruit and vegetables to sell from across the border, priced in Syrian lira. But many can't afford to buy anything and are completely dependent on the aid they receive.

Overcrowded and under-resourced, Zaatari was intended to house a maximum of 60,000 people. As more and more flooded in, humanitarian agencies struggled to respond. Funding appeals suffered shortfalls and donor pledges came late, causing cut backs in service provision. In any case, Zaatari's residents were sceptical about the allocation of aid. Hassan, a refugee from Deraa in his mid-twenties, expresses the discontent: 'If the money donated in Kuwait [where donor countries pledged US$1.5 billion in 2013] was distributed amongst refugees, we'd all be living in five-star hotels.'[29] Hassan had nearly finished his studies when he escaped Syria with his family. Now he lives in a caravan with his wife and two children – his youngest, a girl, was born in the camp. His father and cousins are also in Zaatari, and many other people from his home town. He spends his days in the caravan with members of his extended family, relieving the boredom by beating drums and singing self-composed songs. The words are sad – memories of the revolution's dreams and of the homes left behind.

Over a third of Zaatari's families are headed by women whose men have stayed in Syria to work, guard the family home or fight. Many women are widowed. Those by themselves, without a male relative, are vulnerable to sexual violence. Rape is common, and fear of rape pervasive enough to constitute a constant background terror. Some girls are married off young to Jordanians or Gulf Arabs, their families either unable to keep them or hoping in this way to protect them from rape. Some child brides are later abandoned or trafficked as prostitutes.

'Wassim' is in his late twenties. He's originally from Homs, but as a human rights activist he was forced to leave Syria before the revolution. Now he lives in Amman, Jordan's capital, but smuggles himself into the camp and lives there for weeks at a time. He's worked with the residents of one of Zaatari's sections to improve living conditions and reduce dependency on aid. Together they agreed to group vulnerable residents – unaccompanied women and the elderly – in a specific area where they can more easily be assisted, and they set up a security patrol to guard that part of the camp. They also encouraged qualified refugees to volunteer their teaching and medical skills.[30]

Most of the 629,000 Syrians in Jordan do not live in camps, however, but in Jordanian towns and cities, often in squalid conditions, many families squashed into one room to share the rent, sometimes without electricity or running water.

Mafraq is a town close by Zaatari which, despite its poverty, at first showed extraordinary kindness, opening its homes to welcome fleeing Syrians. But as time passed, tensions rose between Mafraq's inhabitants and the new arrivals. The influx sent rents soaring, pricing locals out. Food prices shot up, and the water supply ran low long before the usual summer shortages. The schools and clinics were groaning with refugees. Syrians aren't permitted to work in Jordan, but unscrupulous bosses take advantage, working them for long hours on very low wages. This took away jobs from Jordanians, creating further resentment. And while some refugees received assistance, the impoverished host communities didn't. More and more frequently refugees reported being harassed by Jordanians, some of whom held demonstrations calling for all refugees to be kept in camps.

* * *

The 1,172,753 Syrian refugees in Lebanon (as of July 2015) now constitute well over a quarter of the country's population – the equivalent of more than 16 million people entering the UK. In March 2014 the World Bank estimated that the influx was pushing 170,000

Lebanese into poverty.[31] In Lebanon's sectarian polity – a crisis-ridden system of government invented by the French and exploited for decades by Assad's occupation – religious identity is more salient even than economics, and communal demographics are inevitably political. This is the key reason why Palestinians have been excluded from official Lebanese politics – they are Sunnis, and their numbers upset the sectarian-political balance between Christians, Sunnis and Shia. Most Syrians are Sunnis too. Worse, the Syrian war provokes ideological conflict between Lebanon's sects. The tensions are taken out on Syrians.

Refugees suffer harassment, physical assault and so-called 'revenge attacks' for the actions of ISIS or Jabhat al-Nusra. They face community eviction notices and have their informal camps set alight. In September 2014, for example, a camp outside the town of Arsal was burned – allegedly by Lebanese soldiers – during a search for jihadist militants. The government refuses to establish formal camps, so most Syrians move into already impoverished Lebanese communities. Perhaps the most welcoming are the long-suffering Palestinian camps; refugees from Yarmouk go there to stay with relatives, sometimes accompanied by their former Syrian neighbours.

Prices are lower in the camps, but not low enough. 'Life is very expensive here', says a Palestinian-Syrian woman from Yarmouk now living in a rented garage in Bourj el-Barajneh, a camp in Beirut's southern suburbs. 'When we left Syria we only had the clothes we were wearing, nothing else. My husband is trying to find work, but it's difficult. Soon we won't be able to pay the rent, and then we'll have to return.'[32]

Most Lebanese have been less hospitable than the Palestinians. An American University of Beirut survey found that more than 90 per cent of Lebanese supported night curfews and other restrictions on refugees, 90 per cent supported restricting refugees' political freedoms, and 75 per cent thought work opportunities should be denied them; 10 per cent said they 'highly endorse' violence against the refugees.[33] The tensions are inflamed by the xenophobic rhetoric of Lebanese politicians who scapegoat refugees for all the country's problems.

In October 2014, Lebanon terminated its open-door policy and banned Syrians from seeking refuge except in cases approved by the Ministry of Social Affairs. In January 2015, a visa system was introduced.

* * *

By July 2015, there were at least 1,805,255 Syrians in Turkey – a much wealthier and more populous country than either Jordan or Lebanon. Some are housed in formal camps of a comparatively high standard, although Turkish authorities are reluctant to allow in journalists. Many more live in border towns like Reyhanli and Kilis, in rented apartments or shop fronts and sometimes in the streets. The character of such places has been thoroughly transformed by the turmoil. Their populations have doubled. Villas are turned into schools and orphanages catering to refugee children. The hospitals swell with Syrian wounded, and Syrian amputees try their wheels in the back alleys. In the cafés and hotels, Syrian aid workers and gun runners rub shoulders with foreign spies. Syrian restaurants and shops sprout up everywhere.

So too in the larger cities, in Gaziantep where so many Aleppans have relocated, and in the distant cosmopolis of Istanbul – here the huge population makes Syrians less immediately visible, but they are present nevertheless, organising discussion groups, or serving *shawarma*, or studying, or begging for coins.

Anti-Syrian sentiment flares at moments of crisis – after the twin car bombs in Reyhanli in May 2013, for example – and there are regular but small protests against the refugee presence. These demonstrations are as symptomatic of internal Turkish political disputes as of deeply held resentment against the migrants. Prime Minister Erdogan is associated with a policy friendly to refugees; some of his opponents, therefore, aim to whip up enmity.

* * *

By the end of 2014, Iraq housed 241,499 Syrian refugees. Most of them are Kurds, over half from Hassakeh city and its environs, and 96 per cent live in the territory controlled by Iraq's Kurdish Regional Government (KRG). Forty per cent of the total are housed in nine camps set up after August 2013, when a large influx followed fighting between ISIS and the PYD. The KRG has warmly welcomed Syrian Kurds with an open-door policy and permission to work. This despite the worsening humanitarian disaster caused by ISIS's rampage against Iraqi Kurds, Yazidis and Christians. Over two million Iraqis were displaced in 2014; very many sought refuge on KRG land.

Syrians are less welcome in Arab Iraq. A few have sheltered with relatives in Sunni-majority Anbar province, but under ISIS rule and subject to assault by the Iraqi army and associated militias, Anbar is little safer than Syria. The Iranian-backed government in Baghdad, meanwhile, is in effect an ally of Assad.

According to the UN High Commissioner for Refugees, 132,375 Syrians were living in Egypt in March 2015.[34] In its revolutionary phase, Egypt had extended warmth and solidarity to the refugees, seeing them as engaged in a common struggle against dictatorship; counter-revolutionary Egypt suddenly turned much colder. General Sisi's propaganda machine painted Syrians – and Palestinians too – as agents of disorder inextricably linked to Islamism. They were demonised as a side effect of Sisi's demonisation of the deposed Muslim Brotherhood government, and of the Muslim Brotherhood supporters his army slaughtered in Cairo's Rabaa Square. Under the military regime, Syrians suffer discrimination and harassment. Thousands, including children, have been detained without charge. Hundreds have been deported, particularly Palestinian-Syrians. Some have been forcibly returned to Syria – where they risk being arrested as soon as they step off the plane.[35]

Many Syrians have made perilous journeys to Europe – a continent increasingly hostile to migrants – placing their lives (and life savings) in the hands of smugglers. Thousands have perished in the waters of the Mediterranean. In October 2013, over 400 people drowned in two disasters off the coast of the Italian island of Lampedusa. The following year, Italian authorities decided to end the search and rescue operations which had saved thousands of migrants, replacing them with heightened border surveillance. There were reports of Greek coastguards shooting at boats carrying Syrian refugees to ward them away. Bulgaria built a barrier to stem the flow crossing from Turkey.

The numbers only increase. An estimated 103,000 refugees and migrants (from Syria and other countries) crossed the Mediterranean in the first six months of 2015;[36] 1,800 are estimated to have drowned.[37] After 800 died in a shipwreck off Libya in April 2015, several EU member states tasked their navies with intensified search and rescue operations. This seemed to reduce the number of deaths.[38] But the human pressure on southern European shores will not relent so long as Syrians and others find it impossible to stay at home. So long as the bombs fall, so will the boats sail.

Those who succeed in breaching Fortress Europe's walls arrive in a climate of economic insecurity and amid surging xenophobic, anti-migrant and specifically Islamophobic sentiment. Primed by their organisational experience in revolutionary Syria, the refugees often fight their corner hard. In late 2014, for example, over 150 Syrians launched a hunger strike in Greece – where migrants are held in overcrowded detention centres for months on end – calling for their rights as refugees and for better living conditions, or to be allowed to travel to another European country. (The Dublin Regulation requires migrants to apply for refugee status in the first EU country they come to.) Syrians in France have also organised to demand their rights. In Calais they try to reach the UK, alongside refugees from Eritrea, Somalia and Sudan. Many try to cross by strapping themselves to the undercarriages of lorries, and some have been killed in the attempt. Their camps are dismantled by the authorities, they are evicted from the buildings they squat; they are attacked by local fascists and police. In the winter of 2014, around 80 Syrians living on the streets of Calais called on British authorities to grant them asylum. Most spoke English and had extended family members in Britain. 'We ask to claim asylum in the UK,' they wrote, 'in a legal way and for the opportunity to reach the UK without having to use dangerous or illegal methods. As people from Syria we have suffered from war and forced exile. We ask for our right to choose the country in which we can live in safety.'[39]

* * *

Marcell Shehwaro talks of the refugee sensation – or the survivor sensation – of 'constant guilt. How can we enjoy ourselves while those inside are suffering? As a result of this guilt we feel a need for sacrifice. Our need to sacrifice sometimes feels more important than bringing down Bashaar or Daesh. That which doesn't translate into anger and can't translate into hope remains as it is: self-destructive behaviour, sadness, a disequilibrium. It makes some drink too much, some smoke too much hashish, some become workaholics.'[40]

Marcell is still working for the revolution, but now, most of the time, she lives in Turkey. Better put, she – like so many other Syrians – is stranded between Syria and somewhere else. The refugees inhabit one place and aim for another, while their fears and dreams focus on a third. They live in between.

Many will never return. Years away from home changes people, roots them anew, especially when the home has been destroyed. But many will return, either because they have no other option, or because they are still mobilised by their hopes. In this way (and in others), Syrian culture will be entirely transformed, for good and for ill.

'Previously Syrians were among the least travelled of peoples', says Aziz Asaad. 'Now they're present in every country, being influenced by the people there and influencing them in turn. Added to that, a whole generation is growing up in the camps of exile – these children who've lost a father to shelling, a friend's brother to bullets, a sister's husband to torture. When they grow up and realise that life is more than a refugee camp, that it isn't natural to lose everything to tyranny... this generation will bear a culture of revenge and anger, and a permanent sense of injustice.'[41]

8

Culture Revolutionised

The revolution was a positive experience even when I felt pain, hunger or fear. The general feeling was of the truth of the will for change. For example: when I saw an old man in his seventies doing the impossible to protect me while I was living in hiding; when I witnessed people forgetting their old quarrels and working together in the revolution's service; when I saw social solidarity operating in its most dignified form ... Syrian culture has filled itself with the spirit of rebellion and refusal. It's been penetrated by entirely new terms and concepts concerning, for instance, life on the run, demonstrations, coordination, the media, citizen journalism.

Aziz Asaad[1]

In four years we've compensated for what we lost over four decades. I'm optimistic about my people.

Bashaar Abu Hadi[2]

We've been compelled to ask ourselves radical questions about God, religion, relationships, men and women, society, poverty, money. ... Those who participated in the revolution have a new perspective on values, courage, on the country itself. But even those who didn't participate have been asking these deep questions.

Marcell Shehwaro[3]

The land and cityscapes of 'Assad's Syria' were punctuated by statues, altars and slogans to the 'Eternal Leader' Hafez. His name was picked out in white rocks on hillsides. His metal hand and impervious gaze rose over shopping streets, college campuses and city squares. Calligraphed messages on motorway flyovers described him as 'al-Ameen, al-Sadeeq' ('the Truthful, the Trustworthy') – titles previously reserved for the Prophet Muhammad. Official iconography depicted a glowing halo surrounding his mother's head. On such special occasions as the run-up to one of the allegiance referendums, grim-faced newsreaders wore T-shirts imaging the great man's face. Official culture consisted in large part of choreographed spectacles of loyalty and obedience. The largest took place in sports stadiums, and involved thousands effacing their own identities to form enormous representations of the leader. The spectacle echoed down to smaller instances – schoolchildren, soldiers, the newspapers, the land itself chanted for Hafez. An alien arriving in the country would conclude that its people had deified Hafez, his mother and offspring.

But almost all Syrians were pretending. The cosmic myths surrounding the president were not usually believed even by those enforcing their repetition. Lisa Wedeen, an American academic who lived in Syria in the late Hafez years, asked why the regime would invest so much money and effort in continuing a cult which, on the face of it, plainly didn't work. Her conclusion was that the propaganda's real aim was not to convince but to undermine the public space. The fact that the state was able to trumpet such absurdities, and to force the people to rehearse them like infants, was itself a demonstration and establisher of power. It humiliated the people; it proved them dishonest whenever they spoke. The tropes of the ubiquitous discourse set the parameters for discussion, even sometimes for potential resistance (in jokes, for example). According to Wedeen, Syrians spoke and acted 'as if' they loved their leader.[4] This corrupted not only the public realm but the private too; it debased language itself. Parents would praise the president in their children's hearing so the children would repeat these right sentiments at school, thereby avoiding disastrous attention. For people who grew up in this, words meant nothing much; no statement could be trusted. (At the same time, against the enforced grain, people became experts in codes, in the subtle discourses which sort out an interlocutor's political positions and social and sectarian background.) In this environment grand conspiracy theories flourished – some favouring the regime and some targeting it, but all adding to the collective impotence. A culture of hypocrisy and opportunism set in. The most cunning and sycophantic prospered.

Under Bashaar, the country witnessed a contrived simulacrum of official cultural development. The 'quasi-NGOs', often run by 'first lady' Asma, imitated a functioning civil society; the new private but regime-affiliated TV channels imitated an unregulated media.

The supposedly Baathist culture was very far from being socialist. While the masses were fed censored Western and Arab world TV alongside a sanitised 'folklore', 'high' art was confined to the narrowest of social strata. Producer and film-maker Itab Azzam writes that:

> In pre-revolutionary Syria a clear separation of class existed between the sophisticated educated elite and the rest. The cultural scene in Damascus and Aleppo ... was exclusive and detached. Time and time again, I came across attitudes that viewed the ordinary citizen as a threat, an embarrassing non-initiate ... All this, of course, was part of ... a strategy enacted with ruthless efficiency by the regime against its people. Who could wish the overthrow of these socially liberal and outward-looking people by uneducated, socially conservative peasants? Never mind that it was precisely those liberal people who kept the rest uneducated and impoverished. The average Syrian sensibly kept himself to himself.[5]

The visual arts did well – expensive galleries displaying abstract works sprouted in Damascus and Aleppo not far from the new boutique hotels. More accessible, Syria's *muselselat* (TV serials) improved in quality, attracting large audiences at home and throughout the Arab world. These historical and social dramas sometimes aimed to provoke debate, but always in ways favourable to the regime agenda.[6] In general, publication, performance and media attention were privileges granted or withheld by regime-appointed gatekeepers. Access to such closely guarded state institutions as the Arab Writers Union was required for anyone wishing to project their voice.

There were exceptions to the rule. At Damascus's Bayt al-Qasid, for example – half a drinking club, half a poetry meeting – anyone could take the microphone and read; and anyone could be shouted down. The dim basement walls wore pictures of Gandhi and Malcolm X. Such places were signals of an unofficial but undeniably vibrant culture straining to articulate itself – but Bayt al-Qasid remained a pre-revolutionary phenomenon. When the revolution arrived, the club closed itself down.[7]

'Before the revolution, there was no culture in the deep sense of the word,' Salim Salamah laments, 'only a framework empty of meaning populated by hired intellectuals, with the exception of a very few real thinkers, who were marginalised.'[8]

Many of the great figures of the late twentieth century had to produce their work outside Syria. Nizar Qabbani, perhaps the best-loved Arab poet of his generation, wrote much of his erotic and political verse in Beirut, Paris and London. Zakaria Tamer, master of the socially engaged short-story, was pressed to move to London in 1980 when he was dismissed from his editorial position at a cultural journal. The novelist Rafik Schami left as a young man in Syria's first year under Hafez. So he wrote his epic, *The Dark Side of Love*, not in Arabic but German.

Others were able to remain inside the country – Muhammad al-Maghout, for instance, the free-verse poet and satirist from Selemmiyeh. While Nizar Qabbani's narrative personas are self-annihilating lovers, Maghout's are leering lechers, and perhaps more honest to the age. Here, for instance: 'Lebanon is burning – it leaps, like a wounded horse, at the edge | of the desert | and I am looking for a fat girl | to rub myself against on the tram.'[9]

Maghout wrote films – like *al-Hudood* (*The Borders*) and *al-Taqreer* (*The Report*) – parodying the failings of Arab nationalism and the bureaucratic state. These were tolerated 'as if' they were generalised attacks on all Arab regimes, and least of all on the Syrian. Yasser al-Azmeh's TV satire series *Maraya* (*Mirror*) was another that danced near the boundary, pointing up corruption and clumsy *mukhabarat* abuses, but never pointing the finger to the top.

Playwright Saadallah Wannous got away with it too, though he made fewer compromises. He called for a 'theatre of politicisation', rather than a merely 'political theatre'. His proto-revolutionary play, *The Elephant, O Lord of Ages*, was professionally performed in central Damascus – but only to an elite audience. He died in 1997. (His daughter, the novelist Dima Wannous, has taken a firmly pro-revolution position since 2011.)

Some lived inside but their work was banned. Nihad Sirees was a successful scriptwriter, but *The Silence and the Roar*, his Orwellian or Kafkaesque novel against tyranny, is illegal. So too are the works of Khaled Khalifa, probably Syria's greatest novelist. His masterful *In Praise of Hatred* is a multi-layered treatment of the repressions and ideological divisions of the 1980s.[10]

One genre which flourished (underground of course) was the prison memoir. *The Shell* by Mustafa Khalifeh is the best-known example; the poet Faraj Bayrakdar and the political thinker Yassin al-Haj Saleh have also written fine reflections on their long detentions.

So high culture existed within safe boundaries, either experienced safely by the loyal elite, or dancing around the margins of the permissible. Banned books were smuggled into the country from Beirut or Cairo, or read online, and discussed in private gatherings. Many in the non-elite classes, meanwhile, were influenced by the regional religious revival, and followed their preferred clerics online, on the radio or on satellite TV. Islamic discourse became more prevalent, either as solace or by peer pressure, and to some extent as a perceived ideological resistance to the corrupt political realm. But perhaps the foremost expression of popular discontent was through irony and black humour. An endless chain of jokes ridiculed the regime, the security services and the humiliated Syrian everyman.

* * *

In March 2011, the culture's established figures split. Those who'd always publicly supported the regime continued to do so – people like pop singer George Wassouf, a friend of the ruling elite, or the comedian Dureyd Lahham, who once starred in Muhammad al-Maghout's films. Syria's 'state intellectual' par excellence is Bouthaina Shaaban, once a professor of English who translated Chinua Achebe into Arabic, now Bashaar al-Assad's most effective English-language propagandist.

There was no surprise in these positions, but people hoped for more from Adonis, or Ali Ahmad Said, an astounding modernist poet and essayist who for decades had railed against Arab tyranny and backwardness. In 2011 he condemned the regime's violence but provided only very tepid support to the revolution. Some suspected the aged poet feared not only Islamism (for this was before Islamism became a major factor in the revolution) but the Sunni majority itself. Strangely, Adonis even referred to Bashaar as the 'elected president'.

But many more got off the fence and stood firmly on the side of freedom. The wonderful cartoonist Ali Farzat, founder of the briefly permitted *Domari* newspaper, had for years satirised oppressive aspects of the culture alongside state corruption and brutality. His drawn targets had always been generic rich men or generals, but as the protests spread he began depicting a recognisable Bashaar al-Assad. After the fall of Qaddafi in August 2011, he drew Bashaar clutching a suitcase and rushing to catch a lift in the Libyan dictator's get-away car. On the night of 25 August, he was picked up by *mukhabarat*, savagely beaten and his hands broken. Today he lives in Kuwait.[11]

In July 2011, the Syrian-American pianist and composer Malek Jandali performed his pro-revolution song 'Watani Ana' ('I Am My Homeland') in Washington, DC. The *mukhabarat* couldn't reach that far, so they took out their displeasure on Malek's parents, who lived in Homs. 'We're going to teach you how to raise your son', they shouted as they bound and beat the aged couple.

Before leaving the country to embark on a series of benefit concerts for Syria, the oud player and singer Sameeh Shuqair wrote 'Ya Heif'! ('For Shame!') – one of the first revolutionary songs: 'For shame, brother, for shame! Shooting the defenceless – for shame! You are a son of this country but you kill its children. You turn your back to the enemy but assault us with a sword.'[12]

The actress Mai Skaf addressed protests and clashed online with Hizbullah's Hassan Nasrallah (after his militia's intervention in Syria, she demanded back money she'd donated when it was fighting Israel in 2006). She was arrested repeatedly and finally went into exile in Jordan.[13] Novelist and journalist Samar Yazbek threw herself into revolutionary activity, visiting besieged areas, interviewing activists and defected soldiers, and writing and speaking against the regime. Her *Woman in the Crossfire: Diaries of the Syrian Revolution* is an indispensable account of the revolution's first months. Slandered and threatened, she eventually left for Paris, but continued to visit the liberated north – the beauty and terror of these trips are conveyed by her 2015 book, *The Crossing: My Journey to the Shattered Heart of Syria.*

The poets Golan Haji, Ali Safar and Rasha Omran, to pick just a few, took unambiguous positions for freedom, as did the young novelist Fadi Azzam, whose *Sarmada*, published shortly before the revolution, seemed strangely prescient of the oncoming events. 'Creative writing about the revolution was done before it and will be done after or during it', Azzam said in interview. 'Authority now belongs to daily events and the tremendous amount of blood being shed. Writing can only interact with it as it is happening by documenting it, with grief and anger. This is very important to the revolution but it is not creative writing in the sense of artistic beauty.'[14]

The novelist Khaled Khalifa has continued to live in war-struck Barzeh, central Damascus, throughout the revolution and counter-revolution. His arm was broken when *shabeeha* attacked a funeral for the murdered musician Rabee Ghazzy. Khaled also wrote an open letter to writers and journalists calling for global solidarity with the Syrian people 'subjected to a genocide'.[15]

The figures named here are socially liberal; many come from minority communities. Their presence in the revolution was therefore very important in proving the lie of the regime's sectarian narrative.

* * *

In their attempt to explain away the uprising, regime supporters celebrated a national identity which excluded almost everybody. If people were protesting in Deir al-Zor and Deraa, they argued, that's because those regions were tribal and backward. Hama was a centre of religious reaction. The people of Homs had always been stupid. And the suburbs of Damascus were inhabited by ridiculous 'slipper wearers'.

The regime's counter-revolutionary narrative is a continuation of the pre-revolutionary 'as if' discourse. This means it need neither be logical nor compel belief. For those already faithful, it offers a line to salve the conscience; for infidels it functions more as a threat. A particularly grotesque example is the 25 August 2012 visit of al-Dunya TV to Daraya, where over 300 people had just been killed by the regime's army. Accompanied by soldiers, the young presenter prodded survivors – one perhaps dying – to praise their tormentors and blame 'terrorists' for the mayhem. The atmosphere was surreal; the presenter forgot to simulate fear and horror. She even 'interviewed' a shocked infant still in the arms of its dead mother.[16]

For revolutionaries, on the other hand, the uprising was experienced as a conjoined process of national and self discovery. 'I think I personally was liberated from two complexes during the revolution', says Salim Salamah:

> The first was my 'centralisation complex'. Although I'm from Yarmouk camp, I'm also from the capital, and the capital was all I saw of Syria. Today I'm liberated from this delusion, and tomorrow I might even live outside Damascus. The second complex was the belief that we were few – only a few in opposition, only a few who refused the system, only a few who were disturbed by the stagnant situation. I discovered the reality – that the majority rejected the system, that the majority were suffocating, but there was no way for us to know of each other or communicate. Now we do know each other. The friendships established in the revolution will endure, because they are friendships based on awakening.[17]

From Manbij in the rural north, organiser and militia commander Monzer al-Sallal agrees:

> From the start, everyone in opposition to the regime became brothers – Kurds and Arabs, Muslims and Christians. We discovered the geography of Syria for the first time. If Homs was hit, in Manbij we'd chant 'Homs, we're with you until death'. It brought us all together. And now the values and traditions of different regions have been mixed together by migrating refugees. We've got to know each other better.[18]

Many of the revolution's cultural activities concentrated on reclaiming symbols of sovereignty from the Assadist state. For instance, protestors adopted the revolutionary, or independence, flag in place of the variant imposed after the Baathist coup. First designed in 1932 and waved in defiance against the French, the revolutionary flag's three stars represent three anti-colonial uprisings – one led by the Alawi Saleh al-Ali, one by the Druze Sultan Basha al-Atrash and one in Aleppo by

Ibrahim Hanano. The revival of this flag not only expressed rejection of the Baathist interlude, but also drew obvious parallels between colonial and neocolonial rule.[19]

The popular online project called Stamps of the Syrian Revolution had similar aims. When a state prints stamps, it claims the authority to define the nation's self-image, its heroes and its victories. Originally a Facebook page, the project generated hundreds of images untainted by the state, commemorated key revolutionary events or acts of repression, and determined a new set of revolutionary heroes – from the martyred schoolboy Hamza al-Khateeb to the martyred comedian Yassin Bagosh.[20]

Education is another tool by which the state imposes its ideological authority, and a variety of educational experiments necessitated by the state's withdrawal sought to contest the old structures. The Return School in Atmeh camp was run by volunteer teachers – themselves refugees – in cramped, wind-blown tents and under the aegis of the camp's coordination committee. The basic Syrian curriculum was taught, but pictures of the president were ripped out of the textbooks, and the propagandistic 'nationalism' class was dispensed with. School days began and ended with a revolutionary song and a shouted question and answer ('Our Aim? ... Freedom!'). Just across the border in Turkey, the Salaam School for refugee children starts its days with revolutionary chants and Quran recitations. Headmistress Hazar Mahayni, an energetic and determinedly cheerful Syrian-Canadian widow, involves the teaching staff in collective decision making – something they found strange at first, but soon adapted to. Corporal punishment is banned at the school.[21]

To some ears, the mass question-and-response in the revolution's schools uncomfortably echoes the Baathist catechism in regime schools. That's why Aleppo's Kesh Malek is trying to build a non-political alternative. 'The regime brought us up', says the organisation's Zaid Muhammad:

> It takes years to escape from this corrupting influence. The opposition's institutions have failed – but they themselves are the product of Assadism. Their members grew up under Assadism. Our aim now is to build a generation through non-ideological

> education. For this reason we don't accept the revolutionary flag in the classrooms of our schools – even if we're ready to die for it on the streets.[22]

Alongside the schools run by councils in liberated areas, or inside camps, or by exiles and expatriates beyond the country's borders, a host of projects provide educational and psycho-social support to children who don't have access to school. Volunteers with the Karama (Dignity) Bus, for example, drive around the heavily bombed villages of southern Idlib province and screen cartoons, read stories, and discuss safety procedures and the emotional aftermath of bombardment. *Zawraq* (*Boat*) magazine, founded by two teachers from Kafranbel, is aimed at 7–14 year olds who have missed a lot of school. Approximately 2,500 copies of each issue are distributed in the liberated north and in Turkish refugee camps.[23]

Bashaar Abu Hadi, from Aleppo, is part of the Fedaiyat Bukra Ahla (Tomorrow's Better Channel), which makes comic-serious TV programmes. One is *Um Abdo al-Halabiyya*, a series for children in which children act adult roles, discussing the food shortages and power cuts, and the effects of the constant bombardment.[24] 'In Aleppo,' says Abu Hadi, 'the people are determined to live and talk, despite Assad, despite America and the whole world. People get married and have children. I've seen a popcorn seller after a barrel bomb hit. He picked himself up, brushed the dust off his clothes, threw away the top layer of popcorn, and resumed his call to the customers – "Popcorn! Popcorn!"'[25]

Such resilience is particularly necessary for media workers. Targeted by the regime and now by ISIS too, Syria's citizen journalists have nevertheless made this revolution the most documented in history. Several hundred have worked with the LCCs; the total number is in the thousands. The activist Rami Jarrah (also known as Alexander Page) founded the Activists News Association (ANA), which maintains a network of 350 vetted journalists inside the country, providing equipment and training.[26] Reporters born from the revolution – like Hadi Abdullah from Homs, with over half a million online followers – have won an enormous audience.[27] Independent news agencies have been established all over the country, including (to choose a few) the

Sham News Network, the volunteer-run Shahba Press, and the Aleppo Media Center.[28] Photography collectives, such as the Lens Young groups, have been set up in every region. Anonymous and cooperative endeavours flourished in the constrained security environment and as an immediate expression of communal solidarity.

All this in a country where the publication of one independent newspaper – *al-Domari* – a decade earlier had caused a great intake of breath. From 2011, the explosion of revolutionary media threw up tens of radio stations and well over 60 newspapers and magazines – each with its own target audience. *Oxygen*, produced in print and online from Zabadani, a besieged city near the Lebanese border, was – in the words of its founders – 'established with the aim of reaching the segments of the population that chose to remain neutral, or silent, in the face of the historic events that Syria has undergone since March 2011. It attempted to convince them of the importance of taking a stand. *Oxygen* has since evolved into a nuanced and in-depth analysis of the uprising, its evolution, its challenges, as well as its mistakes'.[29] *Dawdaa* (*Noise*) magazine is published by undercover activists in the Druze-majority, regime-controlled city of Sweida. *Nabaa* (*Source*) magazine, distributed in Aleppo and Idlib, focuses on creative civil resistance and frequently criticises opposition militias 'to remind these groups that Syrians are no longer tolerant to injustice'.[30] *Buhar* (*Spring*) magazine is published in both Kurdish and Arabic from the town of Maabada in the Hasakeh region. The women's magazine *Sayyidat Suriyya* (*The Syrian Lady*), distributed in Deraa and among refugees in Turkey, focuses on women's rights. From January 2012, *Enab Baladi* (*My Country's Grapes*), another project with significant input from women, was published in Daraya, a Damascus suburb subject to massacres, gas attacks and a starvation siege. Because most people in the area don't have Internet access, it was distributed in the streets. Remarkably, given the level of violence directed at the township, the magazine focuses on unarmed civil resistance.[31] Rushing to fill half a century of absence, many publications provided forums for discussion and food for debate. Ziad Hamoud was part of a group which set up a magazine called *Tumurrud* (*Rebellion*). 'We didn't report the news but asked questions in order to open debate – for instance, What is liberalism? What is socialism? What did Marx believe? Things which weren't talked about publicly before, not in a serious way.'[32]

* * *

It was a cultural revolution from the bottom up. Artists were judged now not by their prestige value but by what they could contribute to a society in transformation. 'Ordinary' Syrians no longer sought permission to speak; they no longer craved entry to the state's official culture. They expressed themselves in the streets and online through slogans, cartoons, dances and songs, and through endless debate in the liberated areas. In contrast to regime propaganda, and kicking against the years of silence, Syrians insisted on speaking the truth as they perceived it, and on criticising the truths set up by others. Their protests targeted the regime, ISIS, the FSA, the Coalition, foreign states and more. In this they mirrored daily conversation.

The liberated areas – which means free of both the regime and ISIS – were dangerous and terrifying, being bombarded from afar, yet remained truly free in a way that was unthinkable in the old kingdom of silence. Kafranbel, an overgrown village between fig trees and rocky scrub, now bomb-blasted in large part, was unknown even to Syrians before 2011. Today it's known all over the world for the witty and pertinent slogans and cartoons cooked up (in Arabic and English) for every Friday protest. The first banner, in April 2011, declared 'Freedom Emerged from under the Fingernails of Deraa's Children'. Perhaps the funniest was directed at North Korea's Kim Jong-Un: 'Your Attempts to Protect Assad by Diverting the World's attention to You is Childish. You'll Be Spanked for That.' The biggest international hit was: 'Boston Bombings Represent a Sorrowful Scene of What Happens Everyday in Syria. Do Accept our Condolences.'[33]

The banners and cartoons were discussed, phrased and painted by Raed Fares and his fellows at the Kafranbel Media Centre, a place where activists and journalists criticised the news, posted updates, hosted visitors and played the oud. And outside, beyond the main street's revolutionary murals, political and social debate continued in pool halls and cafés until the early hours. The village has its own radio station, and a woman's centre. It's remarkable, but not so unusual; Hass is the next village, just a kilometre or two along the road – creative civil society is thriving there too. And this is in the midst of scorched earth. Shop shutters are buckled by vacuum bombs. The mosques and schools are crumpled.[34]

In the village of Dael, near Deraa, protestors turned the romantic song 'Ya Sari Sar al-Lail' into an anti-regime anthem.[35] In Hama, Ibrahim Qashoush sang his song 'Get Out Bashaar!' accompanied by an immense crowd. The revolutionary poet was murdered shortly afterwards, found in the Orontes river with a gash in his throat. The regime's art is one of symbolic retribution – as they'd smashed Ali Farzat's fingers for drawing Bashaar, now they ripped out Qashoush's vocal chords for singing against him.

Online or pasted on the walls is the chilling poster art of Khalil Younes or Fares Cachoux, and the agit-prop posters of the al-Shaab al-Soori Aref al-Tareeq collective (The Syrian People Know Their Way).[36] A generation of revolutionary artists is at work – like Tamam Azzam, who Photoshopped Klimt's Kiss against a pock-marked and cratered Syrian building, or Wissam al-Jazairy, whose art is tragic and light, wistful and forbidding, in equal measure.

One of the most successful online projects is the Top Goon puppet shows, scripted by the Massasit Maté team. These mock the cult of personality by depicting Assad as a lunatic, often in tears, controlled and spoilt by security thugs and foreign leaders. Aboud Saeed, the defiantly working class 'Facebook poet' from Manbij, on the other hand, mocks everybody and everything. A sample: '"You think you're Baudelaire?" she says to me. | I ask: "Who's Baudelaire, a poet? | fuck | history created them, these people | Homs is more important than Troy. | And AbdelBaset al-Sarout is braver than Guevara. | And I am more important than Baudelaire". | She laughs. She thinks I'm joking/'.[37]

'The street is not an ignorant listener', writes Hani al-Sawah, also known as rapper al-Sayyed Darwish, concerning the new criticism. 'It can distinguish the good from the bad.'[38]

During the revolution, hip-hop was performed in various Syrian cities, including in free Raqqa shortly before it was smothered by jihadists.[39] The Strong Heroes of Moscow delivered the powerful and very professionally produced satire the 'Official Song of Bashaar's Men'.[40] Other loud voices included Aleppo's Abdul Rahman, the

Palestinian-Syrian crew the Refugees of Rap, and our personal favourite, Tartous' Abo Hajar. From Los Angeles, Syrian-American rapper Omar Offendum added his rhymes too.[41]

Often perceived as 'Satanist', a small heavy metal scene was developing before the revolution, and was subject to bouts of state repression. Playing up its 'secular' image, the regime became more tolerant of the genre after 2011. Some groups took advantage of increased opportunities to perform in regime-held areas – so long as they censored themselves; others – such as Anarchadia – performed in liberated territory, or left the country. Monzer Darwish's film, *Metal is War*, surveys groups and fans making their own noise while the guns roar.[42]

Graffitied slogans and stencils have been a key means of communication and protest in regime-controlled areas. Rallying cries and responses to state propaganda appeared on city walls from the revolution's outset, alongside the pictures and names of the murdered. Not only in regime areas – the Freedom Graffiti campaign in liberated Idlib, for instance, called for the release of the Douma Four. And from formerly ISIS-controlled territory, graffiti artists of the non-violent movement declare: 'This is an opportunity to regain the public space that was stolen from us by the militias and that was formerly occupied by the regime.'[43] The image they leave in the street is a quote from the Quran – 'There is no compulsion in religion'.

An abundance of high-quality documentary films have come out of the uprising. Bassel Shehadeh's *Streets of Freedom* is produced by the Kayani media project.[44] *The Return to Homs*, directed by Talal Deirki, is an exhilarating and ultimately tragic account of goalkeeper Sarout and his comrades as their city and hopes crumble. *Shebabs of Yarmouk*, by French director Axel Salvatori-Sinz, follows a group of young people in Syria's largest Palestinian camp before and after the outbreak of revolution. One 'character' – Hassan Hassan, who founded an arts centre in the camp – was arrested while trying to leave. He suffered two months of torture in regime detention before he died. Salvatori-Sinz responded with the short film, *Dear Hassan*.[45] But perhaps the most interesting of a fascinating crop is *Our Terrible Country*, directed by Mohammed Ali Atasi and Ziad Homsi – our interviewee who worked with the FSA in Douma and later fell into

ISIS captivity. The prize-winning film examines the relationship between the young Ziad and the political thinker Yassin al-Haj Saleh. The story should be an inspiring document of the generations pooling revolutionary wisdom, but it takes place amid savage violence, the regime's persistence and the rise of jihadist extremism. By the end, both Yassin and Ziad are in exile, and Yassin's wife, activist Samira Khalil – one of the Douma Four – is abducted, perhaps dead. Ziad asks this uncomfortable question: 'When I was held by Daesh, I started thinking, is it possible that that lot came because of us?' *Our Terrible Country* looks hard at a revolution which is now in many ways lost, one strangled by counter-revolution and currently too weak to hold its own against the savage reaction the counter-revolution unleashed.[46]

* * *

In 2011 and 2012, despite the brutal repression, Syria witnessed an explosion of creativity, expression and debate unlike anything in its history. Since 2013, however, the devastating effects of counter-revolution have dominated.

Most visibly, the country's monuments and heritage have been pulverised or plundered. To take one instance, the beautiful museum at Maaret al-Nowman – Byzantine mosaics housed in an old caravanserai – has been looted and shot at by all sides. Maaret al-Nowman was once home to the eleventh-century poet Abu Alaa al-Maari, a vegan and atheist. 'Humanity follows two global sects', he wrote at a time of constant war between Crusaders and Muslims. 'One, man intelligent, without religion | The second, man religious, without intellect.' When jihadists arrived in town in 2013, they chopped the head off al-Maari's statue. The arrival of Salafist militia is often heralded by such ritual beheadings. The same fate befell the statue of the great ninth-century poet Abu Tammam, in his southern hometown, Jassim. The regime, of course, severs not metal but flesh necks in its dungeons; and by late 2014 ISIS's spectacular beheadings were being relayed around the world almost on a weekly basis.

The country was being steadily depopulated. The greatest tragedy was that revolutionaries were being driven out now not just by the regime and foreign jihadists, but by traumatised or criminal 'oppositional' Syrians too. Aziz Asaad narrates what he calls his most negative experience of the uprising:

> In the autumn of 2012 a friend of mine was kidnapped while on his way to Aleppo to pick up his medical qualifications. He was abducted for over a month. He'd been one of the first to demonstrate against the regime in Selemmiyeh, yet his kidnappers said they'd abducted him because he was an Ismaili, because he was from a minority group and therefore he was supposedly with the regime. After we contacted various intermediaries and sent archive footage to prove he was a revolutionary, he was eventually released, but by then he'd been tortured and forced to learn sections of the Quran by heart. The man was the fiercest of revolutionaries. After this, however, he gave up on the revolution, and on Syria too.[47]

'We were always a society based on sectarianism', says Marcell Shehwaro. 'We lived in separate cantons and villages. When I was at school, although I was in a Muslim-majority city, I didn't have a single Muslim friend. This is the Syrian geographical structure which the regime kept in place and exploited.'[48]

The revolution disrupted social cantonisation with its non-sectarian freedom movement and the links of sympathy and solidarity it generated. This was almost a miracle in a country with such deep and carefully nurtured divisions; it was a sign not of the end of sectarian consciousness, but of a striking level of political intelligence. But divisions were reinforced and redoubled by the counter-revolutions.

Creativity and self-organisation met enforced conformity and authoritarian control. Often there was direct confrontation between the two tendencies. Kafranbel's Raed Fares was shot in the back by ISIS operatives in January 2014 – and survived. In January 2015, Jabhat al-Nusra fighters stormed the town's media centre, the Radio Fresh office, and the Mizaya Center for women. The famous citizen journalist Hadi Abdullah was beaten during the attack. Interviewed later on Radio Fresh, Hadi said he'd only been beaten twice in his life – once in regime detention, once at the hands of the Nusra thugs.

Nusra leaders later apologised. To distinguish itself from ISIS, the organisation was still trying to project 'soft power', but local commanders were increasingly letting the mask slip. In early 2015, women accused of adultery were summarily shot dead, and reports came of the supposed 'conversion' of some of Idlib's small Druze community. At the same time, anti-Nusra protests spread in the north, and the militia was forced to withdraw from Beit Sahem, a Damascus suburb, after a fortnight of protests.

Demonstrations were held against the sharia courts in Saraqeb and Aleppo. When Marcell Shehwaro was briefly detained by Islamists for refusing to wear the hijab, popular pressure released her.[49] In June 2013, when the 14-year-old coffee seller Mohammad Qatta was asked if he'd give a free cup, he replied off the cuff, 'Even if the Prophet Muhammad returned to life, I wouldn't!' The remark was overheard by a group of foreigners connected to ISIS. Considering it blasphemous, they first whipped the boy, then shot him dead. Aleppo's activists launched the Enough is Enough campaign in response, organising demonstrations against the jihadists and calling on the FSA to do more in the people's defence.[50] In Raqqa, schoolteacher Suad Nowfal bravely continued her daily one-woman protest against ISIS, and when the entire armed opposition declared war on ISIS in January 2014, they did so in response to popular demands.[51]

Women have been at the frontline of social change. Yara Nseir is confident that the overall pattern is one of progress. 'Women's centres spread during the revolution', she says:

> Before, a women's centre was a ridiculous place controlled by the Baathist Women's Union. Now they are amazing. Razan Zaitouneh started the Women Now for Development centres; Samar Yazbek's Soriyat organisation runs them now. I'll give you the example of the women's centre in conservative Maarat al-Nowman. As well as providing a place for women to meet and discuss their rights, it teaches work skills, including in fields traditionally considered unsuitable for women. There's a course in presentation skills, and a subject called 'scientific research'. These centres are still running even in areas under Nusra control, much more successfully and safely than in areas under regime control. This couldn't have happened without the revolution, and I don't see how it can be stopped.[52]

Lubna al-Kanawati, on the other hand, believes that the devastating humanitarian conditions have reversed whatever progress was made: 'Ultimately there hasn't been much change in gender relations, as a result of the hunger and unemployment. In this issue, we have to consider the men as well as the women. When men are humiliated, some will humiliate their wives and children.'[53]

In ISIS-controlled areas, women are permitted to leave home only heavily veiled. In the refugee camps, financial pressures mean girls are at risk of being married off early, often to much older men. The stifling boredom and lack of employment in the camps often results in a reinforcement of traditional gender roles. For women sharing tents with their extended families, there is no escape from abusive relatives. And many women have been raped in detention or at regime checkpoints. ISIS has turned women of the Yazidi sect into sex slaves. In conservative communities (not only Muslim ones), rape is considered a fate worse than death. Many victims do in fact kill themselves later; others escape their rapists only to be murdered by their relatives for reasons of 'honour'. Yet the fact that so many have suffered has catalysed a public discussion of the taboo, and in some cases a break with old shame-and-honour traditions.[54]

Conditions for gay people are undoubtedly worse under the jihadists than they were under the regime. Though the regime did sometimes imprison people on charges of homosexuality, in general it left them alone – as did the larger society – so long as they did not publicly identify as gay. ISIS, however, actively hunts gays, arresting and torturing those it suspects, and executing many by hurling them from high buildings. As a result, people who walk or talk 'differently' must live in permanent fear. Yet alongside this repression, some gays have insisted on speaking out. A group of Syrians in exile, for instance, have created an online magazine called *Mawaleh*.[55]

The irrepressible urge to speak is perhaps the revolution's greatest legacy, one that will outlast both regime and jihadists. According to Serdar Ahmed, 'People talk about their rights now – political and economic, rights for women and children. People have more independence. There's less family supervision, so there are more sexual relationships. These days it's common for girls to choose their own partners, and to refuse the husbands proposed by their families.'[56] For

Ahmad al-Agyl, 'Ours is a revolution against all forms of patriarchy – against the state, the tribe, even against the self-proclaimed leaders of the revolution. In 2011 the tribal structures were weakening and people dared to contradict the tribal elders – but Daesh is turning this around again.'[57]

When revolution blows the lid off, all kinds of steam rush out. 'People are becoming more extreme', says Abo Hajar from exile. 'And who am I to judge them? I'm in Germany now. I'm not inside – Everybody's focussing on the religious extremism, but there's all kinds. Syria has lots of extremist atheists now'. Because politicised religion has become a key player – and simply because people are thinking and speaking more than they used to – it's now easy to find openly atheist or agnostic Syrians. One such is Ziad Hamoud, who contradicts the notion that strong faith is an inevitable corollary of revolutionary courage. 'In December 2012,' he says, 'I was injured by a cluster bomb, and I was ready to die, not for heaven, but for my rights. I don't believe in life after death. If I'm going to die tomorrow, I may as well express myself today.'[58]

Wartime culture also means a greater prevalence of recreational drugs. Anecdotal evidence suggests hashish and even MDMA are easily available and are used by revolutionaries and regime supporters alike. Fighters on all sides are said to use the amphetamine Captagon to stay awake for days on end – the drug's export brings in money for more weapons.[59]

Zaid Muhammad calls the events of the last years 'an emotional revolution' changing relationships inside families. 'Children still respect their parents but no longer behave with blind obedience. They went out to protest even if their parents told them not to. That changed everything, on every level. Even our love stories today are not as they were before.'[60]

The revolutionary culture of disobedience and questioning is no longer confined to revolutionary communities; the 'loyalists' now must be described as anti-revolution (or more specifically, anti-Islamist) rather than pro-regime. Increasingly their voices are raised in complaint against the conduct of the war. In August 2014, bereaved Alawis in Lattakia protested against Assad, chanting 'God Willing We'll Attend Your Son's Funeral'. In October, hundreds of Alawis called for the governor of Homs to resign after a car bomb in their neighbourhood killed 17 people, most of them children. In the same month, ISIS's slaughter of conscripts at the Tabqa airbase provoked the 'Where Are They?' and 'Speak Up Against Assad' campaigns, and a group called the Syrian Alawi Congregation called for regime change. Many Alawi men are fleeing the country rather than serve on the front. This doesn't mean the community en masse is about to make common cause with Sunnis; it does mean that Alawis won't continue to bear in silence the enormous death rate among their conscripted sons, and that Assad's absolute control of the community is no longer a feasible option.[61]

* * *

'My four-year-old son plays war games constantly', says Bashaar Abu Hadi. 'This is a generation that will seek revenge.'[62] And it's a generation that's seen its friends shot, that's woken in the night to fire and screams. A generation of typhoid and leishmaniasis, of no education, of the camps and the urban ruins. A hungry generation, reared on the apocalyptic Signs of the Hour. But it's a generation also reared on freedom – on the slogans of freedom, on the lived experience of freedom too, if only for a brief passage. A generation necessarily self-organised, preparing not for the end of time but for the practical business of living. A generation of speech to replace the generation of silence.

Syria's future, like its present, will exist in the space between push and pull.

9

The Failure of the Elites

You will find Syria difficult to govern. Fifty per cent of Syrians consider themselves leaders, twenty-five per cent think they are prophets, and ten per cent imagine they are gods.

President Shukri al-Quwatli, handing power to Gamal Abdul Nasser at the foundation of the United Arab Republic in 1958

The West didn't want a true national army to develop in Syria. When the Free Army first liberated Aleppo, some of its soldiers had shaved the word 'Freedom' in their hair. They weren't Islamists, but they were abandoned. What happened is an international crime. There are still very many people – whether secularists or Islamists – who believe in the freedom of the other, but they are dying, they are being murdered. The West knows this but abandons them anyway. I believe that if Russia hadn't vetoed action against Assad in the UN Security Council, America would have.

Zaid Muhammad[1]

The international community is responsible for the desperation that leads people to Daesh.

Yara Nseir[2]

As Syrians rose up against the regime, the old oppositional elites inside the country and in exile scrambled to catch up. Of the three main projects which resulted, one depended on the empty hope that the regime would negotiate itself out of existence, and two threw themselves to the mercy of foreign states. None were able to establish deep roots in the revolution on the ground, neither among activists nor the armed resistance.

The first was the 'national opposition', an umbrella term for those parties and individuals (usually) tolerated by the regime and therefore able to operate – under tight constraints – in Damascus. It included organisations that were not properly oppositional – such as the Popular Front for Change and Liberation, led by Qadri Jamil, the recently fired deputy prime minister for economic affairs, which had no popular base whatsoever – as well as the National Coordination Body for Democratic Change (NCB), which contained a range of genuine oppositional figures. Created in June 2011, led by Hassan Abdul Azim and Haytham Manaa, the NCB called for dialogue with the regime, even countenancing Bashaar al-Assad's continuation as president during a transitional period. Revolutionaries on the ground overwhelmingly rejected any dialogue while the army was deployed against the people. Those who paid attention to elite politics put their hopes, at first, in the Syrian National Council (SNC), founded in August 2011.

One way to understand the split between the NCB and the SNC is to recognise that it echoed the earlier split in the Damascus Declaration between those following traditional party-led nationalist and socialist models on the one hand, and those who focussed on civil activism on the other. The NCB was generally secularist, while the Muslim Brotherhood was well represented in the SNC. The NCB opposed foreign intervention, while the SNC eventually pleaded for it. Crucially, NCB members such as AbdulAziz al-Khayyer, one of its leading lights, believed militarisation would inevitably Islamise the opposition, exacerbating sectarian conflict. In retrospect this seems remarkably prescient; the problem was that the revolution was militarising whether the NCB wanted it to or not, and inevitably, given the scale of regime repression. While the LCCs, for instance, who had opposed militarisation on principle, still did their best to adapt to the armed reality, the NCB only repeated its rejection of arms, again and again, from its state-sanctioned platforms – and became more irrelevant each time. Later it wobbled somewhat. Some members said they'd support arming the FSA, and even foreign intervention, if Kofi Annan's March 2012 peace plan failed (the plan for a ceasefire and then a Syrian-led process to address the concerns of the Syrian people did of course fail – both regime and opposition failed to hold their fire). By September 2012 the NCB was calling for the regime to be toppled, but by then Syria was suffering total war and the window for NCB influence – if it ever existed – had firmly closed.

The NCB originally included four Kurdish parties, but in January 2012 three withdrew to join the KNC, leaving only the PYD – the organisation that would take over Syria's Kurdish-majority areas.

The NCB's presence inside the country was both an advantage and a disadvantage. In theory it allowed for greater contact with the grassroots, and certainly for closer observation of the situation. In practice, it allowed the regime to monitor closely and to control NCB figures – AbdulAziz al-Khayyer, for example, was detained in September 2012. The organisation was rendered insignificant by the fact that it had no partner. The regime clearly wasn't willing to negotiate seriously; nor were its state backers – NCB visits to Russia, China and Iran changed nothing at all for Syrians. In the eyes of most revolutionaries, therefore, the NCB, wittingly or not, played only a walk-on role in the theatre devised by the regime and its international allies.

The SNC was set up in Istanbul, and at first won recognition on Syrian streets – the next Friday protest was titled 'The Syrian National Council Represents Me'. The new body included Damascus Declaration and Muslim Brotherhood exiles, the Kurdish Future Movement led by the soon-to-be-assassinated Meshaal Temmo, the Assyrian Democratic Organisation and various independents, as well as members of the LCCs. Its first leader was Burhan Ghalioun, a professor at the Sorbonne who for decades had worked for Syrian democracy and Palestinian liberation. Accused of autocracy and sometimes incompetence, he certainly gave some rousing and intelligent speeches, addressing the people at the Muslim Eid al-Adha and at Christmas. He rejected images of the Syrian people as a 'mosaic' of sects and ethnicities. 'We talk of one people', he insisted.[3]

Soon, however, the SNC was beset by internal bickering. Three leading figures – Kamal Labwani, Haytham Maleh and Catherine al-Talli – resigned in March 2012, citing corruption, Muslim Brotherhood domination and a failure to make progress in arming the FSA.

Despite its absence from Syria when the revolution broke out, the Muslim Brotherhood held over a quarter of SNC seats. The 'Group of 74', containing ex-Brotherhood or Brotherhood-allied figures, many of them businessmen, added to the Brotherhood's weight. In its March 2012 'Pledge and Charter' the Muslim Brotherhood sought to relieve suspicions by reiterating its commitment to democracy, the equality of all citizens, and freedom of speech and belief.[4] But the suspicions remained – why was the Muslim Brotherhood setting up front organisations if it shared the democratic aims of other SNC members?

One of the SNC's most serious strategic errors was its failure adequately to embrace the Kurds. In April 2012, it recognised the 'national rights of the Kurdish people', but still resisted federalism or other forms of decentralisation.[5] At this point, the KNC departed.

Ghalioun was followed as leader by Abdul Basit Sida, a Kurd, and then by George Sabra, a communist of Christian background. Given the disproportionate Muslim Brotherhood voice in the Council, this was perceived in some quarters as tokenism. Some accused the SNC of missing opportunities to appeal to religious minorities. This seems somewhat unfair, given Ghalioun's efforts and the fact that the SNC, having no presence inside Syria, was in no position to offer guarantees. Still, considering that 70 per cent of Syria's career soldiers, and an estimated 80 per cent of officers, are Alawis, the SNC should have been addressing this community in particular on a daily basis.

In November 2012, after threats, promises and cajolements from the Gulf, France and America, the SNC agreed to subsume itself into the new National Coalition for Syrian Revolutionary and Opposition Forces. The KNC joined the Coalition, which was expanded in May 2013 to include 15 representatives of the FSA and a liberal block led by Michel Kilo. This meant that the Muslim Brotherhood was somewhat diluted.

The Coalition's first leadership trio gave cause for great optimism. All three were in Syria when the revolution started, all had suffered imprisonment by the regime, all were respected by, and linked to, the grassroots. The two vice presidents were secular feminist and leader of the SRGC Suhair Atassi, and key Damascus Spring figure Riad Seif. The president was Muaz al-Khatib, a widely loved cleric and public intellectual who appealed across the spectrum to moderate Islamists, liberals and worried revolutionaries from minority communities. A speech delivered in revolutionary Douma – a largely Sunni area – in April 2011 gives some idea of Khatib's rhetorical skills:

> All of us are one same body. I say to you: the Alawis are much closer to me than many people. I know their villages, their impoverished villages where they live under oppression and toil. We speak for the freedom of every human being in this country, for every Sunni, every Alawi, every Ismaili, every Christian, every Arab and every member of the great Kurdish nation.[6]

One of the Coalition's first actions was to appoint Mounzir Makhous, an Alawi, as ambassador to France. The new organisation was welcomed with even more enthusiasm than its predecessor. The LCCs – who had left the SNC – gave their firm support:

> This entity was established independently and outside the purview of any other nation. Moreover, the National Coalition was established in accordance with the principles and objectives of the Syrian revolution and activists' demands to: Oust the regime (including its symbols and pillars of support); Dismantle the security services; Unify and support the military councils of the FSA; Reject dialogue or negotiation with the criminal regime; and Hold accountable those responsible for killing Syrians, destroying our country, and displacing our people.[7]

Khatib resigned after only six months. The refusal of world powers to properly arm the FSA, undercutting the relevance of his role, seemed to be a factor in his decision. Later he cited the interference of regional states – doubtless a reference to Saudi Arabia and Qatar, which were backing their respective factions in the Coalition as they were on the battlefield.

Aziz Asaad, who approached the Coalition from the grassroots, found it as hopeless as the SNC before it:

> We hoped the Coalition would play a major role, but it failed. I attended several meetings as a representative of the Selemmiyeh

> local council, and unfortunately I discovered that it represented anything but the revolution. It was a wrangling of factions and parties, of conspiracies and empty dramas. It didn't carry the responsibility of the people's suffering. Instead of being a comrade and support for the revolution, it became a political liability.[8]

By May 2013, a statement by four major revolutionary bodies including the LCCs expressed disgust at the Coalition's failure adequately to represent the Syrian people, and demanded – but didn't receive – at least half of the seats in the organisation and its leadership offices.[9]

The Coalition, like the SNC before, produced the ugly spectacle of factions and personalities squabbling over the throne of a country which was going up in flames. Perhaps the politicians shouldn't be blamed too much for this. The ability to put aside personal and factional interests for the sake of a common goal, to adapt, to accommodate the other's point of view, requires a background level of trust in the national community and its institutions, and long experience in democratic collaboration. Syria had been a cast-iron dictatorship for four decades, so these conditions did not apply. Beyond that, the Syrians had no Benghazi in which to base themselves, no field on which to enact transitional authority.

Lacking on-the-ground power, the Coalition put almost all its eggs in the basket of a foreign military intervention which was never going to happen. Indeed, the promise or threat of intervention was the most persistent red herring of the conflict.

'The Coalition was never meant to be the leader of the revolution', says Basel al-Junaidi. 'Its function was only to bring support – humanitarian or military – from abroad. This is why people recognised it. It certainly wasn't meant to negotiate with the regime on our behalf. Perhaps when it became clear there'd be no intervention, we needed political representation, but the Coalition couldn't do it. They didn't control the ground; they had no militia.'[10]

Without an armed force or the mandate of a loyal activist constituency, in the end the Coalition nevertheless found itself badgered into negotiating. Regional and global states arranged a series of theatrical peace efforts as Syria deteriorated. The Arab League sent monitors in December 2011. Savage repression continued even in the monitors' immediate vicinity, and revolutionaries derided their work as a farce. They left after only a month, citing the regime's decision 'to escalate the military option'. Then came two joint Arab League-UN ceasefire plans, the first headed by Kofi Annan, who started work in March 2012 and despaired by May. In August, Lakhdar Brahimi was appointed in Annan's stead, and he won a brief lull for a few days in October, but nothing more.

In June 2012, an 'Action Group' conference in Geneva brought together high-level American, Russian, Chinese and British officials. It called for a transitional government to include both regime and opposition figures, and prepared for a conference in which the two sides would talk directly. This finally happened – at 'Geneva 2' – in January and February 2014.

By now the Coalition was headed by Ahmad Jarba, a relatively successful leader who had increased coordination with the FSA and would later persuade the US to deliver a few TOW anti-tank missiles. He also achieved an upgrade of Coalition offices in Paris, London and Washington to 'foreign mission' status. This was of course no more than a symbolic step, but it did further impede Assad from rekindling official relations with those states.

Jarba's team won a string of diplomatic victories at Geneva 2. The Assad regime and its Russian backer were obliged for the first time to recognise the Coalition as a representative interlocutor. The Coalition also succeeded in blocking a last-minute invitation for Iran to join the conference. It showed itself to be a far more responsible partner than the regime, which was blamed by Brahimi for refusing to discuss the Action Group's call for transition – supposedly the basis for the talks. In Brahimi's presence, the regime's UN ambassador Bashaar Jaafari accused Jarba's team of treason – a crime punishable by death. During the second round of talks, meanwhile, the Coalition exposed the 'Caesar' torture photos described in Chapter 7. Security Council Resolution 2139 in February 2014 – not only demanding an end to regime sieges, but also mentioning barrel bombs – was a direct result of the Coalition's engagement. It was the first time that Russia had refrained from using its veto to protect Assad.

The Coalition followed up at the European Union and in Washington by pushing for serious humanitarian support, for further pressure against Assad's barrel bombs and on the issue of detainees. It also warned incessantly that the FSA was being left alone to fight ISIS, and that the situation was likely to deteriorate further.

But however well the Coalition performed under Jarba, it continued to collide with the Obama administration's obsession with reaching a nuclear deal with Iran. This meant appeasing Iran in Syria and the region, and in the end, nothing practical was achieved at Geneva 2. In the first nine days of the conference, meanwhile, at least 1,870 people were killed in Syria.

This was a 'peace process' ultimately as illusory as the Israeli–Palestinian version. Enjoying superiority of arms and superpower backing, the regime was no more likely to negotiate its end than Israel was about to dismantle its West Bank settlements. No power was going to force it to refrain from slaughter, and so the slaughter continued. In the year after Resolution 2139, hundreds more barrel bombs were dropped, killing thousands more civilians.

So despite its hard work and diplomatic progress, all the Coalition won on the ground from its participation was the heightened disgust of activists. According to Yassin Swehat, the Coalition 'failed when it went to Geneva and sat with the regime. They entered the lobbying game of the international community, and when the international community failed them, they had nothing else. They had no relation with the grassroots.'[11]

This is the sin for which the politicians must ultimately be judged – the failure to build their legitimacy bottom up, from the committees and councils inside. In this respect, nothing much separated the Istanbul-based Coalition from the Damascus-based NCB. Both oppositions were 'external' to the revolution's civil organisations and militias; neither, therefore, were able to prevent the Islamisation of the armed resistance, and they even contributed to widening divisions between Syrian ethnicities. 'The biggest divide isn't between Kurds and Arabs,' says Serdar Ahmed, 'but between those on the inside and those on the outside. The politicians outside think as they thought twenty years ago. People inside, on the other hand, are more practical in making alliances and working together.'[12]

* * *

Alongside the careerists and oversized egos, the Coalition contained some of Syria's brightest, most committed exiles. Its top-down approach was fruitless, and in the revolutionary context quite ridiculous, but here it was only following the global political norm. Fundamentally, the Coalition failed because it had no serious and wholehearted state backing. If its function was to bring support from abroad, and foreign states did not wish to support the revolution, there was little more it could do than fall to bickering.

Some commentators assumed from the start that the United States was hell-bent on regime change in Syria. Some described it as a rerun about to happen of Iraq in 2003. This notion was based on old history, not present evidence. The Iraq invasion, famously, was hubristic. America easily destroyed Saddam Hussain's unpopular dictatorship, but was ultimately defeated politically and economically. The American public and elite recognised this; they had no appetite for further adventurism, particularly as the American economy was fragile after 2008. If it was a rerun, it was not of 2003 but of 1991, when US and allied forces in Kuwait and southern Iraq watched as Saddam Hussain savagely crushed a Shia uprising. The mass graves and sectarian rhetoric of this episode polluted relations between Iraq's sects. This, coupled with twelve years of grievous sanctions, incubated the sectarian breakdown which followed the 2003 invasion and occupation.

Weeks into Assad's mass killing of unarmed protestors, Secretary of State Hillary Clinton said, 'There is a different leader in Syria now ... Many of the members of Congress of both parties ... have said they believe he's a reformer.'[13] Later the American position hardened. In August 2011, President Obama expanded already existent sanctions on Syria to include the energy sector and to freeze Syrian assets in the United States (the EU, the Arab League and Turkey imposed sanctions too); Obama and other administration officials also called repeatedly for Assad to resign. The calls were not backed up by action, and naturally were ignored in Damascus.

Later still, selected FSA brigades were sent 'non-lethal aid', that is, ready-meals, tents, a few uniforms, some satellite phones and so on. As for arms, for a long time the only American move that actually made a difference was to veto other powers from giving the anti-aircraft and other heavy weapons essential to defend liberated areas from Assad's blitzkrieg. In the summer of 2012 small numbers of portable anti-aircraft weapons (MANPADS), some originating from Libya, were being donated by regional states, particularly Qatar, and smuggled from Turkey. At this point the CIA beefed up its presence on the border to stop the flow. They did permit the passage of small arms – Kalashnikov rifles and rocket-propelled grenades – but not anything that could alter the balance of power.

Supplies from US-allied regional states were in any case intermittent. Syrian fighters describe it as the tap being turned on and then off again as soon as any progress was made. In late 2012 the Americans sent some light weaponry to a few FSA formations in Deraa province, and Croatian anti-tank weapons – probably bought by the Saudis – came too. When progress was made, the supply was cut. American diplomatic policy was fairly constant: to encourage Assad to stand down while keeping the regime – expanded to include a few safe oppositional faces – in place. This policy, which fundamentally misunderstood the nature of both regime and revolution, was reflected in the on and off flow of arms. When the FSA won a victory, the weapons dried up; when Assad surged back off the ropes, the supply was resumed. The (unrealised) aim was to bring Assad to the negotiating table, never to end his failed regime.

From April 2014, the US did start to send a handful of TOW anti-tank missiles to a handful of vetted FSA brigades, but this came in the context of the FSA's war against ISIS, launched in January 2014. The Americans had always insisted that the FSA had to first attack jihadists before it would send weapons.[14]

One justification for the failure to support the FSA was the fear that Islamists might benefit. In the end of course, Islamists benefitted beyond their wildest dreams from American reserve. Starved for funds, guns and ammunition, the moderate leadership was unable to win loyalty or establish central control and discipline. Many of its fighters either despaired and left the country or gravitated towards the much better-funded Islamist brigades. Unhindered, Assad's barrel bombs and scuds implemented his scorched earth strategy, traumatising Syrians and producing the vacuum in which jihadism flourished.

The cross-cultural incompetence of American officials meant that commanders using Islamic vocabulary might be disqualified from help, while anyone clever enough to throw around secularist buzzwords might qualify. 'The American vetting is very strange', says Basel al-Junaidi. 'Jamal Maarouf, for example [leader of the US-backed Syrian Revolutionaries Front] is a thief. If I go to a Jamal Maarouf checkpoint, I hide my mobile phone.'[15] In any case, the vetted fighters didn't profit much from American approval. According to the *Wall Street Journal*, 'One of the US's favorite trusted commanders got the equivalent of sixteen bullets a month per fighter.'[16]

Then Obama's disappearing 'red line' over chemical weapons boosted Islamists and devastated the credibility of those Coalition and FSA officials who had tried to work with the West. 'We have been very clear to the Assad regime,' Obama told the press on 20 August 2012, 'but also to other players on the ground, that a red line for us is we start seeing a whole bunch of chemical weapons moving around or being utilized. That would change my calculus. That would change my equation ... There would be enormous consequences if we start seeing movement on the chemical weapons front or the use of chemical weapons.'[17]

At the time, the statement outraged Syrian revolutionaries because its implicit message to Assad seemed to be that aerial bombardment, scud missiles and hunger sieges were fair game. But as we saw in Chapter 5, on 21 August 2013, almost a year to the day after Obama's threat, the regime did launch a mass sarin gas attack on the Damascus suburbs – and the red line was erased.

For a few days it looked as if Assad had overstepped a mark. There was a panicked rush of defections from the regime, and revolutionaries debated whether or not to welcome the coming Western strike. Some rejected it, holding firm to their belief that they should bring Assad down alone, accepting weapons out of necessity but never direct intervention. Others, probably the majority, though no less anti-imperialist, hoped the strike would provide some relief to the tormented Syrian people. Their perspective was eloquently articulated by Aziz Asaad:

> Our number one goal is to oust the regime. Am I for or against a US strike? It's a difficult question. Anyone who wants to strike my country I'm against, in principle. But the problem is that someone within our country is using everything he has to attack Syrians – chemical weapons, rockets, everything. For this reason we agree with the strike to take out Assad. We have air strikes on us every day and every hour. We have shelling every day. We have death every day. Nothing will be particularly different when American bombs come down. We expect the US is going to hit the airports and centers of military leadership and administration. In our area we don't have either, so we're not expecting it to hit our area. But what we're expecting is some chaos and anarchy in the regime's ranks in response to the strike. If that happens we're going to try to make gains from that.[18]

The British parliament voted against action on 29 August. In early September the US Congress debated it, though voting was postponed indefinitely. On 9 September, US Secretary of State John Kerry told a journalist that US strikes could be averted if Assad handed over his chemical weapons. Hours later, Russian Foreign Minister Sergei Lavrov announced that the Syrian regime would agree to this.

So the threat of action was removed. Not only was Assad off the hook, the fact that his regime was signatory to a year-long decommissioning process gave it implied continuing legitimacy – at least for a year. More than that, responsibility for the Syria file had been symbolically handed to Russia – the regime's superpower sponsor. Assad's position was stronger after the chemical massacre than before.

Raising his hands in exasperation, Ziad Hamoud asks, 'Would the Daesh problem be solved if they hand over the knife with which they killed [American freelance journalist] James Foley? Of course not. But Assad gives them back some chemicals, and they're pleased to watch him continue killing.'[19]

At this point, Syrians lost all hope in the 'international community'. It now seemed clear that the world's states would never act, no matter what atrocities Assad committed. The conservative Gulf states, on the other hand, were a partial exception; so too were wealthy Muslim individuals, usually Gulf-based, who thought in terms of jihad. In the months following the gas attack, opposition militias increasingly distanced themselves from the Western-connected Coalition and the FSA's Supreme Military Council. The formation of the Islamic Front in November 2013 was a direct result.

As Sarah Palin declared 'Let Allah sort it out', and Obama referred to the tragedy as 'somebody else's civil war', thousands more fled the country every day. In 1948, three-quarters of a million refugees were driven from Palestine; the result was decades of wars and destabilisations. Ten times this amount of dispossessed wouldn't remain 'somebody else's' business for long.

In June 2014, ISIS conquered the Iraqi city of Mosul, captured the Iraqi army's American weapons, and returned in force to Syria. On 19 August it beheaded James Foley. Revelling in its cruelty, it filmed the murder and incorporated it into a propaganda piece. Those in the West who hadn't cared or noticed suddenly paid attention to Syria.

Enter the supposed 'realists'. Calls were now raised for tolerance and even cooperation with Assad against the ISIS threat. Leslie Gelb and Frank Wisner, for example, argued that 'Washington must pressure moderate rebels and Assad (with Russian help) to set aside their mutual hatreds and focus on what they both see as the much larger long-term danger to them both – the jihadis'.[20] But this isn't realism at all; it's unadulterated fantasy. Assad plainly doesn't consider ISIS a greater threat than the FSA – if he did he wouldn't have pursued his undeclared non-aggression pact with ISIS for so long; nor would his air force bomb the FSA while it was fighting ISIS. And the revolutionary militias, much as they hated ISIS, hated Assad much more. Assad, after all, had murdered a hundred times more Syrians than ISIS had. The overwhelming majority of bombings, rapes and tortures had been perpetrated by Assadist forces.

In the name of realism, America refused to arm the democratic opposition properly. The result was unhindered scorched earth and the rise of jihadism. In the name of disengagement, America ended up bombing both Iraq and Syria, and reverting to the neoconservative discourse of decades-long war.

As already established, America didn't just bomb ISIS; it also struck at the jihadist groups which were actually defending people from Assad, groups which – up till that point – claimed not to have a global agenda. Worse, American fighter planes shared the sky with Assad's, and hit infrastructure as well. Syrians soon heard of Obama's letter to Iran's Khamenei, assuring him that Assad wouldn't be targeted.[21] To many this looked like a Western–Shia–Assadist alliance. No jihadist could have cooked up more effective anti-Western propaganda.

'The religious think it's a war on Islam', says the secular Kurd Serdar Ahmed:

> The secularists think it's a war on the Syrian people. We hate Daesh, but you must compare them to Assad. Daesh's worst crime in Syria was the massacre at the Tabqa airbase where they killed 220. Assad has killed at least 200,000. He's committed thousands of massacres. When the people saw the coalition leaving Assad alone and attacking Daesh instead, some started saying, 'we are all Daesh'. Every bomb the coalition drops, the more popular Daesh becomes.[22]

The common thread between neoconservatism and 'realism' is an abiding refusal to work with the people on the ground directly concerned by the outcome. In 2003, neoconservatives backed Ahmad Chalabi's Iraqi National Congress, an exile organisation with even less relevance than the Coalition in Syria today (Chalabi was later revealed to be spying for Iran). And now Obama's realists undermine the Coalition with tepid rhetorical support, pay no attention to the grassroots committees and councils, and mock the resistance militias. 'When you get farmers, dentists and folks who have never fought before,' breezed Obama, 'going up against a ruthless opposition in Assad, the notion that they were in a position to suddenly overturn not only Assad but also ruthless, highly trained jihadists if we just sent a few arms is a fantasy.'[23] But it's Obama who was fantasising, not only because a high proportion of FSA fighters were in fact defected soldiers, nor because every man in Syria has undergone compulsory military training. Compare the FSA's victories over ISIS in northern Syria in January 2014 to the US-armed, US-trained Iraqi army's defeat by ISIS in Mosul in June.

Kafranbel, the small town in Idlib province known internationally for the intelligence of its weekly protest slogans, gave the best response. That Friday's banner read: 'Yes! Mr. President Obama, Dentists,

Farmers and Students Are the Ones Who Lead Dignity Revolutions; Criminals Kill While Idiots Talk'.

* * *

While Obama was ignoring Syria, his administration was engaging with Iran.

In the dispute over its nuclear programme, Syrians generally supported Iran. Given the international lack of concern over Israel's nuclear arsenal, they saw the sanctions imposed on the country as unjust. In normal circumstances they would have welcomed the Obama administration's easing of sanctions in favour of negotiations with Tehran. But these were not normal circumstances. 'Syria is occupied by the Iranian regime', said former Syrian prime minister Riyad Hijab after his defection. 'The person who runs the country is not Bashaar al-Assad but Qassem Soleimani, the head of the Iranian regime's Quds Force.'[24] Why, Syrians asked, was America dealing with the Islamic Republic now, just as its regional policy took a fiercely sectarian, expansionist and anti-democratic turn?

Before the 1979 Islamic Revolution, the Shah's Iran was a firm Western ally. Later, George W. Bush's 'war on terror' unwittingly strengthened Iran by removing two of its enemies – the Taliban in Afghanistan and Saddam Hussain in Iraq. Iran increased its influence over both countries, but particularly over Shia-majority Iraq. This outraged Iraq's Sunnis and sparked a regional proxy war, sometimes cold but increasingly hot, between Iran on the one hand and Saudi Arabia on the other. Iran – strategically located, resource-rich, with an educated population – is more developed than any Arab country. Perhaps this is why Obama saw the need to engage it, and why he seems to consider a nuclear deal (signed in July 2015) as the crowning achievement of his presidency. But his engagement involved turning a blind eye to Iran's pernicious behaviour in Iraq and particularly Syria. By the summer of 2014, Obama also felt he needed Iran to help him take on ISIS, but Iranian policy in both Iraq and Syria had vastly increased the Sunni sense of victimhood. Iran was one of the factors behind ISIS's rise, and will continue to galvanise Sunni extremists after ISIS's fall.

At first Iran's support for Assad was rhetorical. While it had welcomed the other Arab uprisings, even painting them as repeats of its own revolution – later captured by conservative clerics – in 1979, in the Syrian case it repeated Assad's conspiracist propaganda. It offered Assad the expertise in cyberpolicing which it had employed to crush the Green Movement of 2009. Then its military advisers started arriving. By the summer of 2013, Assad's battles were increasingly directed by Iranian military experts, and Iranian-funded and trained Shia militias fought in great numbers on Assad's frontlines. These include the Iraqi organisations Kata'ib Hizbullah and Asa'ib Ahl al-Haqq, as well as the Lebanese Hizbullah, and the Abu Fadl al-Abbas Brigade, which contains both Lebanese and Iraqi fighters. By 2014, Syrian opposition forces were capturing Afghans on the battlefield too. Some of these were Sunnis, not fighting for ideological reasons but because they were illegal immigrants in Iran, and had been promised money and Iranian nationality if they joined up. Lebanese Hizbullah led the May 2013 fight for al-Qusayr as well as the battles on the Qalamoun in the following months. During the regime's February 2015 offensive south of Damascus, activists and Free Army fighters claimed not only that foreign fighters were leading Assad's forces, but that they even constituted a majority.[25] This is one reason why revolutionaries continued to be irked by the 'civil war' designation. The regime's growing reliance on such militias made it seem much more like a war against foreign occupation.

The Iranian Revolutionary Guard also trained the regime's new National Defense Force, a militia of at least 70,000 drawn from Syria's Alawi and Shia communities. But perhaps Iran's greatest gift to Assad has been financial. In July 2013 it provided a $3.6 billion credit line, separate from military aid and discounted oil deliveries. This means, in the words of analyst Scott Lucas, that 'Iran has been vital in propping up a Syrian regime that can no longer provide for its people'.[26]

Why would theocratic Iran risk so much on a supposedly secularist and Arabist regime? The Alawi identity of the ruling security clique makes little difference, since orthodox Shia like orthodox Sunnis consider the Alawi faith heretical. The alliance, originally struck between Hafez al-Assad and Ayatollah Khomeini, was political. Assad senior, at odds with other Arab powers, supported Iran (rhetorically at least) in its war with Iraq. And since the 1980s, Iran had projected its influence as far as the Mediterranean through Hizbullah, investing billions in the Lebanese Shia organisation. The Assad regime had been an essential link, transporting weapons through its territory and coordinating intelligence. When Hizbullah was perceived as an Arab frontline resisting Israeli occupation, it was wildly popular in Lebanon, Syria and throughout the Arab world. On its back, Iran too won wide admiration.

But the Syria intervention fatally undermined not only Iran's reputation with the Arabs, but Hizbullah's too. The resistance to Israel now looked like a cover for Iranian domination of the Arab region (or, by the sectarian reading, for Shia domination of Sunnis). By 2015, Iranian media was exulting in pictures of Qassem Soleimani leading the battle in both Syria and Iraq, and Iranian officials openly boasted their state's expansion. 'Three Arab capitals have today ended up in the hands of Iran and belong to the Islamic Iranian revolution', trilled Ali Reza Zakani, an MP close to Supreme Guide Ali Khamenei.[27] He referred to Damascus, Baghdad and Beirut, and added that Sanaa would soon follow, after Iranian-backed Houthi fighters took power by coup d'état in Yemen.

Iran's Lebanese proxy Hizbullah, meanwhile, suffered losses on the Syrian battlefield on a scale that couldn't be long sustained. And in fragile Lebanon, the sectarian tensions rose. 'We disagree over Syria', Hassan Nasrallah challenged militant Lebanese Sunnis in a 25 May 2013 speech. 'You fight in Syria; we fight in Syria – then let's fight there. Do you want me to be more frank? Keep Lebanon aside. Why should we fight in Lebanon?'[28] Some of his Sunni opponents obliged, which may have saved Lebanon from another bout of war – though the war frequently spilled over in gun battles in the border areas, and a series of bombings of Shia targets in Beirut, and in a contained but sometimes fierce battle between Sunni and Alawi neighbourhoods of Tripoli.

There was of course dissent among Lebanese Shia. Sheikh Subhi al-Tufayli, who had led Hizbullah between 1989 and 1991, fiercely opposed the Syrian adventure. He blamed Iran: 'I was secretary general of the party and I know that the decision is Iranian, and the alternative would have been a confrontation with the Iranians. I know that the Lebanese in Hizbullah, and Sayyed Hassan Nasrallah more than anyone, are not convinced about this war.'[29]

He warned, furthermore, that the entrance of Shia powers against the Syrian revolution would provoke a regional sectarian conflict. 'Iran and Hizbullah bear responsibility for every Syrian killed, every tree felled, and every house destroyed', he went on.[30] Unfortunately, Tufayli has been confined to the Bekaa valley since leading a 'hunger revolution' against the Lebanese government in 1997. His influence is currently as limited as his movement.

Sayyed Hani Fahs was another highly respected Shia leader who opposed Hizbullah's intervention, but he died in September 2014. A statement in 2012 called on Lebanese Shia to 'support the Arab uprisings ... particularly the Syrian [one] which will triumph, God willing ... Among the [factors] that guarantee a [good] future for us in Lebanon is for Syria to be stable, free, and ruled by a democratic, pluralist and modern state.'[31]

Beyond the clerics, a combination of Lebanese, Syrian and Iranian activists and citizen journalists formed the Naame Shaam campaign against Iranian and Hizbullah intervention.[32] But they were facing a party and militia deeply rooted among Lebanese Shia. According to Hanin Ghaddar, a Lebanese journalist of Shia origin who has argued repeatedly against the organisation:

> Despite individual voices here and there, there is still no collective resistance by the Shia community against Hizbullah's role in Syria. There are two reasons: One, there is no viable alternative for the Shia in Lebanon – such a figure will not be allowed to flourish. Two, the Shia are afraid of the sectarian tension and feel that Hizbullah, although not ideal anymore, can still protect them against Daesh, Nusra and other Islamists.[33]

If Iran acted as the Syrian regime's banker and military strategist, Russia was its superpower sponsor. In the UN Security Council, Russia played the role with regard to Assad that the United States plays with regard to Israel, protecting his regime on several occasions from international condemnation. In October 2011, for instance, Russia vetoed a resolution condemning regime repression and calling for targeted international sanctions. So did China. Both powers had reason to fear any such precedent; one day the United Nations might focus on their abuses in Chechnya, Tibet or Xinjiang.[34] Russia, in addition, has preserved a web of business and military relationships with Syria since the Soviet Union era. The Syrian port at Tartous houses Russia's only naval base outside Russia and the Ukraine. Still, it's a small base. A greater motivation seems to be the Putinist desire to project Russian influence and prestige after the humiliating collapse of the Soviet Union.

Russia shipped billions of dollars worth of arms and ammunition to the regime, provoking Western censure. At one point Putin denied Russia was sending any weapons 'which can be used in a civilian conflict', deliberately missing the point – Assad was using weapons fit for an interstate war against unarmed civilians. Barrel bombs were dropped on residential tenements, for instance, from Russian-supplied helicopters. This prompted a response from Amnesty International: 'Anyone supplying attack helicopters – or maintaining, repairing or upgrading them – for the Syrian government displays a wanton disregard for humanity.'[35] Russian military advisers trained regime soldiers; Russian fuel shipments arrived at Tartous. And there was still more direct intervention. In October 2014, when opposition forces captured a strategic hill at al-Harra in Deraa province, they found evidence that Russian military intelligence was operating a communications monitoring centre there, helping to coordinate the regime's attacks.

* * *

Certain regional states – not so much allies of the popular revolution as opponents of Assad – have provided support to the opposition.

Despite a history of disputes over water, territory and the Kurdish PKK movement, Turkey and Syria enjoyed excellent relations in March 2011. Partly as a result of Turkish Foreign Minister Davutoglu's 'Zero Problems with Neighbours' policy, visa requirements between the two countries were cancelled and a free trade zone was being set up. Syria, for its part, had quietly dropped its claim on Wilayet

Iskenderoon, or Hatay to the Turks, a territory awarded to Turkey by the French occupation.

In the first months of the revolution, Davutoglu engaged in intense diplomacy, seemingly winning Assad's agreement to ease the repression. But Assad's promises were empty. This outraged Turkish prime minister Erdogan, as did a series of Syrian aggressions. In November 2011, Syrian soldiers opened fire on a bus carrying Turkish pilgrims home from Mecca. In June 2012, Syria shot down a Turkish reconnaissance jet flying near its airspace. In October 2012, in the first of several such incidents, Turkey returned fire at Syrian troops after mortars killed five people in southern Turkey. Then in May 2013, two car bombs exploded outside the town hall in Reyhanli, killing at least 43. Blamed on the Syrian *mukhabarat*, it was the worst terrorist attack Turkey had ever suffered.

Turkey has been the most generous of neighbours in permitting Syrian charities and political activity to operate on its territory, and allowing the free passage of refugees and resistance fighters across its border. Very damagingly, however, it has until recently also neglected to police the passage of foreign jihadists adequately. One of this book's authors crossed over illegally in June 2013 – right next to the official Bab al-Hawa border post. There were no cameras, and the soldiers nearby weren't paying attention. The Kurdish boys in charge of the smuggling remarked that they'd taken Chechens across at the same spot.[36]

Was this carelessness or a deliberate anti-Kurdish policy? It's sometimes claimed that Turkey turned a blind eye to jihadist traffic in order to create problems for Syria's PYD-managed Kurdish-majority areas. The PYD is, after all, closely linked to the Turkish Kurdish PKK – designated a terrorist organisation by Ankara (and the US). In late 2014, Turkey provoked outrage by refusing to allow PYD fighters from Hasakeh to transit through Turkey to aid their comrades in Kobani, though it did allow Iraqi Kurdish *peshmerga* – with whom it enjoys much better relations – to travel to the battle through its territory. Until July 2015, Erdogan refused to join with the United States and its Gulf Arab allies in bombing ISIS, because he (logically) held that any action against ISIS would be futile if it is not accompanied by action against Assad. Turkey (with French support) has repeatedly called for a no-fly zone to be established at least over northern Syria. Conspiracy theories of outright Turkish collusion with ISIS, meanwhile, are unfounded. What remains of Turkey's military 'deep state' tends towards radical secularism, while Erdogan's Justice and Development Party follows a moderate Islamist and economically liberal policy, and is loosely allied with the Arab world's Muslim Brotherhood. This is one reason why the SNC, and to a lesser extent the Coalition – both based in Istanbul – have over-represented the Brotherhood. It also explains the suspicion harboured towards Turkey by some non-Islamist revolutionaries.

On 20 July 2015, a ISIS suicide bomber struck the Turkish border town of Suruç, killing 32 people, mostly young Kurds affiliated with the Federation of Socialist Youths who were preparing to take aid to Kobani. Three days later a Turkish officer was killed in a cross-border firefight with ISIS. On 24 July, Turkish F16s began bombing ISIS targets in Syria, and government officials announced that American planes would be permitted to launch missions against ISIS from the Incirlik airbase.

Although ISIS's terrorism provided the pretext, the timing of Turkey's intervention had more to do with the PYD victory over ISIS at Tell Abyad, strengthening Syrian-Kurdish power along the border. In July 2015, Turkey spoke of a 'safe zone' for civilians in northern Aleppo province between Marea and Jarablus – an Arab-majority area. Its presence there would disrupt potential PYD plans physically to link up the Rojava cantons.

At the time of writing it is not yet clear to what extent and in which direction the Turkish intervention will push events. Any truly secure 'safe zone' will also have to be a no-fly zone, to protect the people there from Assad's planes as well as ISIS's guns – but American officials seem no closer to agreement with Turkey on this point. On the other hand, activists in Aleppo reported a dramatic reduction in regime bombing in the first days of Turkey's action.

Direct Turkish involvement provokes many questions. Will Turkey now arm the Free Army and Islamic Front militias much more intensively than before? Will this lead to an early assault on ISIS in Raqqa? And will Turkey end up in direct conflict with the PYD? Given the US Air Force's battlefield coordination with the PYD, this eventuality seems unlikely, but on the first day of bombing the PYD had already accused the Turkish army of striking its positions as well as ISIS's. Turkey's raids come simultaneously with strikes against PKK bases in Iraqi Kurdistan.

Then there are the Arab Gulf states. In March 2011, Assad's relations with the Gulf Cooperation Council (GCC) powers were reasonably warm. Qatar in particular was friendly towards the regime, which extended its period in the Gulf's good books by supporting the GCC intervention against the democratic uprising in Bahrain. It should be noted that the GCC combatted the Bahraini movement as Assad would the Syrian – by playing the sectarian card. Where Assad described his challenge as a foreign Sunni conspiracy, the GCC described the one in Shia-majority Bahrain as having an Iranian-inspired anti-Sunni character.

As Assad's repression intensified, however, and as Iran swung its weight behind him, the Gulf began supporting segments of the Syrian opposition politically, financially and with arms. Often simplistically described as obedient clients of the Americans, Qatar and Saudi Arabia fund who they fund in Syria for their own reasons, which are to do with the Saudi proxy war with Iran, and the conflict between Qatar and Saudi Arabia themselves – the former supported the Muslim Brotherhood across the Arab world; the latter, the key backer of General Sisi's anti-Islamist junta in Egypt, vigorously opposed them. Qatar donates to Islamist groups; Saudi Arabia works with militia leaderships previously known to the kingdom. These are sometimes Islamist, but more often it is the more secular and American-friendly groups (such as the Syrian Revolutionaries Front) that benefit from Saudi largesse. No Gulf state funds ISIS, an organisation which aims to destroy them, though none have done enough to prevent their wealthy citizens from sending it money.

Neither the Saudi nor the Qatari rulers desire democracy (as the Bahrain example, and the repression of protests in Saudi Arabia's east, amply demonstrate). Motivated by influence-projection, responding too to a groundswell of popular sympathy for the Syrian cause, they sought to neutralise the more radical and democratic impulses of the revolution.

Saudi Arabia's greatest contribution to the fall of Assad may well turn out to be its oil policy. Global oil prices halved in the latter part of 2014, in part as a result of fracking and a slowdown in the Chinese economy, but also because the Saudis refused to cut production. Both Russia and Iran are dependent on high oil prices to keep their economies afloat. Revolutionary Syrians hope that financial constraints will make these states less able to bail out the regime in the medium and long term. At the same time, they fear the ramifications of the July 2015, US–Iran nuclear deal. Supporters of the agreement argue that improved economic conditions will empower Iran's democrats and curtail its hardliners. Syrians respond that any eventual changes in the Iranian polity will come far too late for Syria. In the meantime, sanctions relief will mean that Iran has much more money to lavish on Assad.

In January 2015, King Salman ascended the Saudi throne following the death of his half-brother Abdullah, and a new tone was immediately adopted by the kingdom. Responding to a changed environment characterised by Iranian expansion and American distance, Salman dropped his predecessor's hostility to the Muslim Brotherhood and reconciled with Qatar and Turkey. The increased supply of anti-tank weapons for the rebels in northern Syria, and the string of victories in Idlib province in the spring, were an early sign of greater Saudi assertiveness.

In Yemen, meanwhile, the Iranian-backed Houthi movement, based within the country's Zaidi Shia minority, had allied with ex-President Ali Abdullah Saleh – who still controlled parts of the army despite having being pushed out in the popular uprising of 2011 – and together seized power in the capital. As the Houthis expanded their control into southern Yemen, Saudi Arabia was spurred into precipitous action. On 27 March 2015, alongside Bahrain, Qatar, Kuwait, the United Arab Emirates, Egypt, Jordan, Morocco and Sudan, the kingdom launched Operation Decisive Storm – a bombing campaign still continuing at the time of writing in October 2015. Apparently President Saleh spent billions on arms and ammunition; endless ammunition dumps have been spectacularly destroyed by Saudi bombs, along with residential areas, an aid warehouse and a camp housing displaced people. Yemenis – inhabiting what was already the poorest of Arab states – are suffering enormously. But Decisive Storm has as yet achieved no decisive political effect. On the campaign's first day, the Saudis announced Pakistan's involvement. The Pakistanis later demurred. It may be that the Saudis had expected Pakistan to provide men for a ground invasion. Unable now to send in troops to beat back the Houthis, Saudi policy in Yemen seems to be adrift.

By bombing Yemen, King Salman hoped not only to confront Iran but also to undercut the appeal of extremist Sunni identity politics at home. Until the Saudi bombs started falling, al-Qaida in the Arabian Peninsula and ISIS (whose suicide bombers killed 142 people in Houthi-aligned mosques on 20 March 2015) looked like the most organised 'resistance' to Iranian/Shia plans in southern Arabia. This illustrates the discomfort of Sunni Arab powers in the Gulf, squeezed between Sunni Islamists and an imperial Iran.

Saudi commentators have suggested that once a clear defeat has been registered on Iranian-backed forces in Yemen, the Saudi-led coalition will turn its attention more fully to Syria, perhaps even providing air cover for a Southern Front offensive against Assad's Iranian-backed forces south of Damascus. Saudi clumsiness in Yemen, however, does not give cause for optimism.

* * *

Of all Syria's neighbours, Israel has involved itself the least in the conflict – although this may change. Until Israel returns occupied territory and Palestinian rights are realised, most in the Arab world will consider it an enemy. In this context, the Assad regime is the devil Israel knows. A column in an Israeli newspaper went so far as to describe Assad as 'Israel's favourite Arab dictator'.[37] Despite its anti-Zionist rhetoric, the regime had not only preserved peace on the border with the occupied Golan Heights since 1973, it had successfully repressed Syrians and Palestinians who had called for confronting the occupier, and had limited the fight – such as it was – to Lebanon. When Assad's cousin Rami Makhlouf told the *New York Times*, 'If there is no stability here, there's no way there will be stability in Israel', he was reminding the Israelis that a dictatorship on their border was preferable to either Islamists or revolutionary nationalists.

So Israel largely kept out of it, though it struck at weapons destined for Hizbullah on several occasions. Its most grievous blow against the Lebanese organisation and its sponsor was on 18 January 2015, when it destroyed two vehicles on the Syrian side of the Golan Heights, killing several Iranians and Lebanese including an Iranian general. Israel may become more involved in the future as a result of the increased presence of Iranian forces and their proxies in southern Syria, and perhaps even to offer 'protection' to Sweida's Druze community from jihadist attacks.[38]

* * *

At the time of writing, the United States had finally begun a three-year training programme to turn out a supposed total of 15,000 Syrian fighters to serve as an anti-ISIS force. So far the programme has been bedevilled by logistical setbacks including the resignations and mass disqualifications of potential recruits. In July 2015, 54 US-trained fighters finally entered Syria. Eighteen were immediately abducted by Jabhat al-Nusra, which accused 'the filthy US-backed group' of calling in airstrikes on Nusra targets. The Americans retaliated by bombing a Nusra target north of Aleppo, killing twelve. Nusra retaliated to that attack by attacking the Free Army's 30th Division, which hosted the trainees. Most other rebel forces in the area pointedly declined to come to the 30th Division's defence.[39]

The episode illustrates the meaninglessness of the American endeavour. After years of war, Syrian fighters need effective weaponry, not training. Since the US chose not to act against the regime, US-backed troops are seen on the ground as American mercenaries, not as Syrian patriots. Assad is the first enemy of revolutionary Syrians; ISIS is a symptom of Assad's scorched earth. Any plan which does not work against Assad as well as ISIS, and which ignores Iran's Shia jihadists, will gain no traction.

So the stalemate continues. Even if the opposition encircles and besieges central Damascus, it will find it impossible to storm the capital. Regime forces are so well dug into the mountains above the city, and in the strategic regime-dependent Alawi suburbs around it, that a final battle would lead to its total destruction. At the same time, the regime is incapable of clawing back the two-thirds of the country it has lost, even with intensified Iranian help. Propped up by foreign money and desperately short of men, time moves against it.

The regime, in any case, is no longer the regime of 2011. That has already fallen. In its place is a collection of militias, both foreign and domestic, loyal to external players or to substate leaderships. It's likely that some of these will last longer than the regime core. But when the Assadist inner circle does fall, new domestic alliances will become possible. Freed of the regime's weight, Alawis will be able (and will find it necessary) to reach out to the more moderate revolutionary forces.

Current international diplomacy is reduced to vague hopes that the battle lines can be frozen through local ceasefires. This might produce some temporary respite for civilians, but Syrians, longing for a long-term solution, are often dismissive of the idea. Yara Nseir, for instance, says, 'Well, we've experienced this before and we know what happens. In Yalda, in Moadamiya, or even in Homs where the UN and the Iranians were involved, the regime went in after the ceasefire and arrested men who've never been seen again.'[40]

Talk of freezing the battle feeds into potential partition scenarios. One such envisages the regime retreating to the coast, where most Alawi families originate, but this too would only be a temporary solution. Though the rural hinterland has an Alawi majority, coastal cities such as Lattakia and Banyas are majority Sunni. The creation of an Alawi state would require an ethnic cleansing on a far greater scale than that yet seen. The remainder of Syria would be cut off from the coast; Alawis would be cut off from Damascus, and stuck once again in their economically undeveloped corner of the country.

By 2015 the UN seemed to have abandoned Annan and Brahimi's proclaimed quest for a transition. 'President Assad is part of the solution', said envoy Staffan de Mistura in February, a few days after attending the Islamic Revolution anniversary party at Damascus's Iranian embassy. Millions of Syrians disagreed so vehemently as to render the UN, once again, irrelevant. The largest rebel groupings suspended cooperation with de Mistura after his comment.

* * *

Syria presents serious issues for consideration by revolutionaries everywhere. First, revolutions in the real world (as opposed to ivory towers) are always messy. As soon as state power is weakened, external state interests will enter the fray in the attempt to influence potential future governments, to compete with rival states, and to manipulate, reshape and tame revolutionary energies. Second, states – sometimes even supposed enemy states – will come to each other's rescue, directly or indirectly, if there's a real possibility of power slipping from elite hands. Third, they will often be aided in this by commentators, including supposed 'leftist' and 'dissenting' ones, whose obsession with states leads them to see conflicts as a chess game between 'better' and 'worse', and to ignore the people suffering under and struggling against these states.

10

The Start of Solidarity

I am afraid that it is too late for the leftists in the West to express any solidarity with the Syrians in their extremely hard struggle. What I always found astonishing in this regard is that mainstream Western leftists know almost nothing about Syria, its society, its regime, its people, its political economy, its contemporary history. Rarely have I found a useful piece of information or a genuinely creative idea in their analyses. My impression about this curious situation is that they simply do not see us; it is not about us at all. Syria is only an additional occasion for their old anti-imperialist tirades, never the living subject of the debate ... We, rank-and-file Syrians, refugees, women, students, intellectuals, human rights activists, political prisoners ... do not exist ... But honestly I've failed to discern who is right and who is left in the West from a leftist Syrian point of view ... Before helping Syrians or showing solidarity with Syrians, the mainstream Western left needs to help themselves.

Yassin al-Haj Saleh[1]

Videos of tens of thousands of people demonstrating against tyranny gave way to the images of deserted streets in derelict towns. Of tanks driving up main streets and planes bombing villages. The cynics who didn't bat an eyelid for the thousands of innocents who were shot like dogs now nod their heads knowingly and speak of a revolution 'hijacked'. They can go to hell. This revolution was not about an ideology or a religion, and it wasn't about grand political scheming, it was about normal people who stopped what they were doing to stand up for what they believed in, and they did that even though they were afraid and, in many cases, would lose their lives. Injustice can only sustain itself through fear, and on that day we broke fear forever.

Wassim al-Adl[2]

The Syrian revolution didn't receive the international support and recognition it deserved. And not for want of information. Syria's citizen journalists, as well as foreign reporters, struggled and even died while attempting to communicate Syrian terrors and hopes to the world. Journalists Marie Colvin and Remi Ochlik were killed in Homs in February 2012. The photographer Paul Conroy was injured in the same attack. 'The regime gunners', he wrote, were 'bracketing in on us, which is adjusting fire with the use of a drone, until they had precisely targeted the building. They then fired four rockets directly into the media center ... Why? What was happening in Baba Amr was wholesale slaughter, Marie had the audacity to report live from the scene. We had witnessed the butchery and that crossed the boundaries as to what the regime would tolerate. We rattled too many cages in Damascus.'[3] Ali Mustafa, a Toronto-based activist and freelance photojournalist who'd worked previously with the Landless Workers Movement in Brazil, was killed by regime bombs in Aleppo in March 2014.[4] Journalist Kenji Goto and aid workers Alan Henning and Peter Kassig were beheaded by ISIS. Activist and aid worker Kayla Mueller also died in ISIS captivity.[5] These were people – and of course there are many others, including the great journalist Anthony Shadid – who chose to go to Syria out of a profound sense of human solidarity, and who paid the greatest price.[6] The Syria reportage and analysis of writers like Martin Chulov represent investigative journalism at its very best.[7] Weapons expert Eliot Higgins leads the field of those who cross-reference and examine YouTube videos and satellite imagery to build a picture of the forces and arms in play on the battlefield.[8] And the wonderful novelist Jonathan Littell contributed a perceptive account of his 2012 visit to revolutionary Homs.[9]

Many others near and far have done the Syrian people great service in activism, in collecting and delivering aid, by volunteering in refugee camps or advocating for refugees in Europe. Sadly, however, these were a small minority, and they frequently found themselves swimming against the tide. The dominant narrative on Syria was often terribly flawed, beset by false assumptions, red herrings and sensationalism. The start of solidarity is to correct the narrative.

* * *

The consistency and volume of citizen journalist videos and reports left little doubt concerning the scale of the regime's repression. This presented a problem to regime propagandists. Their response, given that they couldn't hide the violence, was to at least establish a functional doubt as to its nature and its perpetrators. In this way they hoped to render everything grey and cloudy so that responsibility remained unclear and meaningful solidarity with the victims would become impossible.

Their first channels of misinformation were the state's newspapers and TV stations as well as private but regime-affiliated stations like al-Dunya and al-Mayadeen.[10] Their propaganda was then repeated and amplified by the official media of the regime's state sponsors – foremost among them Iran's Press TV and the Kremlin's Russia Today. These two stations were very useful because their stories were often picked up in the West, first by conspiracist websites and then by sections of the mainstream media.

Sometimes Western media did the job without the mediation. Journalists like Colvin or Goto risked everything for the freedom to report beyond regime control. Others – very understandably – obeyed their visa conditions and stayed in regime-run territory, accompanied by regime minders. Some of these appeared to forget the constraints they were working under, and accepted what the regime offered at face value.[11]

Some commentators proved remarkably vulnerable to regime tricks. Blame-the-victims conspiracy theories abounded after the May 2012 Houleh massacre, and again after the August 2013 sarin massacre. Falsely assuming that the US or NATO were hell-bent on regime change, several 'dissenting' journalists produced implausible claims of regime innocence in both incidents, seeing them as proof of a supposed 'information war' waged by Western capitals against Assad.[12]

* * *

Some Western sympathy is generated for the Assad regime by the sense that it – alongside Iran and Russia – stands in opposition to hegemonic

US-led imperialism. By this reading, the Syrian state (rather than the Syrian people) represents the underdog. A closer examination of the regime's neo-liberal policies and security collaboration with the West, and of American willingness to tolerate the regime's destabilisations, soon demolishes the foundations on which the reading is built. Yet it persists, and leads some ever deeper into conspiracism. For such people, not only the Syrian revolution but the whole Arab Spring was a foreign plot, the English-language slogans at Kafranbel are proof of a CIA presence, and Egypt's uprising is best explained by the American donation of $250 million to democracy programmes in the country (ignoring the $7.8 billion donation to the Egyptian army). These narratives remove the agency of the peoples concerned, casting the Arabs as innocents pleased to suffer poverty, torture and humiliation until some devilishly clever Westerner whispers in their ears.

The two-campist method of thought, an archaic legacy of the Cold War, also leads its adherents into a selective and morally inconsistent anti-imperialism. 'Anti-imperialist' supporters of Russian and Iranian policy in the Arab world should consider this: with its massive military involvement on the side of a client minority regime, Iran is to Syria what the United States once was to Vietnam. And Russia – providing weapons, deflecting sanctions, shielding from blame – is to Syria what the United States is to Israel.

* * *

More specifically, the Syrian regime markets itself with considerable success at home and abroad as a 'resistance regime', a friend of the Palestinians constantly engaged in existential struggle against the Israeli occupier. Resistance was the pretext for its decades-long 'Emergency' that suspended due process and political life, for its smothering of civil society and for the financial prioritisation of the military over all else. Resistance justified the airfields and bases outside every town which Syrians assumed constituted a complex defence against Israeli invasion, but whose real function was revealed during the counter-revolutionary war. And the resistance label is one reason why so many foreigners have seen the regime as victim rather than beneficiary of foreign machinations.

But how resistant was the regime in reality? True, it assisted the Iranian-backed Hizbullah militia in Lebanon, which did indeed strike grievous blows at Israeli expansionism. The 22-year occupation of southern Lebanon was ended by Hizbullah's armed resistance, not by a one-sided peace treaty. And when Israel launched a ferocious assault on the country's civilian infrastructure in 2006, moving troops back into the south, it met much fiercer resistance than expected, even suffering missile barrages on Israeli towns. Syria's bit-part in this drama must, however, be weighed against Hafez al-Assad's original intervention in Lebanon, when he threw Syria's weight behind right-wing Christian militias to halt the imminent victory of the Palestinian-Muslim-Leftist alliance. The thousands of Palestinian civilians slaughtered in Tel Zaatar in 1976, and in various other camps in the 1980s, must also be considered. Syria in Lebanon played factions and sects against each other to serve diverse temporary priorities and the one consistent policy of attempting to assert total control, particularly over the Palestinian movement. And the battle with Israel always remained in Lebanon. The regime policed its own frontier with the occupied Golan Heights so obediently that it remained more peaceful than the borders of states that had signed peace agreements with 'the Zionist enemy'. Whenever the enemy chose to strike deep inside Syria – destroying a suspected nuclear reactor in 2007, for instance, or assassinating Muhammad Suleiman, 'Special Presidential Advisor for Arms Procurement and Strategic Weapons', in 2008 – the regime announced its attention to respond 'at a time and place of its choosing'. The time never arrived.

It's true too that Palestinians in Syria, though not fully integrated, enjoyed far greater freedoms than their compatriots in Lebanon – though they were welcomed first and foremost by the Syrian people rather than the state, and decades before Hafez al-Assad established his dictatorship. But Palestinians were certainly no more free than their Syrian neighbours; they were subject to the same impoverishment and repression. And beyond the state's propaganda framework, neither Syrians nor Palestinians were permitted to direct their social, cultural or intellectual energies towards Palestinian liberation. The (Syrian) blogger Tal al-Malouhi, for example, was arrested in 2009 (when she was nineteen) for publishing poems and articles in support of the cause. She was held until 2011, and then sentenced to five years in prison.

Very many supposed supporters of the Palestinian cause, including some Palestinians, continued to view Assad as a victim of Western imperialism even as he tortured Palestinians to death and starved them in Yarmouk. Palestinian-American writer Talal Alyan laments their silence:

> Yarmouk stands as a kind of historic curiosity, an exception to the numerous massacres Palestinians have endured over the years. Not because it is uniquely brutal, Palestinian history ensures that that particular distinction be almost unattainable. What makes it stand out is the lack of public reaction many Palestinians have had to this catastrophe. There has been a decidedly muted response and coverage of the slaughter of this segment of Palestinians. Additionally, there has been a tacit accommodation of those who blatantly cheerlead for the culprits of this siege. The gamble represented with this silence, this neutrality, contains a much broader calamity. The destruction of the Yarmouk refugee camp signals a severe, perhaps unprecedented, disruption in Palestinian collectivity.[13]

* * *

'Zooming out' is one of the worst habits of an oversimplifying media. We see presidents, kings and warlords on our screens, alongside maps and flags, but seldom the people in all their diversity. In the Syrian case many commentators slipped into a generalising Islamophobia, one of 'al-Qaida' terrorists explaining all, and of all Sunni Islamists representing a monolithic enemy. Against the grain of reality, the phrase 'jihadists armed and funded by the West' came very easily to columnists' pens. Little distinction was made between moderate Islamists and extreme jihadists, between those willing to accommodate democratic forms and those not, and ISIS was casually and routinely conflated with 'the Syrian opposition' – even when they were at war with each other. Instead of examining how deliberate political decisions by key actors brought sectarian identity to the fore, Orientalist opinion-formers portrayed sectarian conflict as fated and inevitable. In this way they became unwitting carriers of Assadist propaganda, and contributed to the manufacture of popular assumptions in the West concerning Syria – that a secular regime stands on one side and fanatical Islamist extremists on the other, with nothing in between.

Some commentators have been so fixated on the evils of Sunni Islamism that they reverse cause and effect as well as chronology to understand Assad's repression as a defensive response to Islamist violence.[14] And journalists of the left and right frequently agonise over the potential fate of Alawis and Christians in a future Syria while ignoring the actual fate of the Sunni majority today. Syrian philosopher Sadik Jalal al-Azm bemoaned this narrow focus:

> The Sunni majority of the country is getting a savage beating from the storm troops, militias, and scud missiles of a small militarized minority that monopolizes the power and wealth of the country. The cities that have been destroyed are Sunni cities, while minority communities have remained relatively safe and calm. The large majority of the more than 200,000 killed so far, of the wounded, of the permanently impaired, of the disappeared and vanished, of the imprisoned and tortured are Sunni. Most of the millions who have been exiled and internally displaced are Sunni.[15]

ISIS's theatre of atrocity demonstrates an accurate understanding of Western media prejudices. The beheading of one American is headline news; the tens or hundreds killed daily by Assad's war go unreported. The immolation of the Jordanian pilot Muaz al-Kasasbeh creates global outrage; the routine incineration of women and children by Assad's barrel bombs doesn't.

* * *

The Muslim world did show some solidarity, sometimes in useful ways. As individuals or in groups, Muslims donated a great deal to refugees and those suffering inside. Muslims came from around the world to deliver aid, to provide medical care and to fight in moderate, Syrian-led brigades.

The transnational jihadists who joined ISIS, on the other hand, those who impose their ideology on the Syrians under their sway, are of course taking advantage of Syrian suffering rather than showing solidarity. And the ever-ready angry crowds so easily mobilised and manipulated by the beneficiaries of a politics of offence have been resoundingly silent. Syrians reacted with tired cynicism to the manufactured furore over the *Innocence of Muslims* YouTube film. Protests over the obscure insult led to at least 50 deaths around the world. No such upheaval followed the destruction of countless Syrian mosques or the rape of countless Syrian Muslim women. A banner unfurled at one Friday protest read: 'Is This the Same Prophet Who is Insulted Every Day in Syria?'

Still the fact remains. Syrians know that Muslims sent them money and weapons, and sometimes came to die for them. Much of the international left, on the other hand, slandered them as fools, barbarian jihadists or agents of the West.

* * *

The Kurds were a partial exception; they did enjoy a good deal of popular support in the West, particularly during the battle for Kobani in late 2014. Some anarchists and leftists even went to fight for the PYD against ISIS. Syrians – Kurds as well as Arabs – were bemused by this selective solidarity. Why, they asked, did the West (its warplanes more than its activists) care about the small town of Kobani but not the enormous city of Aleppo, where the liberated area was hard pressed by both ISIS and Assad? Some of the answer must lie in the poor media coverage of the revolution discussed here. All Western readers knew of Arab Aleppo was that it was ruled by 'Islamists' of some stripe or another; they knew nothing of the grassroots activists, the committees and councils or the extraordinary 'ordinary' men fighting to defend their communities. Even more important than the misreporting was the hard work done by well-established Kurdish communities in Europe, often linked up to trades unions and leftist parties. Turkish Kurds in particular have been very enthusiastic about PYD rule in Syria – understandably, given the scale of the national accomplishment – and have worked hard to relay the PYD's leftist and egalitarian rhetoric to the West. Syrian Kurds, who have witnessed the gap between rhetoric and reality, tend to be much less enthusiastic. But most still welcome the attention and support.

Here it's worth quoting the Syrian-Kurdish journalist and activist Shiar Nayo:

> It was heartening to see all that international solidarity with the Syrian Kurds' struggle in the wake of Daesh's attacks on Kobani in 2014. But it was disappointing that this solidarity remained largely confined to that one particular battle, and that it was often expressed in uncritical, naïve ways. Many Syrian revolutionaries and rebels in other parts of the country had also been fighting Daesh and had also been experimenting with self-administration initiatives for four years. But their incredible efforts have gone largely ignored internationally, both by governments and by supposed leftists.
>
> Even when the momentum was high around Kobani, international expressions of solidarity with Syria, especially in the West, did not grow more mature. Culturally, they often fell for simplistic Orientalist stereotypes spread by mainstream media about beautiful women fighters, barbaric Islamists and so on. Politically, they often failed to distinguish between the aspirations and rights of a group of people and a specific model that claims to embody these aspirations. Then there was all that hype around the PKK's and PYD's claims that they were changing into an 'anarchist' movement. The PKK is a highly ideological, nationalist party based on a strict military regime and blind loyalty. It still thrives on the apotheosis of the leader and the notion of one party leading state and society. It is not very different to so many leftist parties that have been riddled with these Stalinist-Leninist plagues. I would like to believe that the party is changing and is rethinking its ideology and practices. But until it really changes, I cannot understand how anyone can call it an anarchist movement, or even a legitimate representative of people's struggle for freedom and justice.
>
> So, while more solidarity is needed, it should be a critical solidarity – which should be distinguished from conditional solidarity. Critical solidarity means you support a struggle as a matter of principle (with real material support) but maintain an

active, critical stance toward a particular version or force that claims to represent people's aspirations and capitalises on them for political ends. Without such solidarity, it is likely that the promising self-administration experiment in the Kurdish areas of Syria will end with the strengthening of the PYD's dominance and an increase in its oppressive practices against other Kurdish forces and activists in the name of protecting what has been achieved so far, along with a gradual squandering of these achievements in exchange for narrow political interests.[16]

* * *

The European far right has in general been very supportive of Assad. British National Party leader Nick Griffin visited Damascus in support of the regime in June 2013. The European Solidarity Front, with strong fascist connections, has been prominent in anti-intervention demonstrations, and has sent various extremist delegations to Damascus. The Greek fascists of the Black Lilly organisation – a member of the European Solidarity Front – have gone so far as to fight in Syria alongside Assadist forces. It is interesting to note that the far right's position is motivated by the same factors galvanising sections of the left – an inchoate anti-imperialism/anti-globalism, and the perception that Assad is resisting both Zionism and Islamism.[17]

* * *

In 2011 and 2012, Syrians launched a popular revolution of enormous consequence and reach. New forms of organisation and expression emerged which reconfigured social relationships away from those based on hierarchy and domination towards the empowerment of individuals and communities. From 2013 on, however, these experiments were increasingly submerged by fiercely counter-revolutionary trends, both Assadist and regional. War dismantled the country's infrastructure and social fabric. Over half the population fled its homes.

What does this mean for revolution as a desired end? Revolutions erupt when people cannot breathe. And if they cannot breathe, by definition they haven't been able to build an alternative to save them when the system smothering them falls. Does this mean that revolution must inevitably end in the counter-revolution's victory? Not necessarily in the victory of the old regime but in some new hierarchy built from its ruins – a Frankenstein rising? In revolution, every energy is liberated, the good and the bad, energies people never knew they contained. And in our social soul the bad may overwhelm the good, in our social soul everywhere, not only under dictatorships – at least it overwhelms us at the point at which we cannot breathe. The hungry fight each other in the street over scraps of bread. The best armed win. The most psychopathic win.

This pessimistic reading misses two points. First, there was nothing inevitable in the counter-revolution's victory. Had Assad not received such solid military and economic support from abroad, had the Free Army, the Coalition and the grassroots organisers not been in various ways abandoned and betrayed, it's possible that the regime would have fallen in 2013. Even then it would have been immensely difficult to establish a more democratic and socially just society, but Syria would have been spared the rule of ISIS and the ongoing destruction of its cities. Second, very many decent, forward-thinking Syrians still have stomach for the fight – even if many are in exile. There's reason to hope that when the bombs finally stop falling, when ISIS and regime checkpoints no longer threaten death, these people will return and raise their voices again for a better future.

At the time of writing, more Syrians flee the country every day, and more Sunni and Shia foreign fighters rush in. It's hard in this context to see any light. So it isn't surprising that some question whether Syria did actually experience a revolution. The current beneficiaries of the collapse of the old order are Salafist militias, after all. But if counter-revolution disqualifies the original revolution, then there's been no revolution in modern times. The French Revolution ended up crowning Bonaparte. The Russian Revolution called for all power to the soviets but ended with all power in the Kremlin. The Chinese revolution ended in authoritarian capitalism. The Spanish Revolution was defeated first by Stalin, then by Franco.

Those Syrians whose lives were transformed, who found the strength to say no, to break the silence – these people would say yes, they've certainly lived a revolution. We could ask then: were they wrong to revolt? Did they make a mistake? But if we ask that, we're missing the original point – that people revolt when they cannot breathe. Systems fall when they finally smother the people. Otherwise put, when they smother the people they smother themselves. Syrians did not vote in conference on the decision to revolt. What happened was that a system collapsed, unable to contain its contradictions.

'Developed' or 'advanced' states in which power is diffuse and contested between centres – big business, the monarchy, the parliament, the political parties, the media – are infinitely harder to take down. But it's infinitely easier to work within them – anyone who thinks otherwise should examine their own privilege. Here there are opportunities, though ones which must sometimes be grasped at in peril. Here, if people wanted, in city neighbourhoods and in rural zones, they could work to produce potential alternatives to the dominant system. They could experiment with different ways of living and organising beyond the frameworks offered by states and corporations. Creating workable alternatives would be a million times more useful for revolutionaries elsewhere than misinformed theoretical hectoring. And perhaps people here could learn from those cursed enough, or sufficiently blessed, to have experienced the collapse of a system, those who have been thrown by necessity into the business of building something new.

We hope this book has shown that there are Syrians inside and in exile who are more than worthy of support. We ask the reader to engage with them, with media and creative workers, with the committees and councils, by working with refugees and in the camps. Learning opportunities will arise naturally from such human engagement. In order to truly think globally – rather than to hide from thought behind clumsy globalising paradigms – it is necessary to act locally. We ask the reader, rather than applying the usual grand narratives, to attend to voices from the ground.

Epilogue: October 2015

In the three months since we finished writing this book, the war in Syria has continued to metastasize. The most crucial development has been Russia's direct imperialist intervention.

Nothing much came of the Turkish plan for civilian safe zones. Turkey's limited intervention hit the PYD as well as ISIS and returned Turkey itself to the bad old days of PKK insurgency and state-directed collective punishment. While Turkey was bogged down in its unresolved struggle of nationalisms, and with the Saudis distracted by their seemingly endless bombing of Yemen, the Americans were placing restrictions on the (FSA) Southern Front's offensive to take Deraa.[1] Apparently the US feared sudden regime collapse, and used its observer position on the Gulf-backed Jordanian operations centre – which channels and withholds arms from the Southern Front – to avoid this possibility. The regime, meanwhile, shored up its position in Druze-majority Sweida province, which neighbours Deraa, by killing the Druze leader Wahid al-Balous and 25 others with a car bomb. It paid a short-term price – protestors destroyed a statue of Hafez al-Assad, and gunmen shot six security men – but in the medium term it freed itself of an influential critic of Assad and opponent of conscription who was moving closer to cooperation with the Southern Front.[2]

The most important battle of this period was over Zabadani, a mountain town near Damascus – one of the first to be liberated (in January 2012) and one of the first to establish a revolutionary council. Hizbullah led the three-month assault, pulverising the town and its historical monuments. When the surprising persistence of the defenders led to negotiations, the Islamist militia Ahrar al-Sham spoke on the rebels' behalf. Its interlocutor was not the Syrian regime, but Iran.

Ahrar hoped to win a mutual ceasefire – that Hizbullah would stop attacking Zabadani, and the opposition would stop attacking

Fu'ah and Kafraya, pro-regime Shia towns in Idlib province. But the Iranians demanded a population exchange – that Sunni residents leave Zabadani, and Shia leave Idlib. Between ISIS and the Assadist-Iranian partition scenario, Syria is now witnessing sectarian engineering far worse than under the French.

Zabadani fell, but the talks eventually secured a ceasefire covering 14 northern towns – a potential precedent for calming the conflict – but Russian action soon made this new 'balance' irrelevant.

From mid-August, Russia deployed several hundred troops as 'advisors' to Assadist forces, sent warships to the coast and augmented its Lattakia airbase with drones, attack helicopters and jet fighters. Following this fait accompli, Germany, Britain and the US agreed that Assad could stay for a transitionary period, effectively shifting towards the Russian position.

On 30 September 2015, Russia declared war on the Syrian revolution. Though its public rhetoric was of stopping ISIS, it hit nowhere near ISIS positions. Instead, it struck the communities which had driven ISIS out. The bombing killed at least two dozen civilians, including many children, and destroyed such targets as a building used by a revolutionary council,[3] and Byzantine ruins near Kafranbel.[4]

Further bombing waves did target ISIS, but the vast majority of bombs continued to fall on those opposed to both Assad and ISIS. The liberated Rastan pocket in northern Homs, controlled by the FSA, and targets in Hama, Idlib and Lattakia controlled by Jaysh al-Fatah, were particularly hard hit. US-backed groups like Suqour al-Jabal were also targeted.

The LCCs responded:

> Russian troops are now openly fighting alongside the army of the dictator. Despite international consensus that the attacks have not targeted ISIS positions, we have yet to see any forceful condemnations regarding the killing of civilians, and this leads us to believe that the international community is tacitly approving of these attacks. We believe that any partnership with Russia, which claims to target ISIS and which has the blessing of the Patriarch of the Russian Orthodox Church, will serve only to accelerate the pace of

> killing and widen the circle of devastation. These conditions will inevitably lead to even more extremism.
>
> The LCC calls upon all revolutionary forces and factions to unite by any means and respond to the Russian aggression.[5]

Today Assad, Russia and America share the skies, occasionally bombing ISIS but more usually the struggling Syrian people and their resistance militias. This key event will greatly influence the future transformations of jihadism, both inside and beyond Syria.

It remains to be seen how Saudi Arabia, Turkey and Qatar will meet Russia's challenge. It's likely they will increase weapons supply to the opposition, both to counter Russian and Iranian moves and to prevent ISIS domination.

The Russian air campaign will probably be accompanied by a regime-Iranian ground offensive on northern Homs and elsewhere to shore up Assad's rump state from the coast to Damascus. Like the Iranians before them, the Russians will be unable to claw back the four-fifths of Syrian territory the regime has lost. If the Russian plan goes well and the FSA fighters currently in play are eventually absorbed or conquered by ISIS, then the West may even win the rest of the country back for Assad. Such is the dream.

Russian intervention will be a grievous setback for the rebels, perhaps reversing current trends by another year, but Assad will soon confront the demographic reality once again. He's running out of fighting men; foreign troops, however many arrive, can extend but not win his war. And not only the opposition militias but the majority of the Syrian people too will refuse to cooperate with any plan envisaging regime survival. For them Assad, not ISIS, is the supreme evil, and with good reason: Assad's forces are responsible for the overwhelming majority of civilians killed and driven out.[6]

Sometimes it seems the only Syrian who isn't leaving is Bashaar. Increasing numbers of refugees have been washing up on largely unwelcoming European shores. When emotions were galvanised in September by the photograph of three-year-old Aylan Kurdi lying dead on a Turkish beach, the refugee story topped the headlines for almost three weeks – though commentary focussed on symptoms (immigration/ISIS) rather than the cause.

Clandestine migrants usually slip across borders at night, but Syrians have changed that image. Now European news consumers are treated to the curious sight of hundreds of refugees, trained in the revolution, demanding free passage as they march together towards Germany.[7] (In August, Germany announced it would allow Syrians to apply for asylum regardless of how they arrived.)

Many more refugees will come, for the land under Syrian feet is dissolving. In Palmyra, ISIS has destroyed the tower tombs, the Triumphal Arch and the beautiful 2,000-year-old temples of Bel and Baalshamin. The latest destruction symbolises a total rupture with the country's past and presumed future. A people who dared to demand freedom received annihilation instead.

Further Reading

Background

Hanna Batatu, *The Old Social Classes and Revolutionary Movements of Iraq*, Saqi, 2012.
Alan George, *Syria: Neither Bread nor Freedom*, Zed Books, 2003.
Raymond Hinnebusch, *Syria: Revolution from Above*, Routledge, 2001.
Thomas Pierret, *Religion and State in Syria: The Sunni Ulama from Coup to Revolution*, Cambridge University Press, 2013.
Bente Scheller, *The Wisdom of Syria's Waiting Game*, Hurst, 2013.

The Revolution

Jonathan Littell, *Syrian Notebooks: Inside the Homs Uprising*, Verso, 2015.
Stephen Starr, *Revolt in Syria: Eye-witness to the Uprising*, C Hurst & Co., 2012.
Samar Yazbek, *A Woman in the Crossfire: Diaries of the Syrian Revolution*, Haus Publishing, 2011.
Samar Yazbek, *The Crossing: My Journey to the Shattered Heart of Syria*, Penguin Random House, 2015.

Culture

Malu Halasa, Zaher Omareen and Nawara Mahfoud (eds), *Syria Speaks, Art and Culture from the Frontline*, Saqi Books, 2014.
Ziauddin Sardar and Robin Yassin-Kassab (eds), *Critical Muslim 11 – Syria*, Hurst, 2014.

Aid Organisations

Hand in Hand for Syria: www.handinhandforsyria.org.uk
Karam Foundation: http://karamfoundation.org
Soriyat for Development: www.soriyat.org
Syria Relief: www.syriarelief.org.uk
The White Helmets: www.whitehelmets.org

Activism

Free #Douma4: https://douma4.wordpress.com
Global Campaign of Solidarity with the Syrian Revolution: www.facebook.com/pages/Global-Campaign-of-Solidarity-with-the-Syrian-Revolution/147353662105485
Humans of Syria: www.facebook.com/HumanOSyria
Local Coordination Committees: www.lccsyria.org/en (@LccSy)
Planet Syria: www.planetsyria.org/en
Raqqa is being slaughtered silently http://www.raqqa-sl.com/en/
The Syria Campaign: https://thesyriacampaign.org and www.facebook.com/TheSyriaCampaign
Syria Solidarity Movement: www.facebook.com/syriasolidaritymovement
Syria Solidarity UK: www.syriauk.org
Syrian Nonviolence Movement: www.facebook.com/SyrainNonviolence
Violations Documentation Center in Syria: www.vdc-sy.info/index.php/en/home

News Sites

Aleppo Media Centre: www.facebook.com/AMCenglish?fref=pb&hc_location=profile_browser
ANA (Activists News Association): www.facebook.com/ActivistsNewsAssociation?fref=ts
EA Worldview: http://eaworldview.com
Enab Baladi: http://english.enabbaladi.net
Radio Free Syria: www.radiofreesyria.com
Syria Direct: http://syriadirect.org

Syrian Revolutionary Blogs and Websites (English Language)

The Creative Memory of the Syrian Revolution: www.creativememory.org/?lang=en
Darth Nader: http://darthnader.net
Leila al-Shami's Blog: https://leilashami.wordpress.com
Maysaloon: www.maysaloon.org
Robin Yassin-Kassab's blog: http://qunfuz.com
Razaniyaat: http://razanghazzawi.org
The Revolting Syrian: http://therevoltingsyrian.com
Salim Salamah's Blog: http://salimsalamah.com

Syria Freedom Forever: https://syriafreedomforever.wordpress.com
Syria Untold www.syriauntold.com
Yassin al-Haj Saleh: http://www.yassinhs.com/

Documentary

Bidayyat: http://bidayyat.org/index.php#.VbCcUUV0GLI
Camera Negra Collective 'Ecos del Desgarro': www.youtube.com/watch?v=Bx4PIlwITnU
'Jalila' a documentary about 'Syrian Women' by Adnan Jetto: https://www.youtube.com/watch?v=ydN_a5F3eE8
Kayani Web TV: www.youtube.com/user/kayaniwebtv
Young Syrian Lenses: www.transterramedia.com/media/45580

Notes

Preface

1. From 'Syria, Iran, ISIS and the Future of Social Justice: In Dialogue with Yassin al-Haj Saleh', Radio Zamaneh, 29 May 2015.

1. Revolution From Above

1. Translated by Lena Jayyusi and Diana Der Hovanessian, *On Entering the Sea: the Erotic and Other Poetry of Nizar Qabbani*, Interlink, 1996.
2. The phrase 'revolution from above' (the title of this chapter) is taken from Raymond Hinnebusch, *Syria: Revolution from Above*, Routledge, 2001 – a highly recommended examination of Baathist state-building under Hafez al-Assad.
3. See Malu Halasa's essay 'The Bra in Aleppo' *Critical Muslim 11 – Syria*, edited by Ziauddin Sardar and Robin Yassin-Kassab, Hurst, 2014.
4. Samuel Lyde, *The Asian Mystery Illustrated in the History, Religion and Present State of the Ansaireeh or Nusairis of Syria*, Elibron Classics, 2005.
5. See Tabitha Petran, *Syria*, Ernest Benn, 1972 – a good source of information on the French and post-independence periods up to Hafez al-Assad's coup.
6. Quoted in Hanna Batatu, *The Old Social Classes and Revolutionary Movements of Iraq*, Saqi, 2012.
7. Michel Aflaq, *On the Way of Resurrection*, 1943.
8. The most comprehensive study of the class and regional composition of the original Baath Party (and of Hawrani's ASP) is by Palestinian Marxist Hanna Batatu, *Syria's Peasantry, the Descendants of its Lesser Rural Notables, and Their Politics*, Princeton University Press, 1999.
9. See Thomas Pierret, *Religion and State in Syria: The Sunni Ulama from Coup to Revolution*, Cambridge University Press, 2013.
10. The 2003 film *A Flood in Baath Country*, Omar Amiralay's masterpiece of grim irony, critiques the effect of the dam on the local community, and of Baathism on society as a whole. Available at http://tinyurl.com/k45mc3k (accessed September 2015).
11. The story of Hafez's foreign policy expertise is told in Patrick Seale's somewhat hagiographic biography *Asad: The Struggle for the Middle East*, I.B.Tauris, 1988. A very useful counter-narrative is provided by Bente Scheller in *The Wisdom of Syria's Waiting Game*, Hurst, 2013.
12. Volker Perthes, *The Political Economy of Syria under Asad*, I.B. Tauris, 1997.

13. According to Hanna Batatu in *Syria's Peasantry, the Descendants of its Lesser Rural Notables, and their Politics*, Princeton University Press, 1999.
14. This was nothing new, of course. Dissenters were removed from society throughout Assad's reign – such as, for instance, Palestinian-Syrian leftist Faris Murad, arrested in June 1975 for affiliation with the Arab Communist Organisation and imprisoned (and tortured) for 29 years. Released due to ill health in 2004, he was prevented from seeking medical treatment abroad and died in 2009. A short film about Faris, with English subtitles, can be seen at http://tinyurl.com/ngzxoar (accessed September 2015).

2. *Bashaar's First Decade*

1. Cited in Mohamed Ali Atassi, 'Interview with Riad al-Turk, Syria's most prominent opposition figure', translated by Aimee Kligman, *examiner.com*, 4 September 2011.
2. Mona Shishter, 'Assad lauds Kuwait's role in cementing inter-Arab ties', *Kuwait News Agency (KUNA)*, 4 June 2008.
3. The Vogue panegyric was published – most unfortunately – in February 2011. It's since been taken down from the Internet, but some of it can still be seen at Max Fisher, 'The Only Remaining Online Copy of Vogue's Asma al-Assad Profile', *The Atlantic*, 3 January 2012.
4. In 2011, Moustapha was accused of spying on and threatening Syrians living in the United States.
5. Speech delivered by Bashar al-Assad on his inauguration as President of Syria in 2000, http://tinyurl.com/ndefwc9 (accessed September 2015).
6. Statement of the 99, in Alan George, *Syria: Neither Bread nor Freedom*, Zed Books, 2003.
7. Statement of the 1,000, in Alan George, *Syria: Neither Bread nor Freedom*, Zed Books, 2003.
8. Originally formed in 1989, the CDF collapsed less than three years later following the detention of its head, Aktham Nu'aisah, and several other activists.
9. Sami Moubayed, 'Independent Journalism Slowly Returning to Syria', *Washington Report on Middle East Affairs*, July 2001.
10. Assad interviewed by Ash-Sharq al-Awsat, February 2001, http://tinyurl.com/nhjdvc3 (accessed September 2015).
11. Four other FND members were detained – Kamal al-Labwani, Walid al-Bunni, Fawwaz Tello and the Alawite economist Aref Dalila.
12. For an excellent overview of the Damascus Spring see: Alan George, *Syria: Neither Bread nor Freedom*, Zed Books, 2003.
13. 'Internet Usage and Marketing Report: Syria', *Internet World Stats*, 2010.
14. Committee to Protect Journalists, '10 Worst Countries to be a Blogger', 2009.
15. Suheir Atassi continued the work of the forum online.
16. Interview with Leila al-Shami (LS), July 2003.
17. Interview with LS, June 2003.

18. Interview with LS, June 2003.
19. For more information see Human Rights Watch, 'Group Denial: Repression of Kurdish Political and Cultural Rights in Syria', 2009.
20. Testimony provided to LS by Razan Zaitouneh in Autumn 2003.
21. In September 2008, Aziz witnessed a young Christian man perish under torture in Damascus' Fayha security branch. His home town of Selemmiyeh has an Ismaili majority. The Ismailis are a minority community which in general has supported the revolution. see Robin Yassin-Kassab, 'Aziz's Story', *Qunfuz*, 14 September 2014.
22. Some figures are much higher, over one million Iraqis. The figures used here come from Amnesty International's 2007 annual report.
23. Testimony provided to LS by Razan Zaitouneh in Spring 2004.
24. The signatories to the Damascus Declaration were: the Democratic National Rally in Syria, the Kurdish Democratic Alliance in Syria, the Committees for the Revival of Civil Society, the Kurdish Democratic Front in Syria and the Future Party (Sheik Nawwaf al-Bashir.) Prominent civil society and political figures also signed, including Riad Seif, Michel Kilo and Haitham al-Maleh. The Muslim Brotherhood signed the following day, and later other smaller parties such as the Communist Labor Party joined.
25. In a 2008 interview with al-Hayat cited in Joshua Landis 'The National Salvation Front Folds', *Syria Comment*, 23 April 2009.
26. The term 'civil state' – meaning one run by civilians – though it implies secularism, is usually preferred by Arab activists to 'secular state'. The latter term, much abused by dictatorships identifying as such, has an anti-religious (rather than non-religious) connotation.
27. Liberal and Kurdish groups also participated in The National Salvation Front.
28. The International Fund for Agricultural Development (IFAD), 'Syrian Arab Republic: A Country Fact Sheet on Youth Employment', 2011.
29. Interview with authors, December 2014.
30. For an overview of the Baath party's economic policies and how they contributed to the 2011 uprising, see Omar S. Dahi and Yasser Munif, 'Revolts in Syria: Tracking the Convergence Between Authoritarianism and Neoliberalism', *Journal of Asian and African Studies*, 47(4), 2011: 323–32, and Jonathan Maunder, 'The Syrian Crucible', *International Socialism: A Quarterly Journal of Socialist Theory*, 135, June 2012.
31. Michael Peel and Abigail Fielding-Smith, 'Assad's Family Picked Up by the West's Radar', *Financial Times*, 27 April 2001.
32. Josepf Olmert, 'With Tlass Defection Bashar Assad's Troubles are Mounting', *The Huffington Post*, 7 June 2012.
33. In 2011 the most celebrated of revolutionary songs was 'Irhal Ya Bashaar' (Get out Bashaar!). It was composed and sung to the crowds in Hama by Ibrahim Qashoush, who was soon murdered by the regime. Some lines of the song are directed at the crony capitalists: 'You create new thieves every day | Shaleesh, Maher [Bashaar's brother] and Rami | They robbed my brother and uncles | Go

on, get out Bashaar!' see http://tinyurl.com/qd4ge49 (with English subtitles) (accessed September 2015).

34. Omar S. Dahi and Yasser Munif, 'Revolts in Syria: Tracking the Convergence Between Authoritarianism and Neoliberalism', *Journal of Asian and African Studies*, 47(4), 2011: 323–32.
35. All figures taken from United Nations Development Programme, *Poverty in Syria 1996–2004: Diagnosis and Pro-Poor Policy Considerations*, June 2005.
36. Riad al-Turk Interviewed by Joe Pace, *Syria Comment*, 8 September 2005.
37. In response to both gentrification and the demolition of historical buildings to make way for new construction, there was a surge in campaigns (often youth-led) to preserve the urban heritage. This was one sign of the rising civic activism which set the scene for revolution.
38. 'SYRIA: Drought Pushing Millions into Poverty', *IRIN*, 9 September 2010.
39. Interview with authors, December 2014.

3. *Revolution From Below*

1. Quoted in Taylor Adams, 'When are Violent Protests Justified?' *The New York Times*, 17 December 2014 http://op-talk.blogs.nytimes.com/2014/12/17/when-are-violent-protests-justified/?_r=0 (accessed September 2015).
2. Interview with authors, December 2014.
3. Interview with authors, December 2014.
4. Interview with authors, December 2014.
5. Hamid Dabashi, *The Arab Spring: The End of Postcolonialism*, Zed Books, 2012.
6. Interview with authors, December 2014.
7. Interview with authors, December 2014.
8. Hareeqa Souk demonstration. 17 February 2011, http://tinyurl.com/k57turw (accessed September 2015).
9. Damascus demonstration. 15 March 2011, http://tinyurl.com/oy8z82p (accessed September 2015).
10. Interview with authors, December 2014. The development of the LCCs will be examined in the following chapter.
11. Interview with authors, December 2014. Ziad would later become a film director.
12. Samar Yazbek, *A Woman in the Crossfire: Diaries of the Syrian Revolution*, Haus Publishing, 2011.
13. Deraa al-Balad demonstration, 18 March 2011, http://tinyurl.com/pvo6b3z (accessed September 2015).
14. Security forces fire water tanks on demonstrators in Deraa's al-Balad district, 18 March 2011, http://tinyurl.com/6b54o8z (accessed September 2015).
15. Protests in Deraa on 20 March 2011, http://tinyurl.com/oee4af5 (accessed September 2015).

16. For details of events in Deraa see, Human Rights Watch, 'We've Never Seen Such Horror: Crimes against Humanity by Syrian Security Forces', 2011, and The Damascus Bureau, 'Syrian Revolution Digest, March 23, 2011', 25 March 2011.
17. For details and videos of 'Friday of Dignity Protests' around the country, see The Damascus Bureau, 'Syrian Revolution Digest, March 25, 2011', 27 March 2011.
18. Irish journalist Stephen Starr witnessed the pro-regime demonstration 'that saw over 100,000 people clog the streets of Damascus. But I would say that 90% of the people I saw were either school children, state employees, or the rough, young army conscripts who shouted about how they would "give our blood for you, oh Bashaar." The Damascenes I know watched from their shop doors, from the balconies. They knew the government was carrying out murderous campaigns in the countryside. But they stayed silent.' Stephen Starr, *Revolt in Syria: Eye-witness to the Uprising*, C Hurst & Co., 2012.
19. This articulate young man from Banyas rejects Assadist propaganda claims (in English): http://qunfuz.com/2011/04/29/a-big-lie/ (accessed September 2015). He was later subjected to death threats.
20. 'Syria: Reports of Mass Killings, and a Blogger and a Journalist Disappear', *Global Voices*, 23 March 2011.
21. Al Dunya TV, 'Barcelona Football Club Conspiracy' [in Arabic] http://tinyurl.com/p3fujqw (accessed September 2015).
22. 'Syria: Speech by Bashar al-Assad', 30 March 2011, http://tinyurl.com/o2pkf4s (accessed September 2015).
23. It's likely that al-Sharaa tried and failed to defect in August 2012. The Free Syrian Army (FSA) announced his defection to Jordan. Some days later he appeared at an official function in Damascus, disproving the claim. Between the FSA announcement and Sharaa's reappearance, his home neighbourhood in his home city – Deraa – was subjected to particularly intense bombardment. Revolutionaries tend to believe that his escape was foiled at the last moment, and that Sharaa was coerced into public loyalty by violence done to his neighbourhood, family and friends.
24. A day before his next speech, in June, a Facebook page was set up called (in Arabic) 'Bashaar, if You Laugh Tomorrow, We'll Shit on You'.
25. Interview with authors, December 2014.
26. For details and videos of 'Friday of the Martyrs Protests' see The Damascus Bureau, 'Syrian Revolution Digest, April 1 & 2, 2011', 5 April 2011.
27. Iman Muhammed, 'An Eyewitness Story: The Clock Square Massacre, Homs 18/04/2011–19/04/2011', *rosealhomsi.wordpress.com*, 18 April 2012.
28. Interview with authors, January 2015.
29. Interview with authors, January 2015.
30. This dramatic video shows young men trying to rescue a fallen comrade under fire in Deraa. 'Khawana!' ('Traitors!') they shout at those shooting. http://tinyurl.com/pngxflz (accessed September 2015).

31. For details of events in Deraa, see Human Rights Watch, 'We've Never Seen Such Horror: Crimes against Humanity by Syrian Security Forces', 2011.
32. Mass grave found in Deraa (warning: graphic footage), http://tinyurl.com/nzzbzbj (accessed September 2015).
33. Interview with LS, January 2012.
34. The day after the regime granted nationality, thousands of Kurds took to the streets declaring the unity of Kurds and Arabs in a common struggle for freedom. For instance, this demonstration in Qamishli, 8 April 2011 http://tinyurl.com/mn2f57c, and this Amouda demonstration, 8 April 2011 http://tinyurl.com/nuagpht (accessed September 2015).
35. A Tribute to Mashaal Tammo and footage from his funeral procession here: www.creativememory.org/?p=30557 (accessed September 2015).
36. 'President al-Assad Address the New Government', transcript of Bashaar's speech, *DP News*, 17 April 2011.
37. Ella Wind, 'Inside and Outside', *Critical Muslim*, 11, Syria issue, July–September 2014.
38. Interview with authors, December 2014.
39. The March 2011 Lattakia stories are anecdotal, related in conversations between Lattakia residents and Robin Yassin-Kassab (RYK) at the time. Yassin al-Haj Saleh expands on the *shabeeha* phenomenon in 'The Syrian Shabiha and their State: Statehood and Participation' at the website of the Heinrich Boll Stiftung, http://lb.boell.org/en/2014/03/03/syrian-shabiha-and-their-state-statehood-participation (accessed September 2015).
40. See Samar Yazbek, *A Woman in the Crossfire: Diaries of the Syrian Revolution*, Haus Publishing, 2011, pp. 170–1 and 184–5. Yazbek describes false-flag operations on the coast at length, as well as the slander campaign against her as a prominent pro-revolution Alawi.
41. 'UN Chief Voices Alarm at Escalation of Violence in Syria,' *UN News Centre*, 3 June 2011.
42. The statistics for those detained were gathered from detainee lists, which are noted as being incomplete and representing only a small number of the total. Syrian Human Rights Information Link, 'List of Detainees of the Syrian Revolution', http://tinyurl.com/orzab9j (accessed September 2015).
43. See Human Rights Watch, 'Syria: Rampant Torture of Protestors', 15 April 2011, and Human Rights Watch, 'Syria: Targeted Arrests of Activists Across Country', 15 May 2011.
44. See Shiv Malik, Ian Black and Nedaa Hassan, 'Teenage Victim Becomes a Symbol for Syria's Revolution', *The Guardian*, 31 May 2011.
45. Video of security forces shooting live ammunition at peaceful protesters in Hama, http://tinyurl.com/ofpjt9t (accessed September 2015).
46. Interview with RYK, January 2012.
47. Riad Seif, the independent MP and Damascus Declaration signatory; George Sabra, the Communist who later became a head of the Syrian National Council;

Meshaal Temmo, Kurdish activist and promoter of Kurdish-Arab cooperation, later assassinated.

48. Interview with authors, December 2011.
49. See Hama protest from 1 July 2011, calling for the fall of the regime: http://tinyurl.com/oucyd9t, and this protest from 29 July 2011 http://tinyurl.com/o4jfxxo (accessed September 2015).
50. See, for example, this demonstration in the Salhiyeh shopping precinct in central Damascus. The middle class participants are doing nothing more than singing the national anthem. Within minutes the *mukhabarat* are on the scene. Soon people are seeking refuge in shops, being dragged out, and then beaten in the buses which will take them to prison http://tinyurl.com/mbadjcv (accessed September 2015).
51. Of course, many middle and upper class Alawis also lived in the mixed areas of the capital.
52. Interview with RYK, March 2011.
53. See Ella Wind, 'Inside and Outside', *Critical Muslim*, 11, Syria issue, July–September 2014: 51.
54. For example, see map showing protests which occurred in 14 different locations in Damascus on 10 June 2011, www.lccsyria.org/688 (accessed September 2015).
55. Interview with authors, December 2014.
56. There's no better description of the atmosphere in bourgeois parts of the city in 2011 than Amal Hanano's diaries, available with her other articles here: www.jadaliyya.com/pages/contributors/27141 (accessed September 2015).
57. Aleppo City Development Strategy, 'Madinatuna', 2010.
58. For an overview and videos of protests in Aleppo between March and August 2011 see, 'A Comprehensive Report on Aleppo and its Participation in the Syrian Revolution since its Start', http://tinyurl.com/m3u39mt (accessed September 2015).
59. Mohammed Ali al-Atassi, (translated by Aimee Kligman) 'Interview with Riad al-Turk, Syria's Most Prominent Opposition Figure', *examiner.com*, 4 September 2011.
60. Interview with authors, January 2015.
61. Interview with authors, December 2014.

4. *The Grassroots*

1. Mazen Km al-Maz, 'Horizons for the Syrian revolution', *anarkismo.net*, 23 May 2011.
2. Interview with authors, December 2014.
3. 'Activists: Revolutions Die with the Death of Civil Resistance', *Syria Untold*, 2 August 2013.
4. A graphic mapping non-violent activities in the Syrian uprising in July 2013 listed 198 committees throughout the country. Some sources have listed more

than double that amount. See, Syrian Nonviolence Movement, 'Non-violence Map in the Syrian Uprising', July 2013, www.alharak.org/nonviolence_map/en/# (accessed September 2015), which gives an excellent overview of civil activities in Syria.

5. Interview with authors, December 2014.
6. Interview with authors, December 2014.
7. Interview with authors, December 2014.
8. The National Coalition for Syrian Revolutionary and Opposition Forces, the umbrella group of the external opposition.
9. As the regime's violence increased the LCCs' positions changed to reflect new realities. They recognised the role of the FSA in defending Syrians and working to overthrow the regime, and following the 2013 sarin gas attacks, they hoped for air strikes on Assad.
10. For a round up (with video links) of some of the towns and cities which participated in the first day of the strike (it lasted over a week) see, LCC Syria, 'Dignity Strike 11-12-2011', www.lccsyria.org/3796 (accessed September 2015).
11. According to Assaad, 'Most of the aid from the USA was in kind, whether telecom support, IT support, or equipment. It gradually moved into support for specific development projects such as public health and basic service delivery. The French support was mainly in cash, and went to buy medical supplies and food baskets. Danish and Dutch funding was mainly geared towards media support, to reinforce the LCC media office and newsletter. A lot of the support came as well in the form of media and advocacy training workshops.' Correspondence with authors, July 2015.
12. Interview with authors, December 2014.
13. 'Syria: Interview with Syrian Revolution Coordinators Union leader in Qabon', *Asingleman*, 10 July 2011.
14. Interview with authors, December 2014.
15. 'Founding Statement for the Union of Free Syrian Students', 29 September 2011, www.lccsyria.org/1958 (accessed September 2015). Their English-language Facebook page is: www.facebook.com/Union.Of.Syrian.Free.Students?fref=ts (accessed September 2015).
16. See www.YouTube.com/watch?v=rWqZPyHgiyU (accessed September 2015).
17. Figures from 2008; 17 per cent were employed in agriculture and 67 per cent in services.
18. Jonathan Maunder, 'The Syrian Crucible', *International Socialism*, 28 June 2012.
19. Mazen Km al-Maz, 'Horizons for the Syrian Revolution', *anarkismo*, 23 May 2011.
20. Shabeeha and security forces attack shops in Deraa, 11 December 2011, www.YouTube.com/watch?v=6ABWc3_MEGM (accessed September 2015).
21. Joseph Daher, 'Sectarianism and the Assad Regime in Syria', *Syria Freedom Forever*, April 2013.
22. See www.YouTube.com/watch?v=m0qo1kwpV1c (accessed September 2015).

23. An excellent overview of the group is given by Budour Hasan, 'Damascus' Stifled Voice from the Left', *Open Democracy*, 31 December 2014.
24. *Syria Untold* interviews a female member who states that in Aleppo, more than 70 per cent of the Communist Party's youth left to join the ranks of the revolution, many going on to work in the coordination committees. Article (in Arabic): http://tinyurl.com/k7olcao (accessed September 2015).
25. Interview with authors, February 2015.
26. LCC, 'Freedom is my Sect', 10 June 2012, www.lccsyria.org/8848 (accessed September 2015).
27. See *Kayani Web TV* short documentary, 'Aleppo Ashrifia: National Unity', www.YouTube.com/watch?v=RaDFddXsJ3w (accessed September 2015).
28. Cited in, *Syria Untold*, 'Salamiyah Women Coordinating Committee', 8 May 2014.
29. Interview with authors, December 2014.
30. See for example demonstration in April 2011 www.YouTube.com/watch?v=WsJSu88ylEY and August 2011 www.YouTube.com/watch?v=wb_fudIs0ok (accessed September 2015).
31. See short documentary 'Zabadani Women', *Kayani Web TV* www.YouTube.com/watch?v=Otc6J9EQGiw#t=255 (accessed September 2015).
32. Interview with the authors, December 2014.
33. Razan Ghazzawi 'Back', *Razaniyyat*, 6 August 2013.
34. Interview with authors, December 2014.
35. Cited in Leila al-Shami 'The Life and Work of Anarchist Omar Aziz, and His Impact on Self-Organization in the Syrian Revolution', *leilashami.wordpress.com*, 20 October 2013.
36. A summarised version of Omar Aziz's 'A Discussion Paper on Local Councils in Syria', translated by Yasmeen Mobayed, can be found here: http://tinyurl.com/kxzdglu. The longer version (in Arabic) is online here: http://tinyurl.com/n63go95 (accessed September 2015).
37. Budour Hassan 'Portrait of a Revolution: The Journey of Faiek al-Meer', *Random Shelling*, 13 October 2013.
38. @DarthNader https://twitter.com/DarthNader/status/304015567231266816 (accessed September 2015).
39. Some reports (including the regime narrative) say Omar Aziz died from a heart attack. Others believe he died under torture.
40. Today local councils exist at city and district levels throughout the country and act as the primary administrative structure in areas liberated from the state. Local councils have also been established in regime-controlled areas, where they focus on humanitarian activities and media, and 128 Local Councils were listed in July 2013. Some sources estimate many more. See, Syrian Nonviolence Movement, 'Non-violence Map in the Syrian Uprising', July 2013.

41. The Cathedral of Constantine and Helen was originally a Roman temple to Jupiter, converted to a church in 300 AD. It was shelled by government forces in 2013 and desecrated by militant Jihadi groups in 2014.
42. The town was eventually overrun by militant Jihadi groups despite the efforts of locals and the FSA to keep them out. It was recaptured by government forces with the assistance of Hizbullah in March 2014. During this battle the town was subjected to SCUD missiles and barrel bombs.
43. The quote comes from the excellent short documentary 'Yabroud: Assad is Overthrown, October 2012, by *Kayani WebTV* which looks at life and self-organisation in the liberated town: www.YouTube.com/watch?v=vr3fLh6KosA (accessed September 2015).
44. Ibid.
45. Interview with authors, December 2014.
46. For an overview of the revolutionary struggle in Manbij and the challenges the city's people have faced see Yasser Munif 'Syria's Revolution behind the Lines', *Socialist Review*, October 2013.
47. Interview with authors, December 2014.
48. *The Syrian Observer*, 'Manbij, a Success Story in the Liberated Areas', 22 January 2014.
49. Interview with authors, December 2014.
50. Razan Zaitouneh, 'Urgent Appeal to Support Eastern Ghouta', *Adopt a Revolution*, 5 September 2013.
51. Interview with the authors, December 2014.
52. Joseph Daher, 'We Need to Support Liberation Struggle Unconditonally', *Syria Freedom Forever*, 28 October 2014.
53. A Kurdish Supreme Committee was established in an attempt to unite the Kurdish opposition. It's a coalition between the PYD and Kurdish National Council (comprising 15 political parties). This power-sharing agreement does not function, with both sides blaming the other.
54. See Abdullah Ocalan (imprisoned leader of the PKK) 'Democratic Confederalism', *Transmedia*, 2011.
55. 'The Social Contract of Rojava Cantons in Syria', *civiroglu.net*, http://civiroglu.net/the-constitution-of-the-rojava-cantons/ (accessed September 2015).
56. Cited in Janet Biehl 'Rojava's Communes and Councils', *Ecology or Catastrophe*, 31 January 2015.
57. See Human Rights Watch, 'Under Kurdish Rule: Abuses in PYD-Run Enclaves of Syria', June 2014 and 'Statement by the Kurdish Youth Movement (TCK) about the Latest Events in the City of Amouda, and Videos and Pictures from the Protests and Sit Ins', *Syria Freedom Forever*, 23 June 2013.
58. Many groups strive to promote Kurdish and Arab cooperation. See, for example, information about the work of the Amouda Coordinating Committee here: www.syriauntold.com/en/work_group/amuda-coordination-committee/; and the work of the Kurdish-Arab Coordinating committee here: www.syriauntold.

com/en/work_group/kurdish-arab-fraternity-coordination-committee/. This unity was often echoed on the streets. Here for example: www.YouTube.com/watch?v=53W42QayTeM (accessed September 2015).

59. Interview with authors, December 2014.
60. Bihar website, http://biharorg.com/ (accessed September 2015).
61. Brides of Peace demonstration in Damascus, 21 November 2012, www.YouTube.com/watch?feature=player_embedded&v=Ak0akv5N6nI (accessed September 2015).
62. Bassel Shehadeh's excellent film 'Streets of Freedom' which documents the protest movement in Syria and records the testimony of those who rose up against the regime is available here: www.YouTube.com/watch?v=7v5Rj3AwWy0. 'Syria through a Lens', a film about his life and work, is available here: www.YouTube.com/watch?v=Nem33Ow8wb4 (accessed September 2015).

5. *Militarisation and Liberation*

1. Peter Gelderloos, 'How Nonviolence Protects the State', *The Anarchist Library*, 2007, http://theanarchistlibrary.org/library/peter-gelderloos-how-nonviolence-protects-the-state (accessed September 2015).
2. Interview with authors, December 2014.
3. LCC, 'Statement to the Syrian People', 29 August 2011, www.lccsyria.org/1797 (accessed September 2015).
4. A number of female-only FSA brigades were established. See Robert Asher, 'Meet the Ladies of the Free Syrian Army', *Vice Media*, 10 April 2013. Women also play an important role in providing logistical support to the FSA, smuggling weapons, food and medical supplies.
5. Interview with authors, December 2014.
6. Interview with authors, December 2014.
7. Malu Halasa, 'Mystery Shopper: Interview with Assaad al-Achi', in *Syria Speaks, Art and Culture from the Frontline*, edited by Malu Halasa, Zaher Omareen and Nawara Mahfoud, Saqi Books, 2014.
8. Interview with authors, December 2014.
9. Indeed, following the sarin gas attacks of August 2013 the LCCs dropped their opposition to international intervention.
10. Interview with authors, December 2014.
11. Interview with authors, December 2014.
12. Gilbert Achcar, *The People Want: A Radical Exploration of the Arab Uprising*, Saqi Books, 2013, p. 141.
13. See http://blogs.aljazeera.com/topic/syria/syria-jun-8-2011-1834 for an example of defector testimony (accessed September 2015).
14. Interview with authors, December 2014.

15. The town had bad history with the regime since 1980, when residents had taken over and destroyed the Baathist HQ, and the army executed over a hundred civilians in reprisal.
16. Harmoush's defection video is available here: www.YouTube.com/watch?v=mLAa9NSC9fo; an interview with another defected soldier is available here: http://all4syria.info/Archive/73588 (accessed September 2015).
17. LCC, 'Getting Revenge from Harmoush through his Family', 20 September 2011, www.lccsyria.org/1921 (accessed September 2015).
18. Interview with authors, December 2014.
19. Until his implication in a sex scandal.
20. Interview with authors, December 2014.
21. Paul Wood, 'Face to Face with Abu Sakkar, Syria's "Heart-Eating Cannibal"', *BBC News*, 5 July 2013.
22. '"Surge" in Weapons Sales to Syria', *Al Jazeera*, 11 May 2011.
23. Examples include: http://photoblog.nbcnews.com/_news/2012/10/15/14458274-syrian-rebels-use-catapult-to-launch-homemade-bomb?lite and www.huffingtonpost.com/2012/12/10/syria-rebels-playstation-tank-sham-ii-video_n_2272930.html (accessed September 2015).
24. Interview with authors, December 2013.
25. Interview with authors, December 2014.
26. Interview with authors, December 2014.
27. Interview with authors, December 2014.
28. Interview with authors, December 2014.
29. Interview with authors, December 2014.
30. Interview with authors, January 2015.
31. An example of the shelling caught by mobile phone camera is available here: www.YouTube.com/watch?v=xDGmbjeMMDQ (accessed September 2015).
32. Interview with authors, January 2015.
33. Interview with authors, January 2015.
34. Interview with authors, December 2014.
35. Interview with authors, December 2014.
36. Interview with authors, December 2014.
37. Interview with authors, December 2014.
38. Interview with authors, December 2014.
39. Interview with authors, December 2014.
40. Interview with authors, December 2014.
41. 'Aleppo: Zaino Berri, Shabiha Leader, Captured and Executed', *Brown Moses Blog*, 31 July 2012.
42. Interview with authors, December 2014.
43. Residents of the Mar Elias Christian old folks' home, for instance, told journalists that the FSA was supplying them food and protecting them from jihadists. See Katherine Weber, 'Christians in Aleppo, Syria Claim Rebel Forces Keeping them Safe', *The Christian Post*, 22 September 2013.

44. Even as divisions intensified, so too did revolutionary efforts to stress unity. See, for example, this demonstration (with subtitles): www.YouTube.com/watch?v=RaDFddXsJ3w (accessed September 2015).
45. See C.J. Chivers, 'A Rebel Commander in Syria Holds the Reins of War', *The New York Times*, 1 February 2013.
46. www.YouTube.com/watch?v=WL-UQ6OUjsM&feature=youtu.be
47. www.YouTube.com/watch?v=T5ThMJ5875Y&feature=youtu.be (accessed September 2015) – transcripts at the blog of Syrian anarchist Nader Atassi, 'Remembering Abu Furat', *Darth Nader*, 15 December 2012. See also Mohammed Sergie, 'Social Media Buzz: Rebels Lose a Charismatic Commander,' *Syria Deeply*, 18 December 2012.
48. Bassam Barabandi and Tyler Jess Thompson, 'Inside Assad's Playbook: Time and Terror', Atlantic Council, 23 July 2014.
49. Interview with authors, December 2014.
50. The bombing was apparently carried out by one of the inner circle's bodyguards. Some reports describe it as a suicide attack, though when the FSA claimed responsibility for the operation it claimed the device had been remotely controlled.
51. Qusai Zakaraya, 'I Was Gassed by Bashar al-Assad', *stopthesiege*, 22 August 2014.
52. Interview with authors, December 2014.
53. The PFLP-GC, led by Ahmed Jibril, is a Syrian regime-backed splinter group from the Popular Front for the Liberation of Palestine (PFLP). The mainstream PFLP denounced the PFLP-GC's role in Yarmouk. See: www.al-monitor.com/pulse/originals/2012/al-monitor/pflp-on-defense-in-gaza.html# (accessed September 2015).
54. Correspondence with authors, January 2015.
55. For an example of the political murders of men from Yarmouk, see the case of Khaled Bakrawi – in Palestinian blogger Budour Hassan's words, 'a 27-year-old Palestinian-Syrian community organiser and founding member of the Jafra Foundation for Relief and Youth Development. Khaled was arrested by regime security forces in January 2013 for his leading role in organising and carrying out humanitarian and aid work in Yarmouk Refugee Camp. On 11 September, the Yarmouk coordination committee and Jafra Foundation reported that Khaled was killed under torture in one of the several infamous intelligence branches in Damascus.' in 'Death under Torture in Syria: The Horrors Ignored by Pacifists', *Random Shelling*, 15 September 2013.
56. Palestinian League for Human Rights-Syria, 'Camps Without Water: Legal Report on the Cutting of Water to Yarmouk and Deraa Palestinian Refugee Camps in Syria', see also Salim Salamah, 'Starving the Palestinian Yarmouk Camp,' Carnegie Endowment for International Peace, 28 April 2014.
57. Max J. Rosenthal, 'Syrian Activist Forced from Hometown Pledges to Keep Publicizing Atrocities', *The Huffington Post*, 3 August 2014.

58. Interview transcript at, 'Syrian Activist on Ghouta Attack: "I Haven't Seen Such Death in My Whole Life"', *Democracy Now!*, 23 August 2013.
59. See Hans Hoyng and Christoph Reuter, 'Assad's Cold Calculation: The Poison Gas War on the Syrian People,' *Spiegel Online International*, 26 August 2013.
60. Ibid. The regime's use of gas followed the pattern of steady escalation already remarked upon. The use on a much smaller scale of chemical cocktails, sometimes including low levels of sarin, had been reported in the previous months. A *Le Monde* correspondent reported that 'gas attacks occurred on a regular basis' in Jobar in April 2013. see Jean-Philippe Remy, 'Chemical Warfare in Syria,' *Le Monde*, 27 May 2013.
61. Interview with authors, December 2014.
62. Interview with authors, December 2014.
63. For barrel bombs – cheap concoctions of explosive and shrapnel tipped from planes or helicopters – see for example: www.hrw.org/news/2014/07/30/syria-barrage-barrel-bombs (accessed September 2015).
64. RYK's June 2013 visit to Kafranbel. See Robin Yassin-Kassab, 'Syria: Life in the Rebel Strongholds,' *The Guardian*, 14 August 2013.

6. *Scorched Earth: The Rise of the Islamisms*

1. Correspondence with authors, January 2015.
2. Interview with authors, December 2014.
3. Interview with authors, December 2014.
4. The author of the remarkable text 'Fear of Arrest' – a guide for those facing detention – writes: 'In prison try to adapt to everything except to the humiliation and the blasphemies that you will hear. Pray – no matter in what position – and try to keep your relationship to God strong.' Bassam Haddad et al. (eds), *The Dawn of the Arab Uprisings*, Pluto, 2012, p. 214.
5. The reader is referred to Bente Scheller's book *The Wisdom of Syria's Waiting Game: Foreign Policy Under the Assads*, Hurst, 2013.
6. Interview with authors, December 2014.
7. For example here in Deir ez-Zor: www.YouTube.com/watch?v=xDGmbjeMMDQ (accessed September 2015).
8. Speaking at the Edinburgh Book Festival June 2014. See also Samar Yazbek's new book *The Crossing: My Journey to the Shattered Heart of Syria*, Penguin Random House, 2015.
9. The Sunni woman in question had also been widowed and bombed by the regime. Interview with RYK December 2013. See: http://qunfuz.com/2014/01/14/a-widow-of-bayada/ (accessed September 2015).
10. Perhaps the largest massacre with a specifically sectarian flavour was on 2 and 3 May 2013 at Bayda and Banyas, when at least 248 Sunni civilians were murdered. see Human Rights Watch, *No One's Left*, 13 September 2013.

11. 'Shia' here refers to orthodox Twelver Shia, not to Shia offshoot sects such as the Alawis, Druze and Ismailis.
12. Shia regionalisation of the conflict was met immediately by a regional Sunni response. Apparently the Hatla massacre was instigated by a Kuwaiti Salafist preacher called Shafi al-Ajmi.
13. From her essay 'The Sect as Homeland' in *Critical Muslim 11 – Syria*, edited by Ziauddin Sardar and Robin Yassin-Kassab, Hurst, 2014. The essay offers a revealing account of the organised social ostracism suffered by Alawi revolutionaries, as does Samar Yazbek's book *Woman in the Crossfire: Diaries of the Syrian Revolution*, Haus, 2012.
14. Interview with authors, December 2014.
15. See for example this interview with AbdulAziz al-Khair: 'Syria in Travail: Interview with AbdulAziz al-Khair', *ncbenglish*, 17 May 2012.
16. She addresses a protest in Homs here: www.YouTube.com/watch?v=RjEwoZ6rZlY. Beside her is goalkeeper-turned-revolutionary (and later fighter) AbdulBasit al-Sarout. A translation of her hunger strike declaration is available here: http://qunfuz.com/2011/11/15/fadwa-sulaiman/ (accessed September 2015).
17. Zubaida Al Meeki defection video (in Arabic): www.YouTube.com/watch?v=elq-NUgmR5M (accessed September 2015).
18. See this illuminating interview with an Alawi revolutionary activist, Salam Hafez: 'Syrian Alawite Protester Speaks Out', *Institute for War and Peace Reporting*, 17 November 2011.
19. Alawis used to be described – and still are, pejoratively – as Nusairis, after the foundational figure Ibn Nusair.
20. The Palestinian-Syrian leftist Salameh Kaileh – tortured then deported from Syria in 2012 – argues convincingly that the regime prizes loyalty much more than Alawi identity, that the security predominance of Alawis from the president's home neighbourhood is a result of ruralism rather than sectarianism, but that the regime's counter-revolutionary strategy is certainly sectarian, exploiting the fears of a community which was not loyal en masse before the revolution. See Salameh Kaileh and Victorios Shams, 'Is the Syrian Regime Sectarian? Sectarianism, Part Two', *Syria Untold*, translated by Yazan Badran, 29 October 2014.
21. The poet Hassan al-Khayyer, an Alawi from the president's village, summed up the early 1980s conflict between the regime and Muslim Brotherhood like this: 'There are two gangs: one is ruling in the name of patriotism but has none of it. Another gang claims good faith; and religion forbids their sayings and acts. Two gangs. My people, be aware of both! Both drink from the same evil waters.' Al-Khayyer was arrested for his outspokenness and then murdered in prison. Cited in Robin Yassin Kassab, 'Literature of the Syrian Uprising', in *Syria Speaks, Art and Culture from the Frontline*, edited by Malu Halasa, Zaher Omareen and Nawara Mahfoud, Saqi Books, 2014. It is from the poem 'What Do I Say', https://en.wikipedia.org/wiki/What_Do_I_Say%3F (accessed September 2015).

22. 'The Sect as Homeland' in *Critical Muslim 11 – Syria*, edited by Ziauddin Sardar and Robin Yassin-Kassab, Hurst, 2014.
23. The Islamic revival was part of a global trend in which, for example, Hindu nationalists came to power in India, and Christian identity politics became important in the United States.
24. Interview with authors, December 2014.
25. Thomas Pierret, *Religion and State in Syria: The Sunni Ulema from Coup to Revolution*, Cambridge Middle East Studies, 2013, p. 199.
26. Ibid., p. 27.
27. Pierret using Pierre Bourdieu's phrase.
28. Thomas Pierret, *Religion and State in Syria: The Sunni Ulama from Coup to Revolution*, Cambridge University Press, 2013, p. 241.
29. See 'Suicide Bombers in U.S., UK and France Ready to Strike if Syria Attacked: Grand Mufti', *Al Arabiya News*, 10 October 2011.
30. One version holds that Bouti was killed with up to 50 others in a suicide blast. Revolutionaries have disputed this, pointing to video evidence which seems to suggest he was assassinated by the regime. It's hard to see why the regime would want to get rid of such a reliable servant – unless they thought he was about to change his discourse – but the video certainly raises questions: www.bbc.co.uk/news/world-middle-east-22086230 (accessed September 2015).
31. Thomas Pierret, *Religion and State in Syria: The Sunni Ulema from Coup to Revolution*, Cambridge Middle East Studies, 2013, p. 233.
32. Ibid., p. 164.
33. See the important pieces by Peter Neumann, 'Suspects into Collaborators', *London Review of Books*, 3 April 2014, and Martin Chulov, 'ISIS: The Inside Story', *The Guardian*, 11 December 2014.
34. See Phil Sands et al., 'Assad Regime Set Free Extremists from Prison to Fire Up Trouble during Peaceful Uprising', *The National*, 21 January 2014.
35. Interview with authors, December 2014.
36. Interview with authors, December 2014. As Muslim fighters emphasised religious references, so too did their Christian counterparts. See Darth Nader, 'Formation of a Christian Battalion in the Free Syrian Army', 19 September 2012, http://darthnader.net/2012/09/19/formation-of-a-christian-battalion-in-the-free-syrian-army/ (accessed September 2015) for an account of a Christian Free Army militia (The Supporters of God) in the Damascus countryside.
37. Fifty per cent wanted a civil state, and 18 per cent had no preference. See: http://english.dohainstitute.org/file/Get/44ce127c-5cac-4fe3-9959-579062a19748 (accessed September 2015).
38. Interview with authors, December 2014. Also see interview with a media activist attached to a secular FSA brigade: *Syria Deeply*, 'The State of a Secular Rebel Fighting Force', 8 September 2013.
39. Famously, Syrian-born Shaikh Adnan al-Arur broadcasted from Saudi Arabia. He called successfully for the populace to defy the state by shouting God is Greater

from their balconies; and made the following vow: 'the regime has succeeded in seducing a small number of minorities into supporting it ... in particular the Alawi community: no harm will be done to those who remained neutral; as for those who supported the revolution, they will be with us ... however, those who violated sanctities [a reference to rape], we will chop their flesh and feed them to dogs', www.YouTube.com/watch?v=DnJyqrMngC8 (accessed September 2015). It's a fairly specific threat, but was amplified enough to terrify Alawis and others. State media depicted Arur, with enormous exaggeration, as the mastermind of the uprising, and so increased his influence. In Ziad Homsi's words: 'They accused the people of supporting Arur, so they did.'

40. Interview with authors, December 2014.
41. Such as Hassan Hassan, 'Why Syria's Islamic Front is Bad News for Radical Groups', *The National*, 3 December 2013.
42. See Robin Yassin Kassab, 'Something Worse?', *Qunfuz*, 20 January 2014.
43. In this (Arabic only) sermon, for instance: www.YouTube.com/watch?x-yt-cl=85114404&v=FUNsSaoPVl8&x-yt-ts=1422579428 (accessed September 2015).
44. Human Rights Watch report here: www.YouTube.com/watch?v=U10D0-wiJ8A. See also *EA Worldview*'s response: http://eaworldview.com/2013/10/syria-spotlight-isis-jaish-al-muhajireen-wal-ansar-executed-kidnapped-civilians-latakia-hrw-say/ (accessed September 2015).
45. Interview with authors, December 2014.
46. Interview with authors, December 2014.
47. Jaysh al-Islam denies responsibility for the abduction. Some blame a regime false-flag operation. The revolutionary activists close to the Douma Four, however, and the four's families and friends, are convinced of Jaysh al-Islam's guilt, and emphasise that nothing happened in Douma without the Islamist militia's knowledge.
48. By Assaad al-Achi. Interview with authors, December 2014.
49. Ibid.
50. Interview with authors, December 2014.
51. The terrorist designation provoked angry responses from Syrian activists and protestors, who supported Nusra's fight against the greater terrorism of the regime. See 'Syrian Protesters Slam U.S. Blacklisting of Jihadist Group', *The Daily Star Lebanon*, 14 December 2012. Some forward-looking Syrian commentators opposed Nusra's presence from the start. see Joseph Daher, 'Position Regarding Jabhat al Nusra, Similar Groups and Suicides Bombings', *Syria Freedom Forever*, 27 November 2012.
52. Though defected diplomat Nawaf Fares claimed the regime – manipulating Nusra – was ultimately responsible for the bombings. See Ruth Sherlock, 'Exclusive Interview: Why I Defected from Bashar al-Assad's Regime, by Former Diplomat Nawaf Fares', *The Telegraph*, 14 July 2012.
53. Interview with authors, December 2014.

54. Ibid.
55. See Vera Mironova et al., 'Syria's Democracy Jihad, Why ISIS Fighters Support the Vote', *Foreign Affairs*, 13 January 2015.
56. The British doctor Abbas Khan, for instance, who treated civilian victims of Assadist bombing in Aleppo, and was arrested and then murdered by the regime in December 2013.
57. Chechnya has been struggling against Russian imperialism since the mid-nineteenth-century. Its capital city, Grozny, has been destroyed twice during Putin's rule. One result is a seemingly inexhaustible supply of transnational jihadists. Chechens fought in Afghanistan, Iraq and now in Syria. It is likely that their next major battleground will be Russia itself.
58. Interview with authors, December 2014.
59. RYK's June 2013 visit to Atmeh camp. See Robin Yassin Kassab, 'In Atmeh Camp', *Qunfuz*, 5 September 2013.
60. Interview with authors, December 2014.
61. Daesh is an acronym formed from 'al-dowla al-islamiya fi-l'raq wa ash-sham'. Daesh cadres consider use of the acronym a punishable insult, and prefer that we use 'al-dowla' or 'the state' as the shorter term.
62. For an insightful account of the origins of ISIS, see Michael Weiss and Hassan Hassan, 'ISIS: Inside the Army of Terror', *Regan Arts*, 2015.
63. The informant is Saraqeb resident Yasser Barish. See Robin Yassin Kassab, 'Something Worse?', *Qunfuz*, 20 January 2014. The public whipping is on YouTube: www.YouTube.com/watch?v=GT-xHZFBjmo (accessed September 2015).
64. For a precise account of the abduction of journalist Martin Soder, read Samar Yazbek, *The Crossing: My Journey to the Shattered Heart of Syria*, Penguin Random House, 2015. Yazbek was there, separated only by a wall and a veil.
65. See the 'Raqqa is being Slaughtered Silently' campaign, which documents both regime and ISIS violations: www.raqqa-sl.com/en/ (accessed September 2015).
66. This is an extract from his petition to the Pope: 'Unfortunately, the Syrian regime has been very clever in using a certain number of clergymen, men and women, for its propaganda in the West, in which it represents itself as the only and ultimate bastion defending Christians persecuted by Islamic terrorism. This manipulation of the public opinion has succeeded in discrediting to a large extent the Syrian revolutionary effort, both on the ground and abroad, in the eyes of many citizens around the world, and was thus able to create a paralysis of European diplomacy and politics, which ultimately only strengthens the most extremist groups and weakens the civil society.' See: www.change.org/p/pope-francis-the-syrians-are-in-need-of-your-personal-initiative (accessed September 2015).
67. Ella Wind, 'Inside and Outside', in *Critical Muslim 11 – Syria*, edited by Ziauddin Sardar and Robin Yassin-Kassab, Hurst, 2014, gives an illuminating and moving

account of the personalities and revolutionary activities of Paolo Dall'Oglio and Bassel Shehadeh.

68. Ziad was filming his conversations with Yassin during this bitterly ironic episode. The journey across the desert forms part of the highly-recommended film 'Our Terrible Country', http://dafilms.com/film/9410-our-terrible-country/ (accessed September 2015).
69. Interview with authors, December 2014.
70. Interview with authors, December 2014.
71. For instance, former American ambassador to Syria, Ryan C. Crocker, who wrote, with stunning short-sightedness: 'We need to come to terms with a future that includes Assad – and consider that as bad as he is, there is something worse.' See Ryan C. Crocker, 'Assad is the Least Worst Option in Syria', *The New York Times*, 21 December 2013.
72. A round-up of the day's protest videos can be seen at: www.uruknet.info/?p=m103869 (accessed September 2015).
73. Interview with authors, December 2014.
74. For an indispensable account of the Bush and Obama administrations at work in Iraq, see Emma Sky, *The Unravelling: High Hopes and Missed Opportunities in Iraq*, Atlantic Books, 2015. Reviewed by one of the authors here: www.theguardian.com/books/2015/jun/06/the-unravelling-emma-sky-review-high-hopes-missed-opportunities-iraq (accessed September 2015).
75. For more specific information on how ISIS implanted itself in Syria, see the important article by Christoph Reuter, 'The Terror Strategist: Secret Files Reveal the Structure of Islamic State', *Spiegel Online*, www.spiegel.de/international/world/islamic-state-files-show-structure-of-islamist-terror-group-a-1029274.html (accessed September 2015).
76. On al-Gharawi's crimes, see Andrew Slater, 'The Monster of Mosul: How a Sadistic General Helped ISIS Win', *The Daily Beast*, 19 June 2014.
77. A comprehensive account of the Iraqi Sunni uprising and ISIS's place in it is given by Michael Karadjis, 'Iraq and Syria: The Struggle against the Multi-Sided Counterrevolution', *Syrian Revolution Commentary and Analysis*, 25 June 2014.
78. See Josh Rogin, 'U.S. Ignored Warnings before ISIS Takeover of a Key City', *The Daily Beast*, 10 July 2014.
79. See Leila Al-Shami, 'The Deir Al Zour Intifada against Daesh', *leilashami.wordpress.com*, 4 August 2014.
80. Martin Chulov and Julian Borger, 'Syria: Isis Advance on Aleppo Aided by Assad Regime Air Strikes, US Says', *The Guardian*, 2 June 2015, www.theguardian.com/world/2015/jun/02/syria-isis-advance-on-aleppo-aided-by-assad-regime-air-strikes-us-says (accessed September 2015).
81. Interview with authors, December 2014.
82. Ibid.
83. Ibid.

84. From an interview with Syrian leftist Yasser Munif (son of the great novelist AbdulRahman). See 'Manjij, a Success Story in the Liberated Areas', *The Syrian Observer*, 22 January 2014.
85. Interview with authors, December 2014
86. Interview with authors, December 2014.
87. Interview with authors, December 2014.
88. *Al Arabiya News*, 'Al-Azhar Calls for "Killing, Crucifixion of ISIS Terrorists"', 4 February 2015, http://english.alarabiya.net/en/News/middle-east/2015/02/04/Al-Azhar-calls-for-killing-crucifixion-of-ISIS-terrorists-.html (accessed September 2015).
89. Karim Miské, *Arab Jazz*, MacLehose, 2015.
90. BBC Panorama, *From Jail to Jihad*.
91. Such as the privately-educated Aqsa Mahmood, from Glasgow.
92. When Aqsa Mahmood arrived in Syria she changed her name to Um Layth and set up a blog (now taken down from the Internet) encouraging Western Muslim women to follow. The twenty-year-old advised them to bring a good supply of modest clothing because, she opined, Syrian women were generally ignorant of the rules concerning correct Islamic dress.
93. Research conducted by Voices of Syria Project 2012.
94. Interview with authors, December 2014.
95. See Scott Lucas, 'Syria Daily, Feb 6: As Insurgents Attack Damascus, Regime Kills More than 130 Elsewhere,' *EA Worldview*, 6 February 2015.
96. For news on the situation in Yarmouk, see: http://salimsalamah.com/2015/04/03/rolling-updates-yarmouk-battle-anti-isis-and-assad-insights-by-activits-on-ground/ (accessed September 2015).
97. Quoted in Michael Weiss, 'Inside Palmyra, the Ancient City ISIS Just Sacked', *The Daily Beast*, www.thedailybeast.com/articles/2015/05/21/inside-palmyra-the-ancient-city-isis-just-sacked.html (accessed September 2015).
98. Mastoumeh fell from Assad's grip four years almost to the day after his forces committed a massacre against unarmed protestors, recorded here: www.YouTube.com/watch?v=dPOfSIzyBAw&feature=share (accessed September 2015).
99. Interview with authors, December 2014.
100. Michael Karadjis tackles the Israel-Nusra conspiracy theory in typically comprehensive style at *mkaradjis.wordpress.com*, 'The Israel-Backs-Jabhat-al-Nusra Fairytale and its Deadly Consequences', 29 June 2015.
101. See 'Syria Analysis: The Speech of a Desperate President', *EA Worldview*, 29 July 2015.

7. Dispossession and Exile

1. Interview with authors, November 2014.
2. Interview with authors, December 2014.

3. Syrian Centre for Policy Research, 'Syria: Alienation and violence, Impact of Syria Crisis Report 2014', March 2015.
4. Ibid.
5. The report can be found here: http://static.guim.co.uk/ni/1390226674736/syria-report-execution-tort.pdf (accessed September 2015).
6. Scott Lucas, 'Syria Feature: A Regime "Torture Camp" only 500 meters from Assad's Presidential Palace', *EA Worldview*, 18 March 2015.
7. Syrian Centre for Policy Research, 'Syria: Alienation and Violence, Impact of Syria Crisis Report 2014', March 2015.
8. Ibid.
9. Figures from UN Office for the Coordination of Humanitarian Affairs Syria website as of April 2015, http://www.unocha.org/syria or http://www.unocha.org/syrian-arab-republic/syria-country-profile/about-crisis (accessed September 2015).
10. The Syrian American Medical Society also lists 560 people who have died from siege conditions as of March 2015. See The Syrian American Medical Society, *Slow Death: Life and Death in Syrian Communities Under Siege*, March 2015.
11. Qusai Zakarya, 'Hunger Strike, Day 30: We Will Never Give Up', *stopthesiege*, 25 December 2013.
12. See information gathered by the Violations Documentation Centre in Syria, http://tinyurl.com/qa7r82u (accessed September 2015).
13. See the White Helmets website: www.whitehelmets.org/ (accessed September 2015).
14. Video footage of victims of chlorine attack on Sarmeen, 16 March 2015 (warning: graphic footage): www.YouTube.com/watch?v=dmvVJYQGKnM (accessed September 2015).
15. Correspondence with LS, January 2013.
16. Many humanitarians crossed into liberated territory from Turkey and elsewhere without regime permission.
17. See Julia Z, 'The Struggle for Freedom and Food Sovereignty: A Letter of Solidarity to the Farmers of Syria', *Open Democracy*, 24 June 2014.
18. Interview with authors, February 2015.
19. Nayla Mansour, 'My Name is Kafranbel, and I Do Not Need Trainings in "Needs Assessment"', *Al-Jumhuriya*, translated by Murhaf Fares, 4 November 2014.
20. Interview with authors, December 2014.
21. Interview with authors, February 2014.
22. Interview with RYK, January 2014.
23. RYK's return visit to Atmeh camp is described at 'There's No Hope Left': The Syrian Refugee Camp that is Becoming a Township', *The Guardian*, 18 February 2014.
24. Interview with authors, February 2015.
25. Syrian Centre for Policy Research, 'Syria: Alienation and Violence, Impact of Syria Crisis Report 2014', March 2015.

26. See http://data.unhcr.org/syrianrefugees/regional.php (accessed September 2015).
27. See House of Commons Library, Briefing Paper, 'Syrian Refugees and the UK', Number 06805, 18 June 2015.
28. UN High Commissioner for Refugees figures for 17 June 2015: http://data.unhcr.org/syrianrefugees/settlement.php?id=176&region=77&country=107 (accessed September 2015).
29. Interview with LS, February 2013.
30. Interview with LS, March 2013.
31. World Bank, 'The World Bank and the Impact of the Syrian Crisis', 17 May 2014.
32. Interview with LS, February 2013.
33. *Al Akhbar*, 'Study Sheds Light on High Levels of Racism against Syrians in Lebanese Regions', 20 May 2014.
34. See: http://data.unhcr.org/syrianrefugees/country.php?id=8 (accessed September 2015).
35. Human Rights Watch, 'Egypt: Syria Refugees Detained, Coerced to Return', 10 November 2013.
36. 'Mediterranean Crossings in 2015 Already Top 100,000', UNHCR, 9 June 2015.
37. See 'What's behind the Surge in Refugees Crossing the Mediterranean Sea?', *The New York Times*, 20 April 2015.
38. See 'Mediterranean Migrant Death Rate Slows after Search-and-Rescue Boost', *The Guardian*, 01 June 2015.
39. 'Syrian Letter to the UK', 8 November 2014, at the Calais Migrant Solidarity website, a useful source of information on the refugee struggle: https://calaismigrantsolidarity.wordpress.com/2014/11/08/syrian-letter-to-the-uk/ (accessed September 2015).
40. Interview with authors, December 2014.
41. Interview with authors, December 2014.

8. *Culture Revolutionised*

1. Correspondence with authors, January 2015.
2. Interview with authors, December 2014.
3. Interview with authors, December 2014.
4. Lisa Wedeen, *Ambiguities of Domination: Politics, Rhetoric and Symbols in Contemporary Syria*, University of Chicago Press, 1999.
5. From Itab Azzam, 'Syria's Trojan Women', in *Critical Muslim 11 – Syria*, edited by Ziauddin Sardar and Robin Yassin-Kassab, Hurst, 2014.
6. For an interesting discussion of the political uses of *muselselat* see Maysaloon's essay 'The Complicity of Syrian Drama' in *Critical Muslim 11 – Syria*, edited by Ziauddin Sardar and Robin Yassin-Kassab, Hurst, 2014.
7. Bayt al-Qasid's manager and host was the well-known Kurdish writer Lukman Derky. For more on the club see Frederic Gijsel, 'Not Even the Basement

Escapes', in *Critical Muslim 11 – Syria*, edited by Ziauddin Sardar and Robin Yassin-Kassab, Hurst, 2014.

8. Correspondence with authors, January 2015.
9. From 'When the Words Burn', in *Joy is not my Profession*, translated by John Asfour and Alison Burch, Signal Editions, 1994.
10. Khaled's latest novel. *No Knives in this City's Kitchens*, follows a family through the depredations of half a century of dictatorship. see MLYNXQUALEY, '2013 Naguib Mahfouz Medal to Khaled Khalifa's "No Knives in the Kitchens of This City"', *Arabic Literature (in English)*, 11 December 2013.
11. Ali Farzat's website: www.ali-ferzat.com/ar/comics.html (accessed September 2015).
12. Sameeh Shuqair's Ya Heif: www.YouTube.com/watch?v=jMniqStJGoM (accessed September 2015).
13. Azza al-Hamwi's short film, *A Farewell to Damascus*, shows Mai Skaf reflecting on revolution, repression, sectarianism and exile shortly before her departure from Syria. Available at: www.YouTube.com/watch?v=Ph0MxVRdXxU (accessed September 2015).
14. Q&A with Fadi Azzam: www.arabicfiction.org/news.108.html (accessed September 2015).
15. MLYNXQUALEY, 'Open Letter from Syrian Author Khaled Khalifa', *Arabic Literature (in English)*, http://arablit.org/2012/02/08/open-letter-from-syrian-author-khaled-khalifa/. Matthew Davis's excellent essay 'The Writer and the Rebellion' is available here: www.guernicamag.com/features/the-writer-and-the-rebellion/. See too RYK's account of Khaled Khalifa here: http://qunfuz.com/2014/07/18/syria-speaks-on-tour/ (accessed September 2015).
16. The al-Dunya report, with English subtitles: www.YouTube.com/watch?v=uRBnM8tmMuw. Shortly afterwards the British journalist Robert Fisk would make a similarly embedded visit to Daraya.
17. Correspondence with authors, January 2015.
18. Interview with authors, December 2014.
19. For more information about the revolutionary flag, see 'The Flag of our Forefathers', *sarabiany*, 17 April 2013.
20. Bagosh was murdered at a regime checkpoint. Some of the stamps can be seen here: www.creativememory.org/?cat=27 (accessed September 2015).
21. See RYK's account of the Salaam School, its children and staff at 'The Salam School', *Qunfuz*, 5 February, 2014.
22. Interview with authors, December 2014.
23. 'Zawraq Magazine', *Syria Untold*, 2 December 2014.
24. Episode one of Um Abdo al-Halabiyya is available here with English subtitles: www.YouTube.com/watch?v=QNCU6Y3-EBg (accessed September 2015).
25. Interview with authors, December 2014.

26. www.facebook.com/ActivistsNewsAssociation. There are many excellent reports at the ANA Press YouTube page: www.YouTube.com/channel/UCtuKJMKy__R5ZbmExMMlQbw (accessed September 2015).
27. Amongst his current activities, Hadi Abdullah presents *Spirit of the Revolution*, a series covering the motivations, methods and values of the uprising. Now available with English subtitles here: https://www.youtube.com/watch?v=z9bRLduxm-I&feature=youtu.be (accessed September 2015).
28. The Sham News Network's YouTube channel: www.YouTube.com/user/SHAMSNN#p/a; Shahba Press's English-language Facebook page: www.facebook.com/SHahba.EN, its YouTube channel: www.YouTube.com/user/Shahba2013, and its website: www.shahbapress.com/; information and links for the Aleppo Media Centre: http://alepponotes.com/take-action/aleppo-media-center/ (accessed September 2015).
29. From an interview with *Syria Untold*, an indispensable source of information on Syria's civil and creative resistance. See 'Oxygen Magazine', *Syria Untold*, 23 March 2014.
30. 'al-Nabaa Magazine', *Syria Untold*, 3 July 2014.
31. Enab Baladi's Facebbok page (in Arabic) www.facebook.com/enab.baladi?fref=nf (accessed September 2015).
32. Interview with authors, December 2014.
33. The Kafranbel Facebook page: www.facebook.com/kafrnbl, and the website: www.occupiedkafranbel.com/ (accessed September 2015).
34. RYK's trip to Kafranbel is documented here: www.theguardian.com/world/2013/aug/14/syria-life-in-the-rebel-strongholds (accessed September 2015).
35. For the Dael song and more evidence of the revolutionary carnivalesque, see http://qunfuz.com/2011/11/26/turn-it-up/ (accessed September 2015).
36. Fares Cachoux's portfolio is here: http://farescachoux.prosite.com/ (accessed September 2015).
37. AbdelBaset al-Sarout is the goalkeeper turned protest leader turned resistance fighter from Homs. Aboud Saeed, 'The Smartest Guy on Facebook', in *Syria Speaks, Art and Culture from the Frontline*, edited by Malu Halasa, Zaher Omareen and Nawara Mahfoud, Saqi Books, 2014.
38. Hani al-Sawah, 'The Lure of the Street', in *Syria Speaks, Art and Culture from the Frontline*, edited by Malu Halasa, Zaher Omareen and Nawara Mahfoud, Saqi Books, 2014.
39. The Raqqa concert: www.liveleak.com/view?i=411_1366745218 (accessed September 2015).
40. Here, with English subtitles: www.YouTube.com/watch?v=ILasB53X72o (accessed September 2015).
41. Omar Ofendum's website: www.offendum.com/; Abo Hajar's 'Down with the Homeland' is here: www.YouTube.com/watch?v=gbPkh-Fikt0 www.YouTube.com/watch?v=ILasB53X72o (accessed September 2015).

42. Monzer Darwish writes about his film here: http://norient.com/en/blog/syrian-metal-is-war/; Anarchadia are interviewed here: www.syriauntold.com/en/2013/10/heavy-metal-and-the-syrian-uprising/ (accessed September 2015).
43. Quoted from this short film: www.YouTube.com/watch?v=S8jOh7pJhcc (accessed September 2015).
44. 'Streets of Freedom' can be seen here: www.YouTube.com/watch?v=7v5Rj3AwWy0 (accessed September 2015).
45. More on Hassan's story here: https://syriafreedomforever.wordpress.com/2013/12/18/palestine-and-syria-are-one-in-memory-of-the-palestinian-syrian-revolutionary-activist-and-actor-hassan-hassan/ (accessed September 2015).
46. *Our Terrible Country* is a film of the Bidayyat collective, which produces documentaries and experimental shorts. The trailer can be seen here: http://bidayyat.org/films_article.php?id=146#.VOzfluHpxVc (accessed September 2015).
47. Correspondence with authors, January 2015.
48. Interview with authors, December 2014.
49. In this video interview, Marcell explains why she refused to conform to Islamist dictates: https://vimeo.com/89693687 (accessed September 2015).
50. For more on Enough is Enough, see 'Enough is Enough Campaign', *Syria Untold*, 25 June 2013.
51. In this video interview, Suad Nowfal describes her actions: https://vimeo.com/77826189. For a summary of the protests leading to the war on ISIS, see: https://leilashami.wordpress.com/2014/01/07/the-battle-against-isis/, and for information on campaigns in solidarity with the Christian community, see: www.syriauntold.com/en/2014/08/syrians-stand-in-solidarity-with-christians-against-isis/ (accessed September 2015).
52. Interview with the authors, December 2014.
53. Interview with the authors, December 2014.
54. Yiffat Suskind discusses steps to end the stigmatisation of rape victims in this article: 'What Will It Take to Stop Isis using Rape as a Weapon of War?', *The Guardian*, 17 February 2015.
55. *Mawaleh* magazine is available at: http://mawaleh.net/ (accessed September 2015). See also the activist Joseph Mardelli's report at 'Gays in Syria Risk Execution by IS Militants', *France 24*, 12 December 2014.
56. Interview with authors, December 2014.
57. Interview with authors, December 2014.
58. Interview with authors, December 2014.
59. See for instance: www.theguardian.com/world/shortcuts/2014/jan/13/captagon-amphetamine-syria-war-middle-east (accessed September 2015).
60. Interview with the authors, December 2014.
61. For more information on tensions within the Alawi community, see Oula Abdulhamid al-Rifai's 'Not Alright with Syria's Alawites', *Foreign Affairs*, 3 December 2014. The Druze community is also increasingly resisting

conscription. As an illustration – Druze men attacked a military recruitment centre in Salkhad village, Sweida on 8 January 2015, setting free a man who'd been press-ganged into the army.

62. Interview with authors, December 2014.

9. The Failure of the Elites

1. Interview with authors, December 2014.
2. Interview with authors, December 2014.
3. *Al Jazeera*, 'Bala Hudood: The Future of the Syrian Revolution', 5 October 2011.
4. See 'Syrian Muslim Brotherhood: Pledge and Charter on Syria', available at Carnegie Middle East Center, 1 June 2012.
5. See 'SNC: National Charter: the Kurdish Issue in Syria', available at Carnegie Middle East Center, 25 June 2012.
6. Speech in Douma, 5 April 2011, quoted in Thomas Pierret, *Religion and State in Syria: The Sunni Ulema from Coup to Revolution*, Cambridge Middle East Studies, 2013, p. 224.
7. LCC, 'The National Coalition of Syrian Revolutionary and Opposition Forces', 12 November 2013, www.lccsyria.org/10488 (accessed September 2015).
8. Correspondence with authors, January 2015.
9. LCC, 'Statement Issued by the Revolutionary Movement in Syria', 29 May 2013, www.lccsyria.org/11445 (accessed September 2015).
10. Interview with authors, December 2014.
11. Interview with authors, December 2014.
12. Interview with authors, December 2014.
13. Glen Kessler, 'Hillary Clinton's Uncredible Statement on Syria', *The Washington Post*, 4 April 2011, http://www.washingtonpost.com/blogs/fact-checker/post/hillary-clintons-uncredible-statement-on-syria/2011/04/01/AFWPEYaC_blog.html (accessed September 2015).
14. For an overview of American 'arming' of the FSA, see Michael Karadjis, 'Yet Again on those Hoary Old Allegations that the US has Armed the FSA since 2012', *Syrian Revolutionary Commentary and Analysis*, 28 September 2014.
15. Interview with authors, December 2014.
16. Quoted from Adam Entous, 'Covert CIA Mission to Arm Syrian Rebels Goes Awry', *The Wall Street Journal*, 26 January 2015.
17. https://www.youtube.com/watch?v=LfFeLmYe_BQ (accessed September 2015).
18. Aziz Asaad using the pseudonym 'Bassam' in an interview with *Syria Deeply*. See 'The State of a Secular Rebel Fighting Force', *Syria Deeply*, 8 September 2013. See also the LCC's statement on the potential strike, available here: www.adoptrevolution.org/en/lcc-statement-regarding-a-possible-military-strike/ (accessed September 2015).
19. Interview with authors, December 2014.

20. Frank G. Wisner and Leslie H. Gelb, 'Face the Assad Reality in Syria', *The Daily Beast*, 26 January 2014.
21. Jay Solomon and Carol E. Lee, 'Obama Wrote Secret Letter to Iran's Khamenei about Fighting Islamic State', *The Wall Street Journal*, 6 November 2014.
22. Interview with authors, December 2014. Actually ISIS's worse crime in Syria (so far) was the slaughter of 900 Sheitat tribesmen.
23. 'Obama: Notion that Syrian Opposition could have Overthrown Assad with U.S. Arms a "Fantasy"', *CBS News*, 20 June 2014, http://www.cbsnews.com/news/obama-notion-that-syrian-opposition-could-overthrow-assad-a-fantasy/ (accessed September 2015).
24. Karim Sadjadpour, 'Iran: Syria's Lone Regional Ally', Carnegie Endowment for International Peace, 9 June 2014.
25. See Scott Lucas, 'Syria Daily, Feb 12: Are Hezbollah and Iran Leading Assad's Forces?', *EA Worldview*, 12 February 2015.
26. Correspondence with authors, February 2015. Scott Lucas runs *eaworldview.com*, an indispensable news source on Syria and the region. One estimate holds that Iran spends $35 billion annually on propping up the Assad regime: www.csmonitor.com/World/Middle-East/2015/0427/Why-Iran-is-standing-by-its-weakened-and-expensive-ally-Syria (accessed September 2015).
27. See Mamoon Alabbasi, 'Iran Continues to Boast of its Regional Reach', *Middle East Eye*, 13 March 2015, www.middleeasteye.net/news/iran-continues-boast-regional-reach-944755422 (accessed September 2015).
28. Hassan Nasrallah speech, 25 May 2013. The quoted section begins at 32.25: www.YouTube.com/watch?v=wHHnYwr2044 (with English translation) (accessed September 2015).
29. Samia Nakhoul, 'Special Report: Hezbollah gambles all in Syria', *Reuters*, 26 September 2013.
30. Dr Hamad Al-Majid, 'Opinion: The Oppressor and the Oppressed', *Asharq al-Awsat*, 23 April 2013.
31. Hanin Ghaddar, 'Hani Fahs: The Troublemaking Sayyed', *NOW*, 19 September 2014.
32. See for example their open letter to Hassan Nasrallah: www.naameshaam.org/open-letter-to-nasrallah/ (accessed September 2015).
33. Correspondence with the authors, February 2015.
34. The father of Ibrahim Shayban, a nine-year-old murdered by Assad forces, sarcastically 'thanks' Russia and China for their veto here: www.YouTube.com/watch?v=GQWP4eSCrKw (accessed September 2015).
35. See Amnesty International, 'Syria: Reports of Helicopter Shipments Underscore Need for Arms Embargo', 20 June 2012, www.amnesty.org.au/news/comments/28990/ (accessed September 2015).
36. See Robin Yassin-Kassab, 'Syria: Life in the Rebel Strongholds', *The Guardian*, 14 August 2013.
37. See Salman Masalha, 'Israel's Favourite Arab Dictator of all is Assad', *Haaretz*, 29 March 2011.

38. Israel has also provided medical assistance to injured Syrians on its borders. This has given rise to conspiracy theories concerning supposed Israeli collaboration with Nusra and other groups, as well as to the Druze attack on an ambulance described in Chapter 6. Michael Karadjis examines the issue in 'The 'Israel Backs Jabhat al-Nusra' Fairytale and its Deadly Consequences' here: https://mkaradjis.wordpress.com/2015/06/29/%E2%80%8Bthe-israel-backs-jabhat-al_nusra-fairy-tale-and-its-deadly-consequences/ (accessed September 2015).
39. See 'Syria Daily: US War with Jabhat al-Nusra Escalates', *EA Worldview*, 1 August 2015.
40. Interview with authors, December 2014.

10. The Start of Solidarity

1. 'Interview with Yassin al-Haj Saleh: Syria and the Left', *New Politics*, Winter 2015.
2. 'From The Day We Broke Fear', *maysaloon.org*, 3 June 2013. Deeply humane, and with an eye to culture as much as politics, Wasim al-Adl writes perhaps the best English-language blog – *Maysaloon* – of any Syrian.
3. Quoted from 'We Rattled Too Many Cages: An Eyewitness Account of Journalist Marie Colvin's Death in Syria', *Mother Jones*, 2 January 2014.
4. This website preserves Ali's work: http://rememberingalimustafa.org/ (accessed September 2015).
5. This website commemorates Kayla: www.forkayla.org/ (accessed September 2015).
6. Pulitzer Prize winner Shadid died of an asthma attack in Febrary 2012 while crossing the Syrian border on horseback (he was allergic to horses).
7. Winner of the 2015 Orwell Prize for Journalism, Chulov covers the Middle East for the *Guardian*.
8. Formerly known as Brown Moses, Higgins is the founder of www.bellingcat.com/, an indispensable journalistic resource.
9. Littell is author of the important World War II novel *The Kindly Ones*, Vintage, 2010. His account of his visit to Homs is published as *Syrian Notebooks: Inside the Homs Uprising*, Verso, 2015. Reviewed by RYK here www.thenational.ae/arts-lifestyle/the-review/book-review-syrian-notebooks-inside-the-homs-uprising#full (accessed September 2015).
10. The British politician George Galloway, who'd once delivered a panegyric to Saddam Hussain, took a paid job with al-Mayadeen. He used this platform to argue in favour of President Assad.
11. The al-Dunya report on the Daraya massacre is discussed in Chapter 8. Robert Fisk, embedded with the Syrian army, provided his own report: 'Inside Daraya: How a Failed Prisoner Swap Turned Into a Massacre', *The Independent*, 29 August 2012. For the full LCC response, see 'To Kill and Walk in the Funeral Procession', *Qunfuz*, 28 August 2012. For Yassin al-Haj Saleh's criticism of Fisk and others, see 'What is the matter with Robert Fisk?', The-Syrian.com,

29/09/2012, and 'Raging with the Machine: Robert Fisk, Seymour Hersh and Syria', *pulsemedia.org*, 25 April 2014. And for a comprehensive criticism of the influential journalist Patrick Cockburn's coverage of Syria, see Muhammad Idrees Ahmad, 'Who's Lying about Syria's Christian Massacre', *The Daily Beast*, 27 May 2015.

12. Seymour Hersh wrote two stories for the *London Review of Books* which blamed first Jabhat al-Nusra and then Turkey for the sarin attack. The most comprehensive debunkings of Hersh's conspiracy theory are by Muhammad Idrees Ahmad, 'A Dangerous Method: Syria, Sy Hersh, and the Art of Mass-Crime Revisionism', *Los Angeles Review of Books*, 01 June 2014, and Eliot Higgins and Dan Kaszeta, 'It's Clear that Turkey was not Involved in the Chemical Attack on Syria', *The Guardian*, 22 April 2014. For a summary of these episodes by the excellent Muhammad Idrees Ahmad, see 'The New Truthers: Americans Who Deny Syria Used Chemical Weapons,' *New Republic*, 11 September 2013, and 'On Monsterphilia and Assad', *Guernica Magazine*, 24 October 2013.
13. Talal Alyan. 'The Death of Palestine: Two Years of Siege in Yarmouk', *The World Post*, 16 December 2014.
14. In the opinion of writer Nir Rosen, for instance, Assadist brutality 'was done more out of a fear of Sunni sectarianism than as a result of the regime's own sectarianism'. See David Kenner, 'Rewriting Syria's War', *Foreign Policy*, 18 December 2014, and also Thomas Pierret's rebuttal of Rosen's claims in 'On Nir Rosen's Definitions of Sectarian and Secular', *pulsemedia.org*, 23 December 2014.
15. Sadik Jalal al-Azm, 'Syria in Revolt', *Boston Review*, 18 August 2014.
16. Correspondence with authors, March 2015.
17. For further information and analysis of European fascists in Syria, see Leila al-Shami, 'Who are Assad's Fascist Supporters?', *leilashami.wordpress.com*, 12 December 2013.

Epilogue

1. See 'Syria Daily: Regime Carries Out Another Mass Killing in Douma', *EA Worldview*, 23 August 2015.
2. 'Violent Protests Hit Syria's Sweida City', *Arab News*, 6 September 2015.
3. See 'Syria Daily: Russia Begins Bombing of Rebels and Civilians', *EA Worldview*, 1 October 2015.
4. 'How Russia Bombed a UN Heritage Site in Syria', *NOW*, 1 October 2015.
5. Press Release Regarding Russian Airstrikes in Syria, LCCs Facebook page, 2 October 2015, https://www.facebook.com/LCCSy/posts/1238711152822685 (accessed October 2015).
6. See data from the Syrian Network for Human Rights in 'Syria: The Facts and Figures', *The Syria Campaign*, 23 September 2015.
7. 'Refugees March on Austria after Hungary Blocks Trains', *Al Jazeera*, 4 September 2015.

Index